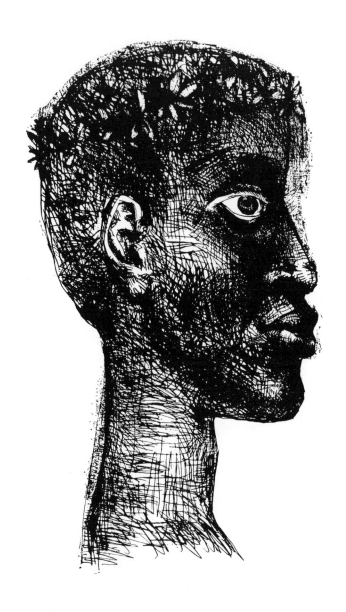

THIS AFRICA

NORTHWESTERN UNIVERSITY African Studies

Number Fourteen

This volume has been published with the aid of a grant from the Program of African Studies, Northwestern University.

THIS
AFRICA NOVELS BY
WEST AFRICANS IN ENGLISH
AND FRENCH

by
Judith Illsley Gleason

NORTHWESTERN

UNIVERSITY

PRESS

Evanston

1965

TO BILL

Ihe kwulu, ihe akwudebe ya.

—IBO PROVERB

ACKNOWLEDGMENTS

My gratitude to all of those who helped me write this book. First to Zimanimoto Kadzamira of Malawi, on whose account we first began to concern ourselves with modern Africa. Then to Mr. Trilling, whose sympathetic imagination could see this topic first as a dissertation and then as a book, whose sense of fun helped to mitigate the exactions of his unrelenting critical standards, his unfailing good sense. Thanks to John Thompson of the Farfield Foundation for much-needed funds for books, to Walter Goldwater of the University Place Bookshop for supplying them with courtesy, to John Thompson again, and to Louis Nkosi for supplying me with the publications of the Transcription Center in London. Without the American Society of African Culture (A.M.S.A.C.) I never could have got to first base; and I would like to thank everyone there for their hospitality, their endless information, and for providing just the right climate in which to work. More particularly, I would like to thank Shirley Branch; John Davis; James Baker, especially for the questionnaires from Lagos; Mercer Cook, United States Ambassador to Senegal and A.M.S.A.C. member, for his prompt intelligence on biographical matters; and most of all, Brooke Aronson, who in a sense shares this book (without, of course, being responsible for it) with me. Lastly, to Catharine Carver, without whom I never could have revised the manuscript—much thanks for such a sensitive and intelligent appreciation of the material, and for sparing me the time. And thanks to Charlie Pratt for the picture.

For the translations, except when specified otherwise, the author is responsible.

PREFACE

Picasso designed the poster. A classical black head in profile, crowned with laurel now—perhaps by implication once with thorns—serenely announced *Présence Africaine*'s First Congress of Negro Artists and Writers, held at the Sorbonne in September, 1956. Picasso's design was created as an illustration for some poems of Aimé Césaire, the black poet from the Antilles responsible for the notion of *négritude*. The Congress made this notion public. In solemn convocation now, as well as in literary forms, *négritude* was the black man's cultural *prise de soi*. United by the historical experiences first of slavery, then of colonialism and racial prejudice, delegates from both hemispheres marked this occasion to take stock of everything about them that was non-European, everything that had been muted or mutilated under Western hegemony. Here began their proud, legitimate dialogue with the West.

All was not unanimity at the Congress. "Our peoples reject assimilation—without at the same time wishing to isolate themselves in their own cultures," said Mr. Alioune Diop, director of *Présence Africaine*, in his opening address, thus defining the particular poignancy of the French-speaking delegates' situation. (They were, of course, the majority, but what they had to say gave Negro writers in English something to think about.) What was the present state of indigenous cultures ruled and educated by France? Aimé Césaire saw chaos and ruin in Martinique, but Léopold Sédar Senghor, the future president of Senegal, saw an original African way of life still extant in the back country, and sensuously, rhythmically remembered in the hearts of assimilated poets like himself. An American delegate, Richard Wright, rather savagely refused to take African culture on faith, saying that for the most part the destruction of the old gods by the colonial powers was a good thing. James Baldwin, an American observer, "perhaps somewhat wistfully" sensed the joyous beauty of the communal art and life that Senghor was talking about, and strained to see just what it was that black and not-so-black Negroes of both hemispheres had in common now. It was not

Africa—the strikingly gowned Yoruba scholar patiently demonstrating the tonality of his language on the drum—so much as "their precarious, their unutterably painful relation to the white world." [1]

When the delegates reconvened in Rome two-and-a-half years later, Nkrumah's Congress of Independent African States had already taken place at Accra, and a revolutionary urgency was in the air. Sekou Touré of newly independent Guinea—with all the authority of his recent defiance of de Gaulle behind him—sent greetings to the artists and men of letters, urging them to subordinate their "personal egoism" (fostered by education under colonialism) to the interests of their emerging national masses. Present this time was a delegate from South Africa, Ezekiel Mphahlele, whose exile to West Africa had marked the beginnings of a cultural exchange between writers of English expression * all over the continent, and a subsequent articulation of their ideological opposition to African writers in French.

Inventories of African cultural accomplishments were taken at this 1959 congress, and concrete suggestions for the future were made. There must be decolonization and Africanization in all things. More specifically, the possibility of linguae francae indigenous to Africa should be given serious attention. The literary commission warned that the prominence of the individual in Western literature had become a snare to the African writer, and hoped that in the future a more African approach to morality, to social harmonies, and to the importance of nature, as well as a more pointed attack on the agents, institutions, and effects of colonialism, would find their way into African books.

The African novels to be discussed in these pages are themselves evidences of the patterns of cultural consciousness manifested by the delegates to the Présence Africaine congresses of 1956 and 1959. And they are here grouped in a way which should make the conditions of this growth of consciousness clear. First there are novels of the African past, to the glorious heights of which contemporary nationalists would like to see the entire continent dialectically return. (I say "dialectically" because European hegemony did intervene, and no one would wish Western influence entirely

---

* This term of art is often used, with its counterpart "African writers of French expression," to stress the voluntary nature of current African cultural affiliations.

away; it is an antithesis to be overcome.) Then there are novels about village life, in most cases, in effect, novels about the author's personal past. But the villages survive, even under the impact of social change, and so remain the basis of the new Africa—the source of social values. Novels of the cities follow. Here, traditional values fight it out with Western notions of personal advancement and material success. The heroes of these novels are preoccupied with a new African style. And finally, there are the novels in which the protagonist's inner life is the real scene—novels of psychic conflict in which traditional Africa and imperial Europe play symbolic parts. But since there are two sides to all of these stories—the objective scene in which the events take place and the author's awareness of the significance of the scene for him personally, for his Western audience, for the emerging Africa he cares about—it is only the relative intensity of the subjective passion which has thrust certain novels out of one of the more objective categories into the more uncertain territory of the enlarged self.

I have dealt in detail with some twenty-five novels, seventeen originally of French expression and eight of English. If novels from South Africa had been included, the English-French linguistic balance would have been about even, but the novels as a group would cease to be related thematically.* Modern literature in East and Central Africa is just beginning to show itself, and it is impossible at this time to predict just what directions it will take. Therefore, with two exceptions, one from Basutoland (a special British colonial case), and one from the Congo, I have stuck to West Africa, where there has always been plenty of a certain kind of freedom. And I have stuck to novels as such: Although the distinc-

* Thematic considerations aside, the forms that South African writing has taken would make it difficult to do justice to here. With the exception of many novels by the Coloured writer in exile Peter Abrahams, and a novel in the Xosa—as yet untranslated—by A. C. Jordan, most of the creative energies in South Africa have gone into autobiography, reportage, and the short story. What Ezekiel Mphahlele says about this situation rings true: "It is not easy for the oppressed African to organize himself for the writing of a novel unless he produces the kind that panders to European 'supremacy.' The short story strikes swiftly and drives home a point (and there is but one point to make now) with economy of language and time." Ezekiel Mphahlele, The African Image (London: Faber and Faber, Ltd., 1962), p. 37.

tion between a tale and a novel cannot be too rigorous when dealing with African literature, I have—with my Western bias—chosen to regard the Nigerian Tutuola as not a novelist but a storyteller; the body of his work might perhaps be dealt with in relation to the collected art tales of the Senegalese writer Birago Diop.

It may be of some interest here to note that many more West African novels have come out of Senegal, and later out of Nigeria, than out of other countries. Conditions peculiar to these territories and apparently conducive to novel-writing will be given some attention later. Also, a group of novels from two talented writers of Cameroun have a certain style of their own, which is closer to the literary products of neighboring Nigeria than of Senegal, with whom Cameroun shares a language, and once a colonial government. Furthermore, although each of the nations formerly belonging to French West Africa has produced at least one or two, Ghana, at the time of this writing, has produced no full length novel at all! All this would seem to indicate that special European influences are important, but not crucial. Without them, however, the novels I shall discuss would never have been written. Colonial conditions both supplied the tools and irritated the authors into the act of art. The end result of colonialism may be that African writers will push themselves back into the vernacular, where we will no longer be privileged to overhear them. But will it be a very different sort of novel that is written then?

Since the novels discussed here arose out of the colonial condition, and since Western literary forms have been used by the authors to describe African spiritual predicaments and ways of life, the first chapter will give some preliminary inkling of what Western rule and education have meant to the average exceptional African of this century. I have taken the liberty of magnifying the particular instance, drawing extensively on the experiences of two men who grew up under these conditions—one in the Ivory Coast and one in Nigeria—to dramatize the necessary facts. The cultural encouragement given by the European powers to their subjects is as much a part of the African picture as the ethnocentric dogmatisms which in effect attempted to take their self-esteem away. And the styles of the conquerors include the styles of their arts.

There is a sense in which colonialism provided its own homeo-pathic remedy. By offering Christianity, classroom education, and employment for cash in the cities, the colonial powers wrenched individuals from their groups and their traditional thoughts and employments, effectually isolating African individuals in ways that they had never been isolated before. European languages and the literary conventions that go with them provided a means of expressing this isolation in detail. But although the possibility of an expanded and articulated consciousness was provided by Western education, the artistic temperament is as native to Africa as to anywhere else. As Mbonu Ojike has written, "He [the artist] is the only individualistic personality in Africa. We the unartistic live communally, think nothing, and act like a crowd." [2] Western influence strengthened the artist's sense of himself, gave his works the respect given their counterparts in Europe, and seduced him into wishing to produce for himself—for fame, rather than for the group. Now, in principle the post-colonial African artist has returned to the pre-colonial view that the only worthwhile art is that related to the ordinary living experience of the community. But the artist in words, in territories where analphabetism is still an enormous social problem, must of necessity find it difficult to keep his communal vows. Furthermore, the nature of words themselves—their logic, their essentiality, their ironic relation to reality—conspires to keep the verbal artist separately talking of himself.

Also, to think that before colonialism all Africans participated in communal activities with equal intensity, or without irony, is to fall into romantic myth. But colonialism gave the dissatisfied, ambitious African who had felt himself too much the "mere spectator" a chance to move out into something else. And in school-rooms and towns and cities, surrounded by a mixture of fellow Africans from all sorts of different clans, villages, and towns, this loneliness was intensified. It was further exacerbated by the stress placed on the individual personality by Western institutions and thought, as well as by the fact that the Europeans, whose lives this lonely African was more or less invited to share, in the end excluded him from their society tactlessly or even brutally, depending on where he happened to be. Through art he could attempt to regain his lost sense of community, the African identity he had been given at birth.

An avowed European—no matter how sympathetic to Africa (and the more sympathetic the more to be suspected of an archly romantic, neocolonialist point of view)—cannot, according to the dictates of the delegates of the Second Congress of Negro Writers and Artists, regard with dismay the resemblance of the new African novels to novels anywhere else. Quite the contrary! Discontented with our own culture perhaps, we have had our own brief *période nègre*. Have we found what Picasso found? That putting on a contemporary African mask is not such a difficult thing for a European to do—that it means no dizzying loss of self, no false, cosmetic *négritude?* For through those hollow, ridged eyes, ringed with intricate incisions, one simply gets a fresh look at it all—the same old human life again, in a clearer style.

Cultural difference, discrimination, and political tyranny: these in Africa have taken the place of the snobberies and class distinctions through which European novels moved at their genesis. But the characters remain the same. The opportunist, the rogue of the cities, is present in the African novels too. He tries, as he has always tried, to beat the system. The romantic hero is also here, his heightened sensitivity and divided consciousness pulling him into lethargy, wild humor, tragedy, or strenuous communal activity, as they have always pulled him. The African environment and the colonial situation are rather new to the novel. The perennial class struggle has been here transposed into a struggle between white conqueror and colored subject, between the technologically superior European and the ambitious African of limited opportunity and unlimited *élan*. The perennial struggle for personal maturity projected into this colonial framework comes out again with Europe as the father, traditional Africa the mother, and modern Africa the son. Of this scene, and of this struggle for the re-establishment of human dignity in the tropical climate from which it was so rudely torn, the modern African novel boldly speaks.

Notes

1. For a complete account of this congress see *Présence Africaine*, Nos. 8–10 (June–November 1956). For brilliant impressions of it by an American observer see James Baldwin, *Nobody Knows My Name*, Ch. 2, "Princes and Powers" (New York: Delta Books, Dell Publishing Co., 1962).

2. Mbonu Ojike, *My Africa* (New York: The John Day Company, 1946), p. 202.

TABLE
OF CONTENTS

THIS AFRICA

I THE STYLES OF THE CONQUERORS

"We are not in the same situation as our ancestors ... there has been the colonial fact."—SENGHOR

The new African novels, like the new African states, are the results of a brief but intensive imposition of European authority and ideology on Africa. The briefness of this experience should not be ignored, nor should the intensity. Strictly speaking, the colonial situation in most African territories lasted only about sixty years. But colonial rule so altered the lives of the new African elites who were able to take advantage of its "possibilities" that their novels often give the impression that there were generations of it.

Part of this sense of remoteness—this yearning way back before the Europeans ever came—can be attributed to complicated personal myths of separation from home and traditional culture; but by no means is all of this hyperbole based on fantasy. The roots of anger against Europeans go deep into the history of the slave trade.*' Against four centuries of depopulation, degradation, and demoralization of African societies, the brief span of outright occupation, where it has been that brief, may even be seen to have had some redeeming features. In *The Mind of Africa*,[1] the Ghanaian W. E. Abraham, hardly a neo-imperialist spokesman, gives rather forthright credit to Britain for stopping the slave trade (which Hawkins under Queen Elizabeth I all but began), for improving conditions of health and communication, and for introducing the Western type of school.

* Contrary to a misconception which persists to this day, the slave trade was not an aspect of traditional African life, although various forms of enslavement were. Nor was it indigenous to Europe, although absolute property rights and the wholesale extraction of and trade in "raw materials" from "underdeveloped areas" are indigenous European patterns.

After the Conference of Berlin (1884–85, with Bismarck "honest broker" again) * set the ground rules for the late nineteenth century scramble for African territory, Britain and France went ahead until each ultimately became responsible for governing about 4 million square miles of continent. The presumptiveness of this task staggers the imagination. The arrogance, the ignorance, the incompetence, and the injustice with which these two powers governed is—despite the schools and the technology they fostered—responsible for bitter African feelings today. The styles of colonial administration established in West African territories by the British and the French at the turn of the century are important determinants of the answering nationalist movements—a part of whose literature, from one point of view, the new African novels certainly are.

The colonial situation did not begin with district officers, however. It began with the missionaries. After the slaver's whip, the Bible was brought to Africa, making this Europe's and Africa's first contact with each other's souls. But that the gun, the dollar, and the desk lurked in the bushes became to the African converts quite clear, and these things came to compromise the position of the missionary, although they did not entirely destroy his influence. Furthermore, although it was through the missionary that the African first became acquainted with ethnocentricity and racial prejudice, with the duplicity of the distinction between European words and deeds, Christianity's message remained an impressive one.

With the double-dealing of those hardy commercial agents, the

* European contacts along the coast of Africa, dating from the fifteenth century, were continued and expanded even after the abolition of the slave trade at the beginning of the nineteenth century. But it was not until the 1880's that the real race to the interior began. Why it should have begun at all, especially then, is still fascinating food for speculation. The specters of the great European explorers and of the greedy and yet supposedly "selfless" fools like Livingston haunt Western schoolbooks still, just as Leopold's ghost haunts Vachel Lindsay's much anthologized Congo. (For a series of "adult" economic arguments, for discussion of the white man's burden and the imperialist mystique which gained popular domestic support for the scramble, see The "New Imperialism," Harrison Wright, ed. [Boston: D. C. Heath & Co., 1962].) The immediate reason for calling the Conference at Berlin was to attempt to make order out of the chaos which Leopold's independent International Congo Association, formed with bold Stanley in 1878, was causing.

traders of the seventeenth and eighteenth centuries who paddled up not easily navigable African streams, realistic Africans had long been familiar. (To turn the other cheek to a thief only means more thievery in traditional Africa—this aspect of Christianity has always seemed nonsensical there.) But the early European men of commerce were not bigoted; they had, after all, to make deals, to get along. They were interested in and sometimes horrified by "native" customs, but on the whole they were rather impressed. They never were indifferent. The missionaries of the nineteenth century and after both had and gave a far different impression. In *The Lonely African*, Colin Turnbull presents a remarkable series of depositions—that of fourteen-year-old Antoine of Stanleyville, for example, baptized and a mission employee:

> I have seen the reverend fathers stub their cigars out in the food left on their plates so we shall not be able to eat it or take it home. They are a heartless people and think only of themselves. I shall never be a Christian. . . . When Sunday comes, go to Mass in the cathedral. There it is, right above us, looking across the river. You may find a few white men there, standing all by themselves. . . . [African services were separate because, as a priest told Turnbull, "Of course we don't believe in segregation, but Africans smell."] It is a lie, the whole thing. There is not a thing that they preach with their mouths and do with their bodies. Their whole life is a lie.[2]

Most missionaries to the Africans, if they did not fear and despise their pupils in this crass sense, did nonetheless refuse to regard them as fully human until they had abandoned their "frightful" or even "disgusting" heathen beliefs. Most converts, however, secretly retained these at some level of consciousness as convictions to be reasserted in times of stress, as world views to be consciously—and occasionally somewhat ironically—cultivated later as a matter of nationalist principle. For Christianity—although the missionaries at the time did not realize this—was an additive rather than a revolutionary spiritual influence in Africa. African societies, as the West has gradually been discovering, are essentially religious societies and to these Christianity meant, as W. E. Abraham has said, an "enrichment." This incremental tendency in African religious life has been discussed by the Reverend Placide Tempels under the ontological rubric Force—spiritual energy of which the white man, with his technological mastery over nature, apparently had the lion's share.[3] But without taking any speculative risks of this sort, one can simply state that most aspects of Christianity were already by analogy familiar to African converts. The rites and moral concerns of the Old Testament were hospitably received by imaginations in which there were already lively precedents for these. The message of brotherhood in the Gospels is after all a universal— and most emphatically an African—hope. Even Western religious music, from Methodist soul-rousers to Catholic polyphony, was received with as much enthusiasm in the African village as African rhythms have been received in our own towns.

The missionaries offered alphabetism partly as an inducement, partly as a necessary preliminary, to developing a Christian understanding of the Word. Schoolboys took a certain amount of religious instruction—and even a certain amount of abuse—in exchange for this convenient means of personal advancement. The lasting effects of the schooling cannot be denied. In most British territories up until after the second world war, almost all schooling was in mission hands. In Ghana, four-fifths of all approved primary and middle schools were still operated by missionary organizations in 1962. In French territories, the traditional hostility between church and state did not apply. "The administration conceived of a French missionary as a sort of colonial agent without pay. It was taken for granted that he would combine Christian teaching with national propaganda."[4] In 1962, even in such a wildly anticlerical state as the Ivory Coast, one-third of primary education remained in mission hands.*

But unlike Islam, which has always fit into traditional African communities without attempting to change their social structures, Christianity does not promise to be of any real institutional or ideological significance in free Africa. The Catholics have latterly

---

* In South Africa certain mission schools provided a decent education for Africans despite the nationalists. One by one, however, they were forced to close down. The most famous of these was St. Peter's School in Rosettenville, which fell victim to the notorious Bantu Education Act in 1956. Both Ezekiel Mphahlele and Peter Abrahams, the writers, attended it. See Mphahlele's *Down Second Avenue* (London: Faber and Faber, Ltd., 1959) and Abraham's *Tell Freedom* (New York: Alfred A. Knopf, Inc., 1961) for accounts of what this education meant to them.

tried to retain their influence by Africanizing Christian ritual to include dancing and drums, by synthesizing traditional dirges and the Western mass, by establishing a sort of halfway covenant with polygamous converts, and by canonizing African saints. African Protestants, on the other hand, have tended to form separatist churches and sects. The Catholic approach is traditional; it is only unfortunate from their point of view that memoranda like that issuing from the Holy City in 1962 with the protasis "Given that the African personality exists. . . ." were not conceived earlier. But the Catholic approach is also a corollary of the French pattern of a unified rule with a good deal of official cultural interest in Africa. The Protestant pattern in Africa, also traditional in its dissent, is appropriately supportive of group expression as the legacy of British "indirect rule."

How Christianity actually came to an African village, its effects on the minds and customs of the inhabitants, has been beautifully documented by Mbonu Ojike in his autobiography, *My Africa*. Akeme is an Ibo village in the town of Ndizuogu, formerly of Owere district in Southeastern Nigeria. In 1842, the first missionary was admitted into Iboland; by 1857, the faith had reached the famous market city of Onitsha, and in 1906 it attained Ojike's district. Four years later the following incident took place: The king of the town of Ndizuogu had a younger brother, Akweke, a man in his thirties who was suddenly struck blind. Determined efforts by African doctors failed to restore his sight. The king had heard of a hospital about thirty miles away, where all manner of diseases had been cured by a strange group called the Church Missionary Society. Eight strong men volunteered to carry Akweke to this hospital on their heads.

Akweke remained in the hospital for two years, during which time he attended chapel every day according to rule, and came to believe that Jesus Christ would hear his prayers and restore his sight. In 1912, he opened his eyes and saw, but not very well. He began to learn the Ibo alphabet, nevertheless, and when a pair of glasses was prescribed he went on to read the Bible and to write letters home.* Upon his return, some praised the Ibo god Chineke, and heaped offerings before Akweke the living miracle; but Akweke, now "Abraham," the future patriarch of his people,

* According to the New York specialist, Dr. Anthony Donn, it is statistically probable that Akweke was suffering from Keratitis, common in that area at the time. Also he was myopic, hence the glasses.

wanted Christianity to come to his town. By 1913, the Church Missionary Society, by Abraham's brother's leave, had established a station at Ndizuogu.

There had been neither churches nor schools in Iboland since the medieval Arab invasion, and the people had forgotten how to read and write. The Christian invaders felt justified, therefore, in raining down contempt on the villagers for their atrociously ignorant pagan way of life. Ojike's elder brother, Abanogu, became the first convert from Akweke Village, and Abraham of the new vision ejected two of his three wives. But the elders of the town did not let the revolutionary movement go unchecked:

> My father called Abanogu to fetch the big jar filled with snuff. Abanogu did not appear.
> "He's gone to school," I reminded him.
> "You see?" said my father to Okoli Onugo. "Since the white man came to this country, no son is a son any more."
> My father, gnashing his teeth to ease off his rage, ordered me: "Go and call Ojii."
> "Father, Ojii went to school along with Abanogu." [5]

When the boys returned in the evening, their father seized their slates and pencils, flogged them, and ordered them put into his dungeon. (He was a powerful man whose compound housed one hundred souls.) The boys were starved for a day (after which their mother secretly brought them a meal at midnight). The next day they were brought to court, questioned, and flogged. But when nothing could make them change their minds, teachers and converts from other villages intervened and a compromise was reached. They could go to school, but when the Sabbath fell on their father's workday, they must work nonetheless—on the day after or on the day before. And they were forbidden to take their third brother, Ojike, to the school.

The Christian community so increased in size that ecclesiastical headquarters in Onitsha sent a specialized African teacher to the town. He was small of stature but he possessed great courage and a dozen English words, which, being more than anyone else knew, gained him enormous prestige. One day, while school was in session, the "long *juju*" procession passed by and stopped to drum at the window while the masqueraders danced energetically outside. Unable to concentrate his class on their lesson, the African teacher ordered the pupils to go out and destroy the procession.

The elders of the town had the teacher and such arch criminals as Abraham and Abanogu arrested. The church house was fired, as was the teacher's. But starvation and physical punishment again could not make the faithful give in, so all parties were taken to court. A white missionary from ecclesiastical headquarters was present at the trial. The judgment given was as follows: The non-Christians were guilty of deliberate nuisance. They were told to repair their costumes and in the future to dance wherever they wished, except on church premises. The Christians were told to rebuild their houses and to refrain in the future from interfering with pagan rites. The visiting white missionary then paid a visit to Ojike's father at the insistence of Abanogu. "Why do you persecute Christians?" asked the missionary. The father pointed to a scar on his forehead. "In 1902 your white soldiers attacked us on our own soil. I led our army against the invaders." (Many villagers had been killed or wounded in this skirmish.) A few years later the soldiers had attacked again. (This was known as the pacification of the tribes of the lower Niger.) "But we are not like those who fought you," said the missionary, "we are your friends. . . . We are going to teach your children many good things." "What things?" Bridge-building, road-building, foreign tongues, and the curing of diseases was the reply.

One year later, the body of the faithful was large enough to attempt a "trial of strength." One Saturday morning, when only children and old people were about, Christians went to the sacred river Anamiri to fish. A girl come down to fill her pitcher reported the river dammed and polluted. On the war drum *iroko*, her ancient father telegraphed the news to the men in the fields, who hastily armed themselves and flew to defend their holy stream. They beat up the Christians and restored the Anamiri to its course. This time, however, there was no hearing. Instead, on the following Sunday, the Christians preached before the king. After the hymn-singing, Abraham-Akweke told the story of St. Stephen, the first Christian martyr, and Abanogu told the story of Saul, who, struck blind on the road to Damascus, repented of having persecuted Christians. "From that day onward," Ojike reports in 1946, "relations between the two faiths have been fairly satisfactory."

It began to be fashionable in Akweke to be a convert, to wear new fashions, take a foreign name, marry one wife, and rest on the seventh day. By 1918, two years after the trial of strength, Ndizuogu had become the center of a newly formed ecclesiastical and political district, consisting of all churches radiating from Abraham's home town. (In 1946, there were 300 churches for a population of over a half million.) But in 1918, Ojike's father was seventy-two years old, and with the arrival of the Pax Britannica his career as an agent supplying mercenary troops to warring parties had been cut short. The "long *juju*," the special divining organization founded by his Ado people, had by British command ceased to operate, except in a ceremonial way. His large, elaborate compound, walled two feet thick along a mile perimeter, had begun to fall into ruins before his very eyes. Most of his sons had already become ardent Christians * and "I," Ojike says, "the only reincarnation of his brother killed in war, I also had gone to school."

Christianity came slightly earlier to the town of Ikenne in Yorubaland, where Chief Obafemi Awolowo, a contemporary of Ojike's, grew up. Awo tells in his autobiography of how his father's (his father was already a Christian) wedding to his mother (the devotee of a river god) was postponed by events following upon a "trial of strength" like the one described above. In this case the Christians fished in the river Uren and the retaliating Yorubas, stronger than the resident police, had to be put down by imported British troops. (The first decade of the twentieth century in Nigeria was not only a time of missionary consolidation. It was the decade of British force.)

II.

France, in the middle of the nineteenth century, was the first European power to establish a government in the interior of West Africa. Interest in the small agricultural colony of Senegal which had dwindled after the abolition of the slave trade was

* The only son who did not become a Christian was his father's eldest. He died of a heart attack in 1926, and his father died shortly after, in his eighty-fourth year.

revived under Napoleon III, *pour la gloire.* The Emperor deliberately appointed a vigorous governor for the colony—General Louis Faidherbe, later known as "power and powder" Faidherbe because of the colonial policy he announced upon his arrival in 1854.

The situation Faidherbe found in Senegal called for exactly the qualities he possessed. The Toucouleurs to the east of the colony, led by El Hadj Omar, were in the process of expanding into the Senegal and Niger valleys. Farther south, the Mandingoes under Samory were pressing towards the Gambia basin. And in so doing, both groups were harassing the Wolofs, upon whom the French traditionally depended for trade, for peanut oil, and for cotton. Faidherbe mobilized the famous Senegalese *tirailleurs* to drive El Hadj Omar and Samory back. But these two heroes had no intention of keeping to fixed frontiers, nor was Faidherbe interested in pursuing them through territory 2,000 miles deep. He devoted himself henceforth to the management of the colony, the reorganization of which at this time provided a model for more recent, comprehensive, French administrative schemes.

The leaders of the Third Republic, however, anxious to expand the commerce, territory, and prestige of a nation humiliated by her defeat in the Franco-Prussian war, decided that the Mandingoes and the Toucouleurs must be defeated at all costs. It took nineteen years to do it, but in the end the Western Sudan had become French. In 1904, the separate military jurisdictions then established in West Africa were united in a centralized administrative system designed to exploit these territories by tying them as closely as possible to France.

From 1904 until the abrupt and final devolution of authority to the Africans half a century later, eight territories (Senegal, Mauretania, Guinea, Sudan, Dahomey, Niger, Ivory Coast, and Upper Volta) were governed directly from Dakar. These territories were each in turn divided into as many as twenty *cercles,* like the *départments* in the mother country, which purposely cut across tribal lines. The "wheel" system of civil service, instituted in 1924, in which no administrator could serve in the same colony for two terms running, reflected the French passion for standardization. In two senses, this discouraged African loyalties of any kind: No civil servant could become so knowledgeable about a territory that he would tend to promote its interests, and similarly, no African could develop regional loyalties.* The *cercles* were to be considered interchangeable parts. Since the territories to be ruled amounted to fifteen times the area of the mother country, chiefs had to be used by the French to collect taxes and to perform other minor administrative functions. But local potentates were required to pass examinations in the French language before they could be officially appointed to take charge of their own people.

At the time of the political formation of the A.O.F., a system of instruction was planned to form a West African elite, capable of assuming minor administrative and managerial positions. A director general of education was appointed, a resident of Dakar, to oversee a program that was to be open, on an equal basis, to talented youths of all races. Certain ground rules were laid down for mission schools to follow in primary education; governmental secondary schools were to be established gradually on a regional basis for those few who proved able to qualify. All instruction offered—at any level—was to be the equivalent of metropolitan instruction, and the language of instruction was to be uniformly French. At the apex of the system was the unique normal school William Ponty, in Dakar, and beyond that lay schools and faculties in Paris, with scholarships for the most highly "evolved" Africans, who at this point became, theoretically, Black Frenchmen—with honors, so to speak.

The status of the populations of this "Greater France" was a vexing question. In what sense could those ruled arbitrarily be considered "French"? Although the Second Empire and the Third Republic inherited the revolutionary notion (announced 16 *Pluviôse*, Year II) that "all men, without distinction of colour, domiciled in French colonies, are French citizens and enjoy the rights assured by the constitution," it was fortunate for later, less egalitarian governments that this enthusiastic bit of doctrine was never really implemented in West Africa. Nevertheless, two Senegalese cities, St. Louis and Gorée, had a history of "citizenship" on a par with French citizenship—of municipal freedom which it was impossible to deny for long to the "mixed" popula-

* This latter situation created tremendous minority problems—in the Ivory Coast, for example, into which neighboring Dahomeans and Togolanders flocked for jobs. These "aliens" were actually preferred by the colonial administration as "buffers."

tions there. Thus under the Third Republic, rights which Faidherbe in effect had taken away were once again restored, and expanded during the first decade of the twentieth century to apply to the newer mixed cities of Rufisque and Dakar.

This was 1914. Blaise Diagne was the first Black African to be elected to the French parliament as a representative of the four Senegalese communes of *pleines exercise*. Also the first of his people to achieve ministerial rank, he became undersecretary for the colonies in 1919, and president of the first Pan African Congress the same year. Straddling these apparently contradictory offices, he proclaimed, "We French natives wish to remain French, since France has given us every liberty." [6] France had given him and those like him these liberties, but the masses of French Africa were still administratively classified as *sujets*.

As *sujets*, the masses were subject to all the abuses of the *ancien régime*—all too easily revived in Africa on a grand scale.* These were the forced labor system (*corvée*), peremptory administrative justice (especially for suspected political crimes—the *indigénat*), and outrageous punishments instantly meted out to those who refused to fight for France (the "grand reservoir" theory of universal military conscription), or to labor for her, or to pay onerous taxes. African villagers ruled according to these institutions were often caught between the necessity of serving on the roads during the rainy season and the equally pressing necessity of working their fields during the same season to raise cash crops for taxes or subsistence. A breach of any of these obligations meant ruin. Famine, flight, depopulation, and degra-

---

* They were revived by men whose imperious and sadistic impulses met with little resistance in these African vasts. Robert Delavignette (in 1950 Directeur des Affaires Politiques and Ministère de la France d'outre mer) tells the story of a young cavalry officer, De la Tour Saint-Ygest, who left a republican France he abhorred to destroy the feudal power of the Tuareg, "whose principles and sentiments he cherished," and of a Freemason and member of the Radical Socialist Party who, as a governor in Africa, became "fanatically attached to old-style hierarchy, using autocratic methods to lead the natives along the path of progress." R. Delavignette, *Freedom and Authority in West Africa* (1950), quoted in Immanuel Wallerstein, "The Search for National Identity in West Africa," *Présence Africaine*, XXXIV–XXXV (December, 1960–March, 1961), 21 (English edition).

dation were the worst results of such a colonial scheme. "There is no doubt," wrote one of the irate observers of the thirties,

> that the Negroes of French West Africa are a dispirited, miserable and resentful people, who can now only be ruled by fear. It is not merely the colonial policy which has brought them to this state, but the brutal and abusive manner in which the French treat them on nearly every occasion, and the systematic way in which they are cheated in every transaction, which the cheaters quite erroneously believe their simplicity prevents them from realizing.[7]

The *sujets* could, of course, become naturalized French citizens. However, the fact that by 1921, for example, only 308 inhabitants of the Ivory Coast and seventeen of the Upper Volta had desired or managed to acquire this liberating privilege is not so surprising when one considers what it entailed. Becoming a citizen meant renouncing one's customary legal status, one's land usufruct, one's extra wives; it meant giving every evidence—tonsorial and linguistic—that one had adopted a European way of life. And yet only in Senegal (where indeed only a minority for religious reasons were willing to take advantage of them) were there educational facilities in any way consonant with the doctrine of assimilation and the mechanics of citizenship.

Under such a centralized system, effective pressures for responsible government could come only from the top. And since it was possible under the French system for certain West Indians (who never lost the "citizenship" privileges secured during the revolution) and Senegalese to rise in the French civil service or to sit as representatives of their people in the French parliament, the political future of French Africa depended somewhat paradoxically upon a small Frenchified elite who would choose, in the system's despite, to put ethnic claims above the interests of an extended metropolitan France. Such a man was Felix Eboué, a remarkable French Guianese scholar and civil servant, who, having served successively as secretary-general of Martinique and as governor of the French Sudan, of Guadeloupe, and the Chad—was appointed governor general of French Equatorial Africa in 1940. From this position he was able to exert pressures for fairer treatment of the exploited peoples under his charge, as well as to advocate a complete overhauling of the Black African system.

Although organized into a centralized system (like the A.O.F.) in 1910, the original manner of occupancy of the territories comprising French Equatorial Africa made any kind of public control of abuses or positive welfare measures impossible.* Under the concessionary system adopted there at the turn of the century (with King Leopold and the British Niger Company in mind), individual entrepreneurs were given exclusive rights over vast areas for thirty years, after which they were to have direct ownership. These companies were to build the roads, extract the rubber, and maintain the peace—to facilitate which companies recruited their own private soldiers or "guards." Tax collecting was supposed to be done by government agents, but in practice the notoriously brutal company guards did this, the civil government in effect abdicating all responsibility for what went on. When individuals failed to pay the taxes, extract the proper amounts of rubber, or work at the proper times on the roads, whole villages might be removed to hostage camps by way of reprisal, and dissenters cruelly tortured or murdered, be they men, women, or children. There was no official means of redress. That the concessions were not renewed in 1927 is due in large part to the strenuous efforts of André Gide as publicist in behalf of the oppressed equatorial African.

The Brazzaville conference of 1944 was Eboué's personal achievement.† In greeting this postwar meeting of governors of all the French colonies de Gaulle's colonial commissioner René Pleven said:

> In greater France there are no people to liberate, nor is there any racial discrimination to abolish. There are populations whom we intend to lead step by step to a more complete individuality, to political freedom, but they will know no other independence than the independence of France.[8]

Even through all this self-satisfied French static, West Africans

* As a result, even after Eboué's reforms, school attendance in regions formerly known as Chad, Gabon, Ubangui-Shari, and Middle Congo lagged way behind developments to the north and west.
† By a cruel turn of fate, Eboué died in that same year.

did get the idea that now at last there would be some changes made. They were right. In 1945, African deputies were present at the constitutional assembly in Paris—only six of them it's true, but their inclusion admitted the principle that indigenous peoples through their representatives could have some part in the forming of the institutions governing them. In 1946, the assembly passed the *Loi Lamine Guèye*,* conferring citizenship on all members of the French Union. In French West Africa, all those who toiled at forced labor quit. They were citizens now. Furthermore, although all African political parties up to that time had been associated with metropolitan blocs, at the end of 1946, encouraged by concessions already made, a number of African deputies formed their own political party. The *Rassemblement Democratique Africain* marked the first step towards independence from France, the first effort to include the African masses in an agitation for responsible rule.

Independence from France was finally achieved for Senegal by Léopold Sédar Senghor, whose contemporary political success has stemmed from a chance combination of intellectual distinction—by French or by any other standards—and the social fact of his Serer (rather than Wolof) origin. Senghor has had the loyalty of the Senegalese people because he was not born in a privileged commune, but rather in the remote fishing town of Joal. But although he began life as somewhat of an *ausländer,* his father was a prosperous merchant and Senghor himself was more than capable of the best that the French educational system had to offer. He received his *baccalaureate summa cum laude* in Dakar in 1926, and from there he received a scholarship to the Lycée Louis-le-Grand in Paris. He also attended the École Normale Supérieure and became the first African *agrégé de l'université.* A professor of French literature at the Lycée Marcellin Berthelot, with a book on Baudelaire's exoticism to his credit, Senghor was drafted into an infantry battalion of colonial troops, only to become a prisoner of war. His first book of poems, *Chants d'ombre,*

* Lamine Gueye returned from the Antilles, where he served for years as a judge, to participate in Senegalese politics. In 1945 he was elected deputy to the French parliament, and shortly afterwards mayor of Dakar as well. But the triumph of assimilation as attained in his law meant his own political decline. Times had changed; self-government rather than assimilation was now the goal. A member of Senghor's rival party unseated him in 1951.

was published the year of his election to the constituent assembly of the Fourth Republic. He has published several volumes of verse and political speculation since that time. To other Africans the French educational system was less kind.

III.

There have been two novels from the Ivory Coast on that system's victims—educational novels in the restrictive as well as in a broad sense. One of these, *Kocoumbo, l'étudiant noire,* by Aké Loba (1959), deals with an unfortunate expatriate in Paris and his various African friends. For Senghor, Paris was a productive experience. It was here, with West Indian friends, that the first discussions of those common intuitions that became *la négritude* were held. For Loba's Kocoumbo, Paris meant loneliness and self-conscious *gaucherie* in the presence of well-meaning Europeans and conceited African *evolués*—then the humiliation of sitting as a twenty-year-old in a class of twelve-year-olds at the *lycée!* His efforts to progress beyond the usual stopping place for provincial Africans—the *certificat d'études* from the district school—might be regarded as a kind of *hybris.* His father hoped he would learn how to make airplanes, and was wealthy enough to get him to Paris, but not to maintain him there. Kocoumbo himself hoped for a professional career—to be a lawyer or a doctor (of the "modern" type, like George Eliot's Lydgate)—not, however, with the idea of provincial service but because he wanted to be able to walk about at home with the new confidence of the educated, his hands behind his back with a flair. But the real Paris meant years of poverty and failure for Kocoumbo, disillusionment with the motives and conduct of his fellow African expatriates, and a paralyzing loss of self-respect. At the end of the story he must be "rescued"—ironically—by the district officer from his home town, now retired to Paris.

Bernard Dadié's *Climbié* (1956) is the story of a provincial African educated in French Africa. His successive moves up the ladder of scholastic success and the series of restrictions later placed upon his career are documentary history of the finest quality. But because of this quality *Climbié* cannot be merely combed for its evidence; the lines of the figure must also be traced, for Climbié's is a parabolic career.

One may suppose that Climbié, like the author of the novel

himself, was born about 1916 at Assinie, where the first school in the Ivory Coast was opened in 1888. When we first meet him, Climbié is being raised by his Uncle N'dabian, whose father had managed to conceal him when scholastic recruitment was going on in his day. However, N'dabian's younger brother, Assouan Koffi, was not hidden; he became educated and is now a clerk in the city. N'dabian himself now feels that Climbié ought to emulate Assouan Koffi, for "in today's world one must know how to read and write in order to be a person of consequence." Climbié's first school experience is disastrous, however, and he flees the schoolmaster's rod. N'dabian does not make him go back to this local school, but having permitted Climbié to help him on the farm for a while—an experience he hopes will "form him as a man"—the uncle takes his charge up to the government primary school at Grand Bassam. Although there are no more places, Climbié, as it turns out, is accepted, but other newcomers are turned away. The director of the school regrets the situation, but the regulations are there, "rigid barriers curtailing life and progress." He can do nothing. This European is portrayed as a sympathetic man.

Throughout this book, institutions rather than individuals are blamed, blind rules of order that squelch happiness and human variety. One of these institutions in miniature is the dread *symbole* —a little cube that a student caught speaking his mother tongue must carry in his pocket until he catches someone else in the act of committing the same sin. In the course of their tours of inspection, educational officers had found the polyglot student populations entirely too cavalier in their attitude towards the French language. This, in fact, was true everywhere, not only in the schools but in the streets, in the casernes, in the stores. For nothing is worse than hearing a language ill-spoken, that tongue "which attests to the existence of a people." [9] (Dadié ironically presents his argument from the French point of view.) Therefore, in the interests of future uniformity and as a testimonial to French national existence, African students caught speaking any African language whatsoever on school premises are forced to carry the *symbole*.

At examination time the students are gripped by the "sole obsession, to succeed." Climbié does succeed in passing his examinations for the École Primaire Supérieure at Bingerville. At this institution the students wore uniforms: khaki suits with dolman collars, a blue cap with a black visor, and white canvas shoes. But "to encourage folklorique manifestations" each Saturday was consecrated to the theatre—a spontaneous exercise.

Given the French attitude towards their language, how unjust of the authorities to permit dictation by French provincials who cannot meet the standards required of African students! As Climbié sits at Bingerville for the crucial examinations that will permit a small percentage of his peers from all the regional schools to pass on to the great federal center, to the École Normale Supérieure in Gorée, he is shocked to hear the special examiner begin: "Attenchion, je commenche . . ." The students can hardly understand what he is saying, and refuse to sit for the following examination in mathematics. But prodded by their equally competitive instructors, whose careers can be made or broken by the number of their native "successes," the students of Bingerville finally give in. But they march in protest to the governor's house afterwards. This authority (although he is the new "smiling" type of colonial administrator) refuses to annul the dictation. Luckily, Climbié just manages to pass.

After three years at Gorée, Climbié graduates and takes an office job in Dakar. Race relations seem to him more cordial in the capital. Is it because of the newly inaugurated Popular Front? Young functionaries from France talk to young Africans at night about Marx and Engels. Or is it not rather that here in Senegal's cities "the European respects the African not so much as a man but as a French citizen, that is to say subjected to the same laws"? [10] In any case, as a *sujet* who keeps this status on principle, Climbié's fancy education is wasted. For ten years he is kept to the lower ranks of the paper-pushers, with no hope of ever advancing himself. Salaries, he observes, are paid to all Africans, no matter what their jobs, in accordance with what the Europeans think any reasonable small-familied man requires—so much for food, for rent, and so on. The African wage earner is in no position to continue his inherited membership in his clan.

After the war, the thaw represented by the generous Popular Front mentality congeals into race hatred as strikes (and other progressive techniques learned from the French left) are put down and even forestalled by iron troops. Climbié decides to return to the Ivory Coast, where he becomes a journalist and agitator, urging the small farmers not to sell their crops at suicidal prices and protecting their interests against those of the

French planters and the large European commercial houses (as indeed Houphouët-Boigny did in his early years). Climbié staunchly regards himself as "unassimilatable, undigestable." The administration regards this as being "anti-French." Under the *indigénat* he is jailed under suspicion of future treason. The proud *sujet* has become an *objet* under an alien law.

Eventually Climbié is released and meets a school friend who, in a grand cynical gesture, had given up painting to become a uniformed *gendarme*. "That's interesting," says Climbié, "for some time now I have had a personal bookstall. I have been trying, most unsuccessfully to sell all my useless books." Dadié's account ends, again ironically, with a letter from an emancipated French photographer whom Climbié met as he was on the verge of leaving Dakar. The letter speaks of fraternal hopes for a peaceful world of the future in which the lion (presumably the African lion) will lie down with the (French?) lamb.

Certain purely African alternatives are given to Climbié during the story—alternative approaches to existence that are counterpointed to the theme of successful action according to European standards, bureaucratic or left-wing. The first, the old superstitious way, is figured forth in the story of his mother, whom we never meet because Climbié never does. He is truly one of the uprooted; weaning for him meant a more drastic separation from home than in most cases. Since three of Climbié's mother's previous children had died of a mysterious malady at the age of four years, she insists that Climbié never be permitted to cross her threshold again. She is afraid that somehow she is the cause of the malady, although rumor has it that her mother-in-law is responsible, through a notorious involvement with certain sorcerers. Nevertheless, Climbié hopes someday to be able to support his mother. Presumably he never is.

In this book, the type of the moral man in an immoral society is represented by Climbié's second uncle, Assouan Koffi, the functionary who assumes responsibility for him when Uncle N'dabian dies. Assouan Koffi appears at a crucial point early in Climbié's school career to show his nephew pictures of Harlem riots in a certain book which, he makes quite clear, is forbidden reading for Africans. Were they caught looking at these pictures they would be arrested at once. Climbié is now aware that the struggle for human rights is a world-wide phenomenon, that cruelty of white to black is not limited to Africa, and that men are everywhere the same. When Climbié visits this uncle while on vacation from school, he finds that Assouan Koffi has made a heroic effort to return to the soil: We have been led up a false path, he says. The European, with his whip, seemed terrifying out in the bush. It became our ambition to placate him by serving him as if he were an evil djinn. To plant, to submit ourselves to *nature* began to seem savage to us. We ran to the cities to escape head taxes and forced labor, yes, but we also ran to escape those very hardships of the soil that bring salvation. "Work! and after work independence, my child. Serve nobody else, this ought to be the motto of your generation."

Dadié's book is filled with significant encounters like this one, with carefully illuminated scenes like that of the inarticulate *dictée*. What holds *Climbié* together is a passionate preoccupation with justice. And it is fascinating to observe to what extent a belief, or concern, can actually provide a sort of emotional structure for a series of cultural documentations. Discreet events are suddenly *seen*—as they must have been first consciously or unconsciously selected—as variations on a common theme. For example, in the early pages dealing with Climbié's childhood a folk tale is told him. This is to be expected; the flavor of African youth could hardly be had without it. But the story told is really relevant to moral concerns of the maturing hero, and this is not always the case in accounts of African childhoods. The story is that famous enigma dealing with God the Creator, Sickness, and Death. Which is the more just? God made creatures of varied complexions, talents, and infirmities. Sickness attacks various people in various cruel ways. Is not Death, then, the most just? (The Creator allowed to each tribe its proper tongue with which to tell itself. French, the great equalizer, was imposed in the classroom. Which is the more just? French is Death.)

European scholars have claimed that Africans have no sense of history, but for Africans to have a sense of history in the Western sense means to have a sense of injustice. As a student, Climbié haunts the caves where slaves were once detained awaiting shipment from the island of Gorée. "No longer the little speck of earth it seemed to him on his arrival, [it was] an island bursting with history. . . . Real men were there in the sweating obscurity of the cells. One feared their escape." The long, proud, tumultuous narratives of France had always impressed Climbié as a schoolboy. In these caves, he realizes, is where the documentary history of Africa begins—in servitude. Gorée, like Africa itself, is still a depot: the land's richness being shipped out, worthless consumer goods dumped in. "And full of sadness he continued his walk, wondering if men would ever give man his proper value." [11]

IV.

The British occupation of West African territories, unlike the French, was a gradual process in which the government followed the lead taken by private companies. Upon the conclusion of the slave trade, initiative was allowed and taken by enterprising individuals or groups of men who often began their operations in West Africa by converting to legitimate commercial purposes of their own the permanent forts or trading stations that British slavers had established. These expanding interests, in the nineteenth century limited to coastal areas, eventually had to be protected, and although British troops were often called upon to "pacify" tribes in the interior, these lands were not occupied until expansion on the part of other European powers forced Britain's hand.*

In 1914, the various pacified territories comprising present-day Nigeria were grouped together in a rather loosely organized federation under governor general Lord Frederick Lugard. The governor general was a professional soldier, well-seasoned in imperial affairs, who espoused the white man's burden as the Dual Mandate: that what was good for Britain was also good for colonized peoples who, under British aegis and in a traditional setting, should with patience learn how to govern themselves. Although Lugard is known as the "father of indirect rule," actually the practice existed before the name was coined to express official policy. It existed in missionary and steamship company negotia-

* Sierra Leone, the first British colony in West Africa, is a rather special case. Originally settled by freed slaves under private British auspices in 1787, this territory was early (in 1808) annexed as a colony because of certain difficulties not foreseen by the humanitarians who thought up the scheme: armed resistance by indigenous tribes, lack of provisions in customary law for the sale of lands to foreigners (Africans or not), even if the foreigners had been wanted there, and the miserable farming conditions in this bit of rain forest—conditions which could hardly have been alleviated by a secure Creole title to the lands.

tions with dynastic rulers in the Uganda area, where Lugard played his earliest African part, and before that in the quasi-political operations of commercial agents in West Africa like Sir George Taubman Goldie, of Royal Niger Company fame. As early as 1879, Goldie gave what amounts to a definition of this policy in advice to his company officers: "If the welfare of the native races is to be considered, if dangerous revolts are to be obviated, the general policy of ruling on African principles, through native rulers, must be followed for the present." [12]

Government administrators, like the entrepreneurs who went before them, naturally tended to work with indigenous institutions as they found them. This is not to say that they left them alone. They "cleaned them up," secured the alliance of those elements tending to support British interests, and upon "loyal" chiefs devolved the partial authority which would mean the eventual ruin of the traditional forms they had more or less intended to preserve. The chiefs (some of whom were not even native to the regions to which they were appointed) were no longer subject to that system of popular checks and balances which African elders had developed through the ages. The system worked pretty well in the northern provinces, to which it was originally designed to apply, but long-established social patterns among the southern Nigerian peoples provided a real challenge to administrative officers there.[13] These independent and enterprising villagers felt, not without justice, that if the fact of their rule (behind the pseudo-chiefs) was British, the forms of their rule should be British also— that they should be responsible and self-governing, *mutatis mutandis*, as they were before the British intervened. They saw in the evolution of municipal democracy in Lagos something of what could be in store for them.* The emancipated business and

* The inhabitants of the "mixed" coastal colonies were always supposed to have some say in their own political affairs. Thus the human realities behind "colonial self-government" in Lagos, Accra, and Freetown were the same as those entailing "citizenship" and communal rights in St. Louis, Rufisque, Gorée, and Dakar. But the rationale was different, and so were the institutions through which white, mulatto, and black bourgeois freedoms were to be expressed. At first it was difficult for middle-class Africans of Lagos and Accra to persuade the British that they were *bona fide* inhabitants of these colonies, and then it was difficult for both parties to determine how much say they should have. The tribal powers of the Gold Coast were represented by a well-organized pressure group

professional classes of Lagos, in turn, saw in India's Congress the kind of party organization and political program that could be made to appeal to cherished British notions of self-determination and fair play.

The British gradually acceded to these pressures, as they had originally responded to shows of real strength from the doughty northern emirs. Institutionalized British ideas of the Dominion and then the Commonwealth (old memories of America and fresh memories of India) prepared the way for independence in West Africa. Already, by 1940, the British could foresee this independence—after about sixty years! It took a younger generation of shrewd West African politicians to organize those mass political parties (according to techniques observed in the United States) which "forced the pace," as the British would say.

The British approach to education in Africa was consistent with their bias in other spheres. They too, like the French, needed semiskilled laborers, domestic servants, men of God, primary teachers, and clerks, but the notion of a culturally assimilated Black Englishman (although in practice to be found, especially in medicine and the law) would inspire such exclamations of horror as "Oh those impertinent natives, those cheeky kaffirs." * No official policy was set in the early days, although there were schools. The belated conclusion of the Calcutta University Commission in 1919 that "Only through the wise use of the mother tongue can clearness of thought, independence of judgment, and sense of responsibility be developed at the start," [14] set an early precedent for the official use of the vernacular in West Africa. Unofficially, of course, English-speaking Protestant missionaries in Africa had already successfully reduced many, many African languages to writing, compiled dictionaries and testaments in the vernacular, and taught.

In 1925, a committee finally appointed by the secretary of state for the colonies recommended specifically that in West Africa

---

which managed to see to it that the British were encouraged in their natural predilection for appointing chiefs as agents of a theoretically "representative" government. In the 1920's, Africans in Lagos and Accra were elected directly to legislative councils which, although "advisory only" in these days, evolved in the 1950's into the wholly responsible legislatures of self-governing states.

* This, with a different cadence, is Ezekiel Mphahlele's phrase.

Education should be adapted to the mentality, aptitudes, occupations and traditions of the various peoples, conserving as far as possible all sound and healthy elements in the fabric of African social life and adapting them where necessary to changed circumstances and progressive ideas in the interests of national growth and evolution. . . .

Every effort should be made to improve what is sound in indigenous tradition in the important field of religion and character training.[15]

This doctrine, as implemented, would mean fewer good schools and many more bad ones in British than in French West Africa. This has had many interesting social consequences in Nigeria. About the scarcity of opportunities for secondary and then for higher education the Nigerians could do very little, but they could and did resist all British efforts to debase the currency of certificates awarded those fortunate enough to qualify at these levels. For example, a proposal in 1929 to introduce a special Nigerian School Certificate (apart from the regular Oxford and Cambridge certificates) had to be dropped because of heated and remarkably well-organized nationalist opposition. In 1934, the administration inaugurated an institution known as Yaba Higher College which, unaffiliated with any British university, would issue its own diplomas to those who, in turn, were expected to occupy posts subordinate to those filled by holders of regular British degrees! Naturally this scheme had little appeal, and it too was dropped. The Lagos Youth Movement, which later became the Nigerian Youth Movement, and still later, under Awo's leadership, the political party of Western Nigeria (The Action Party), was originally formed to protest against these "progressive" educational gestures. They were felt as insults then, but later Africanization of Nigerian education has led to proposals similar to these.

The notorious proliferation of "hedge schools" on the elementary level, in which semiliterate products of the British educational system in West Africa taught illiterates, led British reformers to seek technical training rather than a pseudo-liberal education for the masses. Such training would bring "capabilities" more into line with "national growth and evolution." The needs of developing Nigeria have created the same demand. But efforts to reform the old colonial curricula, not only by substituting technical training for liberal subjects, but by Africanizing subject matter and exams as well, are being resisted by conservatives for the same reasons that radicals once resisted them. There still exists what is called an "examination mania" in Nigeria, a desire to be defined as a person by the possession of a Standard Six, which is a carryover of their scarcity in British times. Furthermore, the highly educated few in Nigeria tend to be scornful (as they are not in formerly French territories) of politics and trade. This snobbery is the legacy of a policy whose sound aspects were discounted because of the condescension on which they were based. Nevertheless, the decentralized nature of the school system in English-speaking territories was psychically advantageous to the young. And even the moral training stressed by the British has its forward-looking as well as its paternalistic side. The policy of meeting local students halfway—although never effectually carried out—is evidence of a fundamental bias towards self-government which presupposes effective government of the self. The self was governed effectually under the old African communal system, but as the novelist Chinua Achebe points out in *No Longer at Ease*, once ties to the clan and village broke under the stress of colonial occupation and colonial opportunity, the rigors of "imported" standards could only, with rather messy consequences, be forgot.

What then, under the British system, was it like for a contemporary of Climbié's to go to school? In 1918, the Nigerian Ojike began school. (Before this time, as mentioned before, his eldest brother Abanogu had wished to take him along; but his father, always opposed to the Christian influence, had insisted that he accompany him to court as a page.) The worldwide flu epidemic hit Nigeria in that year. Abanogu's best friend died and was given the town's first Christian funeral. The devoteés of Chineke wept according to tradition, but the converts rejoiced in the dead man's salvation. "I was so impressed by what I saw," says Ojike, "that I determined to go to church and school regularly." (Although he adopted the European way of doing things, it was not until the third grade that Ojike actually saw a white couple. On a choir tour eighteen miles from Akweke he met Bishop [Lord] Herbert Tugwell and Lady Tugwell. He was impressed by the length as by the sharpness of the noses of this aged and saintly pair.)

The first school Ojike attended was a one-room house, grass-roofed, with walls and floor of red mud, adobe benches, and an imported table for the teacher's use. This building doubled as a church on Sundays. The fees then ranged from thirty-six cents to two dollars, although when Abanogu had begun school tuition as well as supplies were free, in order to attract as many pupils as possible. Ojike supplemented the money Abanogu gave him by fishing, trapping, and tapping and nutting palms.

By the time Ojike graduated from infant to primary classes, the school building had been moved and expanded into a T-shaped structure, still with grass roof and mud walls, but now furnished with modern desks and benches to accommodate three hundred pupils. It had become a "central school." The church house, now separate, had been built with a cement floor and a corrugated iron roof. A bell, rather than drums, summoned the pupils of the 1920's, and the teachers, to distinguish themselves from the pupils, now dressed "tip top"—suits, ties, shoes and sometimes stockings, and always a whip in hand.

In 1922 Ojike was baptized, assuming the European name of "Robinson," after his favorite fictional hero from abroad. He bore that name until the Nigerian nationalist fervor of the thirties "revealed to me how utterly ridiculous it all was," when he returned to the name his father had given him, Mbonu, which means "actions speak louder than words." Although imparted in the vernacular, the primary curriculum had little to do with Ojike's history and customs. The pupils were fed stories of British heroes, beginning with Lord Nelson. Ojike came to mock his father's religion and traditions as heathen, inferior. "He [the African] has been terribly miseducated!" It will take decades, says Ojike, to restore the proper balance again. In the seventh grade Ojike began to learn English, and from that time on he and his peers were not permitted to speak their own language in the school compound.

Actually, the British practice of regarding the vernacular as one of the "sound and healthy elements" in African social and cultural life varied in accordance with the views and capabilities of those in charge of instruction. Often, in Catholic schools and in government schools, the native tongue was not taught at all, either because the teachers didn't know it well enough or because they couldn't bear to teach such heathern gibberish. Chief Obafemi Awolowo, in his autobiography, has given a fascinating description of the Yorubazation of education at Wesley (teachers') College in Ibadan in the twenties. This school bore the imprint of its headmaster's somewhat heterodox views. Although he did not see any reason why African boys should be given instruction in logic, he did think them capable of becoming lesser versions of Tom Brown. And so he encouraged both fagging and football, as did many other masters in Africa at the time. Nevertheless, at Wesley the prescribed dress was *sokoto*, *buba*, and *agada*, rather than trousers, blazer, and shirt. And there was a Yoruba rather than a Latin motto for the school, the meaning of which, however, was the somewhat loaded one of "as he that serveth" from Luke xxii, 27. The Reverend E. H. Nightingale, B.D., made a point of insisting that

> We should be proud of anything that was indigenous to us: our langu̇ ̇̇ʒe, our culture [as well as] our style of dress. The official lȧnguage of the classrooms and in the dining room was English, but in the college compound you could speak any language you liked as long as you were understood. It was believed Mr. Nightingale fostered these policies in order to slow down our progress in the Western sense. I shared this view then, but I now [1960] think he was a great pioneer.[16]

Meanwhile, in Iboland in 1926, Robinson Ojike graduated from primary school with two years of instruction in English. But there was no high school reasonably nearby and his brothers could not afford to send him away. They had felt obliged to concentrate their resources on primary schooling for the numerous children in the family. (At that time, counting nieces and nephews, the family included eighty children of school age.) So Ojike went off on his own for the first time as a pupil-teacher, first in his home town and then at Abagana, thirty miles away. He was successful. In 1928, he was given an infant school to administer, and he continued to study for college entrance examinations on his own.

In 1929, he was admitted to the Church Mission Society Training College in Oka (which the Europeans persisted in misspelling Awka—even on the signpost—much to Ojike's chagrin). The large, permanent buildings—cement block walls, corrugated roofing, concrete floors, and iron pillars and staircases—were erected at great cost by the students themselves. The principal was a former army major and clergyman. Methods of teaching, social service, religion, and games were taught, but no secondary school subjects. Elementary courses in arithmetic, history, and so on were presumably more "their" speed. Fortunately Ojike and three others (among these the famous King Ja Ja's * son) were able to study privately with an interested African teacher for the Cambridge junior exams.

Three years later, Ojike left Oka a certified teacher, with an obligation to serve the Church Missionary Society in this capacity for five years. He returned to Abagana, this time in the Western attire appropriate to his station; but he never carried a whip. In 1933 high school enrollments in the region were two and then three times the expected figures, and Ojike was abruptly transferred to the C.M.S. high school in Onitsha, never having had the honor to attend himself. He spent his savings on correspondence courses from Oxford in order to keep well ahead of his students in subjects he was learning and teaching at the same time—a familiar story in any part of the world! In 1938 Ojike passed the London matriculation exam, and, a newly formed and long-lasting friendship with "Zik" paving the way, Ojike resigned from teaching and prepared to sail for Lincoln University in Pennsylvania, with the promise of reduced fees. This was the pattern of the exceptional Nigerian of his generation. (Nowadays he almost certainly would have had a regular high school education, and might have continued his schooling at an African university, before postgraduate study abroad.) †

However the Nigerians may have felt personally about the condescension of the men who educated them in formal classes, roughly along British lines, and despite whatever efforts are now

---

* Ja Ja, a man of great personal ability, rose from a slave's condition in Bonny, Nigeria, to the kingship of nearby Opobo. A successful trader who refused to surrender kingdom or trade to British merchants, Ja Ja fell victim to one of the more disgraceful little imperialist plots of the era. In 1888 he was lured aboard a British ship for tea and forceably exiled. A British lawyer, Sir William Geary, defended him and eventually he won an indemnity of £10,000 from the Royal Niger Company. He died, however, on the way back to Opobo from St. Vincent in 1897. It was not until 1944 that his descendants were paid.

† It is sad to relate that Mbonu Ojike died in 1956, having served as finance minister in the Eastern Region of Nigeria until then. A hospital in his memory is being raised in his home town, and the donations, so a diplomatic officer here informs me, are pouring in.

being made to make these lines more African, a modified European system of education is still assumed to be the best preparation for any African in the modern world. All the new independent governments have embarked upon crash educational programs, in many cases financed with foreign aid. In 1962, the government of the Eastern Region of Nigeria spent 48 per cent of its budget on education, the Western Region, 45 per cent. Primary schooling is universal in these areas now, and the secondary school population continues to explode. From 1952 to 1959, for example, in the Western Region, high school enrollment rose from 6,775 to 84,374—or about 1,500 per cent!

V.

If the British colonial system implied the eventuality of self-management, for this the French substituted the possibility of self-culture. The assimilated elites were the legatees of a refined and glorious occidental civilization; what more could they reasonably ask? For those forced to remain in the African provinces, France had certain cultural advantages to offer which might be compared with those enjoyed by *amateurs* in the French provinces. There was the inevitable *Alliance Française* even in the remoter corners of "the bush," as well as government-sponsored cultural circles. And not only was French culture fostered, but so was African—preserved, however, rather than taught. The students at the William Ponty normal school at Gorée were encouraged to collect folklore (on vacations home) and turn these materials into short plays. Keita Fodeba's famous *Ballets africains* was originally the product of this kind of sponsorship. African writers were rare in the early days, but were almost sure to be awarded some kind of special colonial prize for whatever efforts they made.

A century-long interest in the antiquities of the Western Sudan was climaxed by the establishment in Dakar, in 1938, of the *Institute Française de l'Afrique Noire*, an outstanding organization of scholars responsible for setting up a museum, library, archives, and a research center in each of the West African territories.* And although, as Senghor admitted to the Grand Council in 1953, few

* It is for this organization that Climbié's alter ego, the writer Dadié, worked—first in Dakar and then back in the Ivory Coast. Dadié is now Director of Fine Arts for his own government.

Africans were as yet willing to engage in such an "arid and unre-munerative career as research," [17] the machinery for safeguarding their cultural heritage had been well established before African ministers of culture officially began their work.

During the colonial period the British also came to show a great deal of interest in African societies—primarily in customary laws and offices, however, rather than in artifacts, philosophical notions, and literary or dance forms, as did the French; for British government-sponsored studies of African societies began as an attempt to remedy a serious defect in the doctrine of indirect rule: Granted that the British, whenever possible, were to rule through existing indigenous institutions, did anyone really know, except in the most superficial sense, what these institutions were? How could alien Britons be sufficiently aware of the "sound and healthy elements in the fabric of African social life" effectively to promote these? How could they judiciously settle conflicting tribal claims? And experience showed that apparently incom-prehensible outbursts of violence, or of atavism, could not pos-sibly be obviated or even effectively controlled without recourse to scientific inquiry.

It was the famous case of the Golden Stool that first dramati-cally exposed the need for research. When the leader of the Ashanti confederation of tribes, Prempeh the Asantehene, was summarily deposed and exiled by the British in 1896, the British governor, Hodgson, tried to find the Asantehene's Golden Stool of office so that Queen Victoria, as Protectress of the Ashanti, could sit on it.

"What must I do to the man, whoever he is, who has failed to give to the Queen, who is the paramount power in this country, the stool to which she is entitled? [So Hodgson harangued the people of Kumasi in 1900.] Where is the Golden Stool? Why am I not sitting on the Golden Stool at this moment? I am the representative of the paramount power, why have you relegated me to this [ordinary] chair?" [18]

But unfortunately for all concerned, the Golden Stool was not a mere throne but a sacred symbol of the unity of all the tribes participating in the confederacy—the appointed container of their several ancestral souls. This sort of ethnocentric arrogance has never been forgiven in Africa. That the Europeans exercised their technical superiority was understandable. But Africans in or out of power have always made a point of knowing those with whom they have to deal. Ill-mannered European incuriosity astonished, embittered, and occasionally provoked outraged retaliations. In this instance the Ashanti were equipped to wage a holy war to avenge the impiety. Eventually, of course, they lost, but the Golden Stool was never found. Twenty years later it turned up during construction of a highway, but by then the climate of opinion had so far altered that the new governor, Sir Gordon Guggisburg, at once renounced all British claim to it and recalled the aged Asantehene to resume custodianship of the souls.

A government anthropologist, R. S. Rattray, whose researches into Ashanti law and custom did influence official policy, was appointed to the Gold Coast. This appointment set a precedent, and when local administrative systems in the southern provinces of Nigeria broke down in 1927, an expert was appointed to head research into social institutions there. Thereafter, land rights problems in West Africa were settled according to traditional precedent. (This did not happen in Kenya, however, where British settlers, even if they had been aware of Kikuyu patterns of land tenure, would not have faltered in their determination to alienate African soil.)

It mustn't be forgotten that the British used these researches in their own interests. For example, no sooner had Rattray demonstrated that the administration should use Ashanti chiefs in certain ways than the forward-looking National Congress of British West Africa protested this as willful anachronism. The fact that a course in British empirical (or "field") anthropology eventually became required of all Colonial Office trainees has retroactively been much praised as the progressive gesture that it in a sense was intended to be; yet it probably did as much harm as good. For in opening the eyes of future field officers to patterns of behavior inherited from the past, such studies tend to obviate a fresh look at present patterns of African thought and behavior. The best preparation for this fresh look would seem to be a predisposition for change at home.*

* See, for example, M. Gluckman's attack on Malinowski's functional analysis of social change (Africa, XVII, 2 [1947], pp. 103–21), where he

Anthropology as a science tends to have reactionary political implications because the observer, often a romantic by temperament, develops a strange proprietory interest in the peoples he studies; he wishes, at some level of consciousness, to preserve the "purity" or at least the "integrity" of their lives and customs.* This new science, however, when turned by African nationalists to their own account, has been of inestimable value. A jurisprudential seriousness characterizes the many monographs that have been and are being turned out by Africans from former

---

shows how "change" for the South African meant, in Malinowski's terms, a reconciliation and adjustment to a colonial rule which he in turn urged to become less hypocritical, to preach less about the brotherhood of man and more about economic interdependence. Malinowski, as Gluckman succinctly says, "lacked a sense of history." This same sense of history was in fact possessed by the French colonial officer and expert writer on colonial philosophies, Robert Delavignette. He entitled his first book, a semifictionalized account of his experiences among the Senufo, *Les paysans noirs*—a revolutionary title for a progressive theory. This book was first published in the days of the Popular Front.

* An amusing illustration of this anthropological point of view is found in the writings of Henri Junod. Junod, a Swiss pastor among the Thonga and an entomologist on the side, became an anthropologist by accident after a visit from Lord Bryce, who said how grateful he would have been if a Roman had chanced to record the habits of his Celtic forefathers. Junod subsequently filled out one of Frazer's famous questionnaires for the *Golden Bough*. His own lengthy and elaborate study of the Thonga (published in 1912) has been much praised by professionals. But nevertheless, Junod had a "let us retain all that is pleasing and moral in the picturesque circle of huts" psychology, which complements the essentially Victorian doctrine of indirect rule. This was a squeamishness that led him to write his descriptions of Thonga sexual practices in Latin, a romanticism that made him oblivious to social change. Once, on a ship coming back from Europe, he chanced to meet three African "been to's": a Zulu newspaper editor, a Christian chief, and the principal of a training institution. When Junod tried to interrogate these people on witchcraft, the principal replied briefly that witchcraft was really the same as mesmerism (then all the continental rage), and at once proceeded to question Junod on the latter until the pastor was quite out of countenance. "How different it was with my Thonga informants," he says wistfully, "Mbozo, Tobane, and even," he adds, with that touching particularity characteristic of the best anthropological writers, "even Elias." Henri A. Junod, *The Life of a South African Tribe*, I (New Hyde Park, N.Y.: University Books, 1962), p. 2.

British territories. This orientation is to be distinguished from Africanism in the superlative, from the more artistic and philosophical concerns of monographs showing the influence of *l'Institute Française de l'Afrique Noire.*

On the personal level, anthropology as a science has helped the Westernized elites to reorient themselves in a brotherly, knowledgeable way towards their own particular societies and towards those of fellow Africans as well. When writer-scientist Davidson Nicol, now president of the University College of Sierra Leone, delivered his unique paper on West African writing in English at the 1956 *Présence Africaine* conference, he could— although he did not have much fiction or poetry to talk about— point with pride to the fact that "For over a hundred years British West Africans have contributed to the study of local customs and law." [19]

In 1961, Senghor was able to flatter a Parisian city hall audience by telling them:

> If Paris is not the greatest museum of Negro-African art, nowhere else has Negro art been so well understood, commented on, exalted, assimilated. By revealing to me the values of my ancestral civilization, Paris forced me to adopt them and make them bear fruit. Not only me but a whole generation of Negro students, West Indians as well as Africans.[20]

Of course there is more than one irony hidden in this statement. Isolated from their homelands and from the white community as well, French colonial students in Paris joined together to make a common cause. As products of the French system, they had a perfect command of that language. They knew not only the geography of the *départments* and the names of all the plants that grow in Parisian parks, but the agonies of Descartes and Pascal as well. In Paris they became more familiar with the rebellious and exotic currents of the artistic and literary avant-garde. Having been taught in the colonies that their ancestors were the Gauls, the elite discovered their own ancestors in the process of receding into the bush whence they, the assimilated (be they the great grandsons of slaves or the sons of free Africans), had come. That the Gauls were not prepared in truth to acknowledge them as descendants created crises of the soul that the various introspective and aesthetic traditions to which they had also been exposed could help them to solve.

Ever since 1907, when Picasso began his *période nègre*, and since Apollinaire, about the same time, declared himself "fed up with this ancient world" and bound for somnolence among the "fetishes of Oceana and Guinea," various forms of African art and the cultural values that those who delighted in them believed them to express had became minor motifs in modern French art. The newly articulate French-African intellectuals naturally aligned themselves with the spokesmen of the new movements (and retrospectively with their precursors, like Nietzsche and Baudelaire) to make common cause against the bourgeois rule of reason and greed. In Africa, this rule was French colonialism. When Senghor combatively rephrased Descartes to read, "I feel, I dance to the other, I am," he was not surprised to have his friend Soulages the painter remark, "But this is the aesthetic of the twentieth century." [21] It was.

French intellectuals in turn interested themselves in the new African artists and supported their efforts to transmogrify ancient fetishes into forms expressive of African contemporaneity. In 1932, students from the Antilles published a manifesto, *Légitime Défense*, which took its title as well as its point of view from a pamphlet André Breton * had published six years before in defense of surrealist Communism against the doctrinaire Party in France. In 1934, under the aegis of three colonial poets, León Damas from Guyana, Aimé Césaire from Martinique, and Senghor from Senegal, *L'étudiant noire*, a literary journal which hoped to unite all tribes under the banner of *la négritude*, was established.

After the war, French men of letters helped black men of letters introduce themselves to a wider audience. In December, 1947, the first issue of *Présence Africaine*, devoted to the originality of Negro culture, appeared. To this issue Gide (who with Sartre and Emmanuel Mounier was one of the members of the founding committee) contributed an *avant propos* in which he recalled two past stages in European relations to Africa: exploitation first, and then a condescending pity and instruction. The third phase, he said, is *now*, when we must "écouter" and "se laisser instruire." This, when the war had further called European

---

* (André Breton was responsible for the publication of Césaire's first extensive work.)

values into question, was a timely utterance. In 1948, an anthology of Negro poetry from the French colonies appeared—*La Nouvelle poésie nègre et malgache*, with a classical analysis of the concept of *négritude* by Jean-Paul Sartre.

VI.

African writers in English were not helped by dissenting cultural forces abroad in the same way. They began to write, borrowing from a variety of sources (the zest of Dickens, the agrarian nobility of Tolstoy, the syncretism of Eliot and Pound) just what they wanted and no more. English publishers, although more interested in lives of eminent Nigerians and off-beat prose, began to print what there was, as they had earlier printed Indian writers.* Later branches of some of the houses especially interested in Africa were set up on the big continent itself.

African writing in English has been encouraged on African soil. It was an Austrian, Ulli Beier, and not an Englishman who inaugurated *Black Orpheus* in 1956—a review published in Ibadan, rather than London, which in the beginning had to fill

---

* Of all the Commonwealth writers, however, the West Indians have been the real rage in England—this probably because West Indian writers in English have tended to play the buffoon, a situation which nicely complements the threatening aspect that the West Indians resident in England have assumed in the popular mind. The following dialogue, broadcast in London, between Andrew Salkey, a Jamaican poet, and J. P. Clark, a Nigerian poet, is telling evidence of why West Indian writers have been so popular, and why West Africans in English write as confidently as they do.

CLARK: I lived in two worlds. Whenever I went home on holidays for instance, I still had my family intact, you know family didn't just mean mother and father, it meant the whole tree, the whole village—the whole clan—the whole tribe, and things pretty much . . . as they have always been. . . . All you really have is the English stream and any other thing you did was thought to be barbaric . . . a throwback to your African ancestors or something like that. . . .

SALKEY: We haven't really got anything to reach out to in our past, we tend to live in our present, you know, it's a strange state of confusion and so on. . . . [Caribbean fiction] is one that has to do with the comic imagination . . . a unique way of hitching tragedy and comedy up together. From "Africa Abroad," a magazine program produced at the Transcription Center, London. Recorded January 1, 1964.

up its pages with many translations of African and West Indian writings in French. These served their cultural purpose, however, and soon a group of young Nigerian poets began to publish their poems in the magazine. These poets, with Ulli Beier, founded the Mbari * publishing house and cultural center, the first of its kind in all of Africa. In 1961, *Transition*, edited by Rajat Neogy, began its career in Kampala, Uganda—financed by the Congress for Cultural Freedom. By 1962 there were enough significant modern African works in English for self-criticism formally to begin. A writers conference was called in the summer of that year in Kampala, sponsored jointly by the Mbari writers group and the Congress for Cultural Freedom. Two American Negro experts were invited to speak, and a gentleman of French expression observed. For the most part, the young Nigerian writers wanted to thrash things out among themselves, with some help from exiled South African colleagues. The writers were disputatious and irreverent. Of the exact nature of their Yoruba, Ibo, and Ijaw personalities they were unsure. But two things were certain. They had never for a moment considered themselves Black Englishmen; they felt that they had practically nothing in common with those Africans, wherever they were, who spoke and wrote in French.

The young man who passed his examinations in the Ivory Coast and the young man who saw Christianity come to the town of Ndizuogu are counterparts. This is not merely to say that they

* "Mbari is a word that's puzzled many people. This club was founded for writers and artists to come together to talk, to publish books, to stage exhibitions—to permit writers and artists to be independent of official support and set their own standards. We were looking for a name which would be a Nigerian word—never mind from what area, from what tribe —which had something to do with creative activity. We hit on this wonderful Ibo term, *mbari*, which is the name used for sacred buildings erected by the Ibos in honor of the creator goddess.

The Ibo Mbari is built in mud. It has 20, 30, 40, or 50 life-sized figures in mud representing the goddess, everything on earth . . . women and childbirth, district officers holding court, anything is represented there. And it is by creating this building that they serve the goddess of creation. The moment the rain washes it away they just abandon it. They don't bother about it and they create a new one. The idea is that the creative process has got to be renewed all the time if a society as a whole is going to thrive." "Conversation with Ulli Beier," *Africa Report*, Vol. 9, No. 7 (July, 1964).

were contemporaries. The one refused to become assimilated, the other saw the folly of his adopted British name. Yet Climbié is a fictional character and Mbonu Ojike is real. Colonial conditions have thus been operative from the very beginning. To attempt to describe them from any point of view involves one in a sort of Uncertainty Principle, in which the viewer is already partially determined by the viewed. Therefore, the discrepancy of genres from which the most extended illustrations in this chapter have been drawn is a reflection of the fact that although there have been many African autobiographies in English, Africans who were ruled by France have tended to express their experiences obliquely in the semi-autobiographical novel, in the highly subjective *récit*, or in poetry. Furthermore, that relative latecomer, the Nigerian novel, tends to be more "objective" than the African novel in French—the voice of the author as a reflective or ironic interpreter being less in evidence, more difficult to detect. (By the same token, Nigerian poetry is more personal, more idiosyncratic than the poetry of *négritude*—on principle, yes, but after the fact.)

The relation of these phenomena to the ruling European attitudes, rationalized into the doctrines of assimilation and indirect rule, should be clear from this discussion of the colonial styles and the responding attitudes that they engendered. What the conquerors hoped to accomplish was, ironically, accomplished in the creative arts of self-assertion. For over half a century, France attempted to impose an idea on an African reality. Britain, meanwhile, navigated the Niger, but kept running aground on mangrove stumps and camping in suspicious villages—by policy warding off continuous attacks. To these presumptuous attempts certain Africans were eventually able to respond in writing. Those of French expression had different notions of psychic reality. Those of English expression had their own views of the facts.

Notes

1. W. E. Abraham, *The Mind of Africa* (Chicago: University of Chicago Press, 1962).

2. Colin Turnbull, *The Lonely African* (New York: Simon & Schuster, Inc., 1962), pp. 133–35.

3. The Reverend Father Placide Tempels, *Bantu Philosophy*, Reverend Colin King, trans. (Paris: Présence Africaine, 1959).

4. *The Educated African*, A Country-by Country Survey of Educational Development in Africa, compiled by Ruth Sloan Associates, Helen Kitchen, ed. (New York: Frederick A. Praeger, Inc., 1962), p. 441.

5. Mbonu Ojike, *My Africa* (New York: The John Day Company, 1946), p. 10.

6. Quoted in Michael Crowder, *Senegal*, A Study of French Assimilation Policy (London: Oxford University Press, 1962), p. 22.

7. Geoffrey Gorer, *Africa Dances*, first published in 1935 (London: Penguin Books, Ltd., 1945), p. 83.

8. Quoted in "Senegal," by Ernest Milcent, in *African One-Party States*, Gwendolen Carter, ed. (Ithaca: Cornell University Press, 1962), p. 22.

9. Bernard Dadié, *Climbié* (Paris: Editions Seghers, 1956), p. 22.

10. *Ibid.*, p. 108.

11. *Ibid.*, p. 105.

12. Quoted in Joyce Cary, *The Case for African Freedom and Other Writings on Africa* (Austin: University of Texas Press, 1962), p. 181.

13. See William Bascom, "Urbanization Among the Yoruba," in *Cultures and Societies of Africa*, S. and P. Ottenberg, eds. (New York: Random House, Inc., 1960), pp. 255–67, and Simon Ottenberg, "Ibo Receptivity to Change," in *Continuity and Change in African Cultures*, W. Bascom and M. Herskovits, eds. (Chicago: University of Chicago Press, 1959), pp. 130–43.

14. Quoted in Lord Hailey, *An African Survey*, rev. ed. (London: Oxford University Press, 1957), p. 92.

15. Quoted in *The Educated African*, *op. cit.*, p. 367.

16. *Awo*, The Autobiography of Chief Obafemi Awolowo (Cambridge: Cambridge University Press, 1960), p. 65.

17. Quoted in Virginia Thompson and Richard Adloff, *French West Africa* (Palo Alto, Calif.: Stanford University Press, 1950), p. 514.

18. Quoted in Donald H. Wiedner, *A History of Africa South of the Sahara* (New York: Random House, Inc., 1962), p. 234.

19. Davidson Nicol, "The Soft Pink Palms," *Présence Africaine* (English edition), XVIII–XIX (June–November, 1956), 109.

20. Quoted by Mercer Cook in his introduction to Léopold Sédar Senghor, *On African Socialism*, Mercer Cook, trans. (New York: Frederick A. Praeger, Inc., 1964), p. xii.

21. Léopold Sédar Senghor, "On Negrohood: Psychology of the African Negro," *Diogenes*, 37 (Spring, 1962), 6 ff.

II THE HEROIC LEGACY IN AFRICA

"... et voilà tes veins charrient de
l'or non de la boue, de l'orgueil non
de la servitude. Roi tu a été Roi
jadis."

—AIMÉ CÉSAIRE

African novelists have in the main concerned themselves with
the contradictions and ambiguities of their contemporary experience, or with descriptions of the profound social life of the
vanishing village. But the historical romance has also had its place
in modern African letters. This genre, unlike the others, might
truly be said to have developed out of oral tradition, specifically a
tradition in which bards or professional chroniclers were held
accountable for the magnificent memories of dynasties of reign-
ing kings. This ennobling of forgotten facts into written legend
will become increasingly important in the preservation and promotion of the heritage of new national states. Two imaginative
"histories" were published as early as the nineteen thirties, before
the African renaissance properly began. A third, written in celebration of independence in the Western Sudan, was published in
1960.

Novels such as these would merit attention if only for the living
sense they convey of African societies at their apogees. But the
novels themselves are history too, and as such are vehicles of
another kind of understanding, another kind of empathy. As we
read of invincible warriors and guilty chiefs, we also read,
between the lines, of certain modern personalities struggling to
resist and at the same time transcend colonial teaching and
Western influence. In recreating heroic moments, these writers
are in effect meeting important, contemporary psychic and
social needs.

Nationalist movements have always used past greatness as
a part of their ideologies, but in no case has the development

of a proud historical personality been undertaken in the face of difficulties so overwhelming as has the African. Founders of new states have not always fooled the world into thinking past accomplishments a necessary index of present capacity, but at least the world has been interested in the romance, if not also in the historicity of their claims, and admired the will to power that produced them. Sophisticated Anglo-Irish writers of the early twentieth century were easily able to seek world sympathy for the Irish independence movement by projecting the forlorn image of Ireland as the immemorial Deirdre, and that of rebellion as the undying Cuchulain (a mythic image of Parnell). But this is because no one ever doubted that the Irish were a soulful people in possession of a cultural legacy, rather dimly remembered by themselves because callously ignored by alien rulers on their soil. But the Africans, and the Negro peoples generally, until quite recently have not been able to give the world a sense of a lost heritage, let alone to revive it with a vengeance when there was a crying moral and political need.

The myth of Negro inferiority and the fact of the lack of written records—itself a contribution to the myth—actually obviated research on the question. There are medieval texts by travelers and scholars of various African ancestries which record, in Arabic, the splendors and complexities of the African kingdoms of the Western Sudan. But even with these in mind, and with such striking concrete remembrances of ancient glory as the Nok figurines of Northern Nigeria or the ruins of Zimbabwe in Rhodesia, Europeans persisted in their myth of white, or of "Hamitic" superiority. The kingdoms in question were simply declared ruled by Berbers or Jews. Nigerian artifacts were attributed to stray Greeks, Egyptians, or even the Portuguese. Zimbabwe was credited to the Phoenecians, or to some "superior" alien race, from Solomon's down to the Arabs of medieval times.

Efforts have recently been made, by Africans and clear-thinking Europeans alike, to eradicate historical ignorance by research in areas where time has spared most striking evidence. Thus Mauny has shown that iron smelting began in West Africa as early as 300 B.C., and Murdoch has traced the independent ennobling of wild plants into cultivated West African agricultural complexes back six thousand years. Oral traditions of kingship have been verified by ephemerides. The economic and political complexities of African societies have been described. And, stimulated by these findings, counter theories of African superiority have finally been advanced. The most ambitious of these, Cheikh Anta Diop's (in his *Nations nègres et culture,* and other books), is based on the same assumption of the identity between Egyptian culture and ancient Negro culture that was once used to show how lacking in invention the Western Sudanese were. One of the most appealing of the direct traverses is William Fagg's assertion that those climatic conditions which cause Nigerian wood carvings to be eaten away by termites every generation demanded that the carving styles be kept alive. Un-Egyptian in this innovative urgency, the carvings become bold products of the necessity to make things anew.

It has been the Hamitic version of the myth of Negro inferiority that has died the hardest. This myth is based on Western fascination for the long, lean, pastoral type of African, long assumed—and in some quarters still assumed—to be the culture bearer from the upper reaches of the Nile. But just as Mungo Park the explorer astonished Europe a hundred and fifty years ago by demonstrating that the Niger flowed from west to east (instead of counterclockwise as had always been supposed), so the American scholar Joseph Greenberg has demonstrated, on the basis of linguistic evidence, that the transmission of culture in Africa has taken directions far different from those supposed to have been taken.

The impact of these new developments on the African imagination is clear. Nationalist movements of the past decade were able to invoke the names of warrior heroes of the past in order to speed peaceful constitutional developments. And with the coming of independence, leaders of government sought to strengthen the loyalties of their citizens by linking the names of new states, like Ghana and Mali, and their own names, like Keita and Sékou Touré, to this newly substantiated and revalorized African past. Not only the names, and inherited or revived royal regalia, proclaim the ancient dignity of relatively unstable infant states, but the famous "one party system" as developed in Africa can be seen as a way of unifying large disparate populations (the legacy of European boundary lines) by analogy to past tribal cohesiveness and the institution of the chieftaincy, which European occupation all but destroyed. Similarly, plans for economic development along the lines of "African socialism" are generally formulated with an appeal to the spirit and practice of traditional communal village life.

But beyond these political uses of the past, these necessary assertions of continuity despite the interruption of colonial occupation, beyond the pride of new schoolbooks based on African materials lies the appeal of the African past to the individual conscience. Were we innocent or guilty before European penetration, occupancy, and "influence"? What is the personal relation of an African with a Western education to a totally African past? How three African writers, from very different ethnic backgrounds, under quite different colonial conditions, project their images of past grandeur may indicate the heroic resources of the African continent.

II.

In 1213, according to a more or less respectable tradition, Allakoi Keita founded the Mandingo state, which was to become famous as the empire of Mali. *Soundjata*, by Djibril Tamsir Niane, published by Présence Africaine in 1960, is the story of Allakoi's brilliant successor, who wrested territorial supremacy from the sorcerer king, Soumaoro Kante of Sosso—a wicked *wori* player who had taken advantage of the waning fortunes of the ancient kingdom of Ghana to terrorize the populace of the lands between the upper reaches of the Senegal and Niger rivers. This "sorcerer" was what we would now call an "animist" (rather than a "fetishist") king, so Soundjata's victory meant, in cultural terms, a decisive establishment of Islam in this territory. Having defeated Soumaoro with the help of allied tribes (according to Niane's version), Soundjata then called together the twelve proud kings of the Savannah and restored to them their ancient territorial rights. Like any feudal potentate, Soundjata presumed upon their loyalty and the force of his arms for the maintenance of a loosely federated empire which, a century later under Kankan Musa, was further consolidated and extended over a territory as large as that of any state anywhere in the world at that time.[1]

The original capital of the federation was Niani, whose name the author of the story bears. That Soundjata was actually born in Niani, or that the town played such an important part in the hero's early history as Niane would have it play, is open to doubt.[2] Perhaps, given the rage for historical linkages, the author chose to make the vagueness of tradition legitimatize his own role as official storyteller.

But Niane allows himself this role only in an indirect, or mediating sense. His tale purports to be the work of a *griot* (bard), Djeli Mamoudou Kouyaté, whose family has been immemorially at the service of the Keita dynasty, the latter-day representatives of which still rule over the modern territories of Mali and Guinea as modern heads of state. The *griot*, like other members of his despised and yet honored caste, is both master and teacher of the traditions of his people. "We are the memory of men, through the Word giving life to the deeds and gestures of kings, for the benefit of younger generations." [3] This educative function of the Sudanese bard may account in part for the pure and perhaps deceptively naïve outlines and style of Niane's story. It may also account for the inscrutable elegance of certain magical occurrences in the story—symbols surely, for the initiated, of truths which the youthful lay listener, or the not necessarily so youthful Western reader, is not supposed to decipher completely.

The hero Soundjata is the son of the ugly woman Sogolon, whose advent from the East is prophesied to Soundjata's father by a wandering hunter-diviner as the king of the modest territory rests under the sacred silk cotton tree. The king too has the gift of seeing beyond the appearances of things. The ugly woman arrives, obviously linked in some way with a famous "buffalo woman" who has been ravaging the nearby country of Do. She is accompanied by two princely hunters who have been unable, it turns out, to possess and therefore to propagate upon her the future marvel of Manding. The gifted king of Niani has his problems with her too. Every time he approaches her she bristles with buffalo hairs. But by a clever ruse he is finally able to separate this woman from her buffalo "double," and Soundjata is at last conceived.

But the hero turns out to be even more of a problem than his mother. Whoever heard of a future king who can't walk at the age of seven (some accounts say seventeen), and who spends all his time with his face in his food bowl, apparently oblivious of the consternation his gluttonous backwardness is causing. Yet, had not the forger-diviner, the magical smith of Niani, wisely said: "When the seed germinates, its growth is not always so easy.

Great trees grow slowly; but they sink their roots deep into the soil"? The king believes the prophecy, accepts the smith's advice, and protects his son. But when the king dies, his wicked eldest widow moves Sogolon and her doltish son to the back courtyard, where they exist on scraps and in rags.

Suddenly Soundjata awakens to his mother's humiliation. The usurping queen mother has been taunting her again: *Other* children fetch leaves from the baobab tree to season *their* mothers' cooking pots. Very well, Soundjata says, today I shall walk. He calls for a cane of iron from the forger-diviner's shop. When the magical implement arrives, Soundjata hauls himself up with it, bending the metal of technical mastery, as he rises, into the significant form of a hunter's bow, while his personal *griot* keeps up a torrent of rhythmical praise. The hero then lets fall the enormous iron bow, and with giant steps walks up to the baobab tree, rips it out, and then lugs it back to his mother's hut, saying, this time in the guise of a "gatherer" hero: "Mother, here are the baobab leaves for you. From now on the women of Niani will come before your hut in order to provision themselves." [4]

Soundjata now grows easily into the powerful, youthful hunter he is born to be at this stage. The jealous queen retaliates by engaging nine sorcerer women, linked to the powers of darkness, to pluck vegetable condiments from Soundjata's private garden so that he in turn will strike out against them. Then, having given offense to the powers of darkness, they can legitimately destroy him on behalf of the queen. But the plot fails because of Soundjata's frank courtesy to the old women caught robbing his garden; the powers of darkness are disarmed by his sweetness. However, in mitigation of this and other triumphs, Sogolon suggests exile. She fears the queen will now proceed to work harm on Soundjata's more vulnerable brothers and sisters, and that she will succeed by taking advantage of the hero's compassionate nature. "But you will return later," Sogolon tells him, "when you are fully grown—to reign." Again the lion must await his strength. Soundjata and his entourage go to the Fouta Djallon, where the Kamara smiths live. King Kamara, afraid to touch these hallowed exiles, hurries them off to the fading kingdom of Ghana. But before they leave, Soundjata and his brother, Manding Bory, have the following exchange with their boyish friend Fran Kamara, who, with other well-bred youths, had been educated with Soundjata at the court of Niani:

SOUNDJATA: When I return to Manding, I'll come by and pick you up at Tabon, and we'll go on to Niani together.
MANDING BORY: Between now and then we'll have grown up.
FRAN KAMARA: I'll have the whole army of Tabon to myself. The forgers and the Djallonké people are excellent warriors. Already I play my part in the maneuvers that my father organizes once a year.
SOUNDJATA: I'll make you a very important general. We'll scour many lands. We will be the strongest. Kings will tremble before us like women before men.[5]

And the exiles take up their road to Ghana. The Grand Meaulnes himself has no more confident childish charm to offer than Soundjata and his confreres. Is it the Guinean *griot* or the French writer that presents little boys' conversations so convincingly and so winningly here?

The hero's boyhood dreams, like his childish accomplishments, foreshadow his future strengths. When Soundjata's time is finally ripe, and he is given plenty of leisure to mature, he fulfills his promises to his friend Fran Kamara; and Kamara, in turn, supplies the promised troops. Together the young leaders go off in quest of the sorcerer king, Soumaoro. But this scourge of the Savannah, when hard-pressed in battle, has a distressing tendency to disappear, and he can be vanquished only by an unknown magical weapon. Soundjata's faithful sister discovers the secret. A special arrowhead made from a white cock's spur will do it! Stung by this arrow, Soumaoro disappears forever into a mountain cavern. At the risk of offending the *griots* with our crude categories, one might hazard that the secret weapon is a symbol of the hero's virility, that by this agency the sorcerer is emasculated of his "animistic" powers, and that their potency is in turn transferred to Soundjata's new dispensation, Islam.

Soundjata and his attendant *griot* visit the sorcerer's secret room afterwards, and find that "all the inhabitants of the chamber had lost all force: The serpent in his jar was in his last agony; the owls from their perch fluttered lamentably on the floor— everything was dying in the house of the sorcerer, everything containing the power of Soumaoro."[6] Here again the decor seems French, *symboliste*, haunted by Edgar Allan Poe, although the idea of demonic strength resident in a magician's macabre possessions is universal in tales of enchantment, and although the force of the ideal fetish-object is perhaps stronger in Africa than elsewhere! Among Soumaoro's possessions in the haunted room is an African xylophone known as a *balafon*, which receives the "strength" of the human word and then speaks out on its own. To play such an instrument is to elicit voices, ancestral voices. We also have known such instruments in the West.

The *griot's* story ends with Soundjata's triumphal return to Niani, the claiming of his rightful kingdom, the summoning of the twelve feudal lords so that they may show their loyalty, and the establishment of the faith, peace, and justice in the Western Sudan. Such a story really has to end here. Just as boyish fantasy gave way to real battles with magical weapons in them, so the pure, practical rigor of Islam displaces the messy, unpredictable terror of Soumaoro's reign; the sorcerer's animated room is silenced into a vision of rational political order, and there is nothing else to be said. The tree, Soundjata, has grown up leisurely, deeply rooted in magic; but it is, finally, a real tree, filling real space, and the hero becomes, according to the wisdom of his people, an active political man. Niane's book was published in 1960, as a kind of affirmation of independence in the Western Sudan. The enchanted heroic world of *Soundjata*, in a strangely Hegelian way, seems to cancel itself out. Words become deeds in the adult world; the fabled world of desire becomes a modern political state.

III.

Doguicimi, by Paul Hazoumé, is a 500-page recreation of life under King Ghezo of Dahomey (1818–58). The society here described and the atmosphere of the book as a whole could not be more different from that of Niane's medieval Mali. The world of legend has become somewhat incrusted with the words of documentation. Numerous European eyewitnesses had described Dahomey as a nineteenth century slaving kingdom before Hazoumé began to turn events back into romance again; ethnologists—including Hazoumé himself—already had written monographs in French on various practices of the Fon people; and Herskovits' monumental two-volume study of Dahomey was published the same year as Hazoumé's novel. There had been no lack of work on the subject; but such diligence had not suppressed all dreams.

The Dahomeans are a non-Moslem West African people that sometime around the birth of Christ migrated across the Niger River to settle just inland from the Guinea, or more notoriously the Slave, Coast. They accompanied the Yoruba people, whose vassals they had been for centuries, and from whom they learned significant administrative techniques, cosmological patterns, and tool (later arms) manufacture. Early in the eighteenth century, the King of Dahomey succeeded in capturing his way to the coast and monopolizing the slave trade in that area. Fixing the price from the inland capital, he performed all the necessary "administrative" tasks himself; thus, although his slave supply was smaller than that produced by the Ashanti network along the Gold Coast (because there were no trade ties with Moslem states along the Niger), he did save the Europeans a good deal of manpower and expense. The novel *Doguicimi* takes place just after the abolition of the slave trade which was to mean an abrupt and radical decline in the fortunes and importance, if not in the administrative and military efficiency of the kingdom.

Hazoumé's purpose in writing his novel is apologetic—an attempt by a French-trained ethnologist of his own people to prove to a skeptical French public in 1938 that, amid all the excesses of the slaving kingdom at its apogee, there was a strong strain of personal loyalty and heroism among the Fon people. Unfortunately, he invented a heroine as the vehicle for his task. Doguicimi (whose name means "distinguish me") is as outspoken in her criticisms of the king's bloody regime as Shakespeare's doughty Queen Margaret, as persistent in avoiding all attacks on her virtue as Pamela, as ghoulishly romantic as Mathilde—in short, too much to take, a heroic bore. Fortunately she is far from being the whole story.

Far more interesting as an exception to the bloody rule is King Ghezo himself, a character that would have intrigued Tacitus. Ghezo is a kind of "deified Claudius," a constitutionally temperate man in an intemperate society, a weak man among powerful female advisors and corrupt male agents. Although prone on occasion to making willfully unwise decisions, Ghezo is a man who, when all the values of his culture are attacked, understandably and solidly affirms them, no matter how distasteful to him personally some of them are. And unlike Claudius, Ghezo widely extended the boundaries of his kingdom. It was Ghezo, although for some reason Hazoumé does not tell us this, who was at last able in 1827 to free Dahomey from the tributary yoke of the Yoruba.

Although opposed to them on principle, at least for rhetorical purposes in his book, Hazoumé is rather skilled in descriptions of immolations. By presenting outrageous or extravagant behavior in a plausible, straightforward manner, he seems at some level to be giving it his assent. Or perhaps it is just that by describing it at all he is bound to become involved and in a way committed, such being the trap into which the writer falls. For example, the novel begins on an average Dahomean day, just before sunrise. The official crier is making the rounds of the grand palace, whose walls stand four cubits high. The palace represents the work of nine reigns, whose rulers the crier praises before the gate built by and sacred to each. To forget one word in this official laudatory history means death for the crier. This particular crier survives and day breaks, as it always does, with the sacrifice of a slave to the king's ancestors as a token of gratitude for a successful living-out of the night. Migan, the Prime Minister and, in this society, the Chief Executioner, tests the soil about the head of the victim and reports to the king that "The face of the dawn has been well washed. Soon dawn will open the door to the sun. The abundance of blood augurs a pleasant day." [7]

A second immolation scene is described, not with the brevity appropriate to the everyday sacrifice, but with the fullness of detail with which a court historian might honor an exceptional feast. A deputation of white men has arrived at Ghezo's court to ask him to go along with Europe in giving up the slave trade. They hope to make other, legitimate arrangements for exploiting the West African kingdom, but they make the great mistake of insisting, at a banquet given in their honor, on the renunciation of all human sacrifice as well. Extolling their own country (Portugal) as a model of sanity and civilization, they deprecate everything about Dahomey as barbarous—except its wealth and its trade, which they would like to share.

The most attractive young girls in the royal entourage are serving at table, flirting with these European visitors, to whom they hope to be given as wives. When they leave the room, the younger Europeans grow impatient for the next course. The older men are impatient for the king's answer, which he insists on delaying until after the feast. Suddenly another set of servants appears, bearing the identical platters the girls had passed before, laden this time with the heads of the charming coquettes. One of the Europeans faints dead away. The others hear the Prime Minister-Chief Executioner speak for the king: You brought the slave trade yourselves, he says; to abandon it now would ruin us. Human sacrifice is a sign of respect to our ancestors; to abandon it would be blasphemous. But we have sent these young girls you liked so much as ambassadors to our ancestors—to tell them of your propositions. Should they agree, they will return our headless emissaries and we will do as they suggest. Will you wait?

Needless to say, the Europeans decamp at once. But the king, far from rejoicing at the good riddance, falls into a melancholy fit, during the course of which he reasons much as Hazoumé must himself have reasoned about the bloodier traditions of his people, to whom an inglorious reputation still clung. Stretched out on his couch, propping his heavy head up with a tired palm and elbow, Ghezo follows his guests with his gaze until they are out of sight. Then he follows them in thought, addressing them in this way:

> My august father, he also was preoccupied with the softening of the customs of this people . . . and I have dreamed of realizing his ideas. I fight only just wars. You reproach me vehemently with the slave trade. But was it not you who gave us the idea, the passion for it. . . . I have not suppressed human sacrifice, but I have curtailed it considerably by seeking a substitution in the slave trade. The majority of our captives are thus spared their lives . . . however far they are sold, however miserable the work imposed upon them. . . . And, by cutting off a few heads, surely I protect those of the masses [an economical way of getting rid of criminals and keeping the public peace]. . . . But *your ignorance of the Dahomean soul made you brutally attack our most sacred sentiments. . . . You have aroused in me, as in my subjects, the redoubtable Dahomean spirit that, most discreetly, I was trying, bit by bit, to snuff out.*[8]

Never at a loss for rationalizations, the suffering king relieves his melancholy by preparing one of his "just wars" against the Mahi city of Hounjroto, where Doguicimi's princely husband has been conveniently held captive for years.

Here Hazoumé transposes his story into another key. The conquest of Hounjroto, the final fifth of the book, is presented in that mode of arch fantasy which traditional (or neotraditional) African storytellers use to convey a moral orientation obliquely. Using the humorous fable for cover, the skillful storyteller surprises the human conscience in the throes of truth. The kings of the Aladoxonu dynasty, of which Ghezo was one, also were most successful in the tactics of ambush, and Hazoumé the storyteller begins his account of the "just war" with a fanciful description of one of these. Secretly advancing through the dense forest, the Dahomean army is able to surround an enemy village and capture stray hunters, foragers, and water carriers for use as spies and informants. Having cut the enemy village off from any possible allies, at the same time keeping in continuous communication with ancestral and other appropriate forces through divination, the army can then move in and take the enemy by surprise. This time, however, when the melancholy Ghezo's army moves into the forest, the animals flee and swarm into the unsuspecting village, a host of clamorous refugees. Hazoumé elaborates his invention with great charm:

> The reptile people ... fled toward the village where roof thatching, cracks in the huts, gutters, big stones, calabashes set out to catch the rain, the merest corners and crevices, in short, provided them asylum against danger. The serpents and lizards who betrayed their immoderate lengths and breadths, or who gave themselves away by causing the chickens to shriek in terror, were smashed by the [astonished] inhabitants of the huts. . . .[9]

One would think, were not disappearing water carriers enough cause for wonder, that all this wildlife seeking domestic sanctuary would have given the ambush away. But only one old man, Dĕĕ, is suspicious of an attack from the forest, and no one ever listens to *his* advice. Mocked by the youth for his ugliness, his garrulity, his impotence, it is only with great difficulty that he can now persuade them, in the hour of emergency, to listen to another one of his pointed tales:

When Dê Messê became the fifth king of Porto Novo, he refused to be king of the aged. Since pessimistic old age tended to chill the martial ardor of youth, Dê Messê suggested that everyone murder his parents. The youths went at this with great enthusiasm. Only one of them, while pretending to go along, hid his old father instead. The old father's name was Ayiwou, meaning "it is by spirit," and the son's name, Gbêtohocouê, meaning "that man has valor," completes the proverb. The king then suggested that it might be nice to send his royal cousin a present of 3,000 rolls of supple and resistant cord spun out of earth. The youths protested that this was an impossible idea of a present. Oh is it? said the king; and, angered at their insubordination, he ordered them on pain of death to produce such a present within five days. Most of the citizens of Porto Novo thereafter preferred to live out their youth in exile, but to the few remaining on the fateful day, Gbêtohocouê brought an answer. Your Royal Highness, said the youth, appears to have in his possession a piece of cord which he, as a young hereditary prince, once succeeded in fashioning out of dry earth. We would like to take this and lengthen it—the product of your princely invention—to produce a length sufficient to encircle this enormous calabash which encloses us here on earth.* The king at once cried: There are still old people here! And he is right, for of course only "it is by spirit" could have told "that man has valor" what to do.

In any case, concludes the old storyteller, like Dê Messê and his youthful subjects of Porto Novo, the young people of Hounjroto prefer to indulge their appetites unchecked by the moderating advice of elders. And since they have impiously ceased to respect age and tradition, they are blind to the obvious signs of the coming conquest.† King Ghezo, meeting Dĕĕ after the real and inevitable surrender of Hounjroto, is significantly kind to the old storyteller, as if in him he saw his own image, reflected in life's other side. Had the historical Dahomeans been true to the principles of King Ghezo, they would perhaps have been able to establish a different relationship with the French. This is Ghezo's posthumous, and Hazoumé's rhetorical hope.

* This is a case of resistance to injustice by placing impossible conditions on impossible demands—a process which at the same time preserves respect for constituted authority. For an analysis of this strategy in African folklore among the Akan, see W. E. Abraham, The Mind of Africa (Chicago: University of Chicago Press, 1962), p. 95.
† Cf. the old Chinese tale about starving villagers who did away with their parents only to find the scarcity growing worse. Luckily someone had hidden his grandfather, and this secretly surviving ancient taught the helpless younger generation how to fight famine by beating seeds out of their roof thatchings and planting them.

The wise, inefficacious storyteller and the reluctant, guilt-ridden, progressive king may seem like curious images of the soul of Dahomey for Hazoumé to project before an imperial European public. Yet there is a deeper, more ambiguous truth in them than in the rampant personality of Doguicimi who, as the "Kathleen" of the conquered Dahomean kingdom, significantly spends the entire span of the book not only in tears but in jail. Dĕĕ would seem to represent the only kind of Africa that Hazoumé felt at that time could be revived. Dĕĕ's wisdom is traditional, unheeded, and linked to physical suffering and decay. That Africans of Hazoumé's generation, inhibited in action by colonial occupation and in thought by European teaching, should have vacillated between intellectual collaboration and retreat into fantasy is no cause for astonishment.

At the end of the story, Hazoumé's alter ego King Ghezo does assert himself in a war, but that war takes place in a climate of unreality. The real war took place later. Historically, Ghezo was the last free Dahomean king. When he died in 1858, the possibility of an ambivalent liberalism, or of a proud Dahomean modernism, died with him. His successor multiplied traditional excesses, and the French, long hovering about looking for an excuse, had a "humanitarian" reason to march in. *Doguicimi*, therefore, is a moving book because it is at bottom a moody book. Hazoumé's situation as an assimilated French ethnologist and publicist of his own African traditions during the colonial period might be compared with that of the Anglo-Irishman of the Revival who projected the national images of "a sad dark man" like Cuchulain and a tragic, mournful Deirdre who was unfaithful to the legitimate king of Ireland—an unpleasant, irascible old man.

IV.

In 1816, Chaka the Zulu chieftain first mobilized his famous *impis*. So great was their invincibility that when the commonsense armies of Britain, with the help of allied South African tribes, were finally able sixty-three years later to defeat the remnants and descendants of Chaka's army under Cetawayo, they went so far as to burn the sacred coil, the *inkata*,* of the Zulu chieftains

* The *inkata* was an enormous python skin stuffed with medicine, mostly rubbings from powerful enemies.

so that the potency of these "people of heaven" could never be revived. This power *has* been revived in legend, however, and unfortunately it has also been vulgarized countless times. The first African novel was written about Chaka by Thomas Mofolo, a Basuto schoolteacher, editor, and entrepreneur. The intensity of Mofolo's imagination, which the missionaries snubbed as too pagan for publication, was in reality a catholic imagination, alone adequate to the immensity of its task.

There can be no doubt that the historical Chaka was a remarkable man. He stood six feet three inches high at twenty-one years of age. He always insisted that his warriors run barefoot across thorns to toughen their feet, and he himself led them. He inaugurated the use of the short *assagai* (stabbing spear) to replace the customary javelin, insisted on the finality of hand-to-hand combat —and woe to him who returned from the battlefield unarmed. He refused to allow his warriors to marry until retirement. He implemented this policy by training female regiments as well. Towards the end of his career, now as superbly corpulent as a successful, cattle-fed chieftain was supposed to be, he kept himself and the members of his council in condition by force-marching them 300 miles in six days. As a disciplinarian and strategist, Chaka has had few peers.

Beginning as the inheritor of 500 men and 100 square miles of territory (he could, on foot, reach any of these boundaries in one hour), Chaka expanded his weak Ifenilenja clan into a powerful nation which eventually included about 300 Nguni clans. All those he conquered and all those who, while unconquered, feared him could become Zulus simply by joining his army. He was careful to spare, for impressment, the young men of defeated tribes. At his death his troops are estimated to have numbered 400,000, and his kingdom to have extended 100,000 miles. Pushed by a simultaneous and persistent European encroachment from the Cape, the tide of Bantu migration as a result of Chaka was turned back upon itself, up again toward the equator and the great lakes.

What sort of energy must have animated this man? E. A. Ritter, who has written an excellent biography of Chaka based on firsthand accounts, has a suggestive "modern" theory to account for him.[10] Not only was he abandoned by his father, under pressure from rival wives (as legend has it), but he also apparently was, as a child, taunted for his stubby penis. He refused to wear his *umutsha* (apron), and went about for a long time unclothed, in order to insist on a physical adequacy which he felt compelled, throughout his life, to assert and reassert in suitably heroic and orgiastic ways. All this might account, in part at least, for Chaka's unremitting athleticism; but in order to account for his remarkable manly success on the battlefield, one's weary imagination leaps to give some credence to an equally suggestive "archaic" theory:

> ... in tribes such as the zulu and tsonga, where the mystical relation of the chief to his people and his powers over nature have to be achieved by magical strengthening and to be renewed periodically, it is largely by means of the magic of the royal regalia that the chief is able to exercise control.[11]

Thomas Mofolo, having schooled himself in the traditions of his own people, as well as in the mission literature of the English (of which Bunyan was probably the most notable example), as a writer was able to synthesize the customary notion of "doctoring" the chieftain with the folk-Christian idea of a pact with the devil. This fusion gives a strong spinal column of credibility to his Chaka story. The double necessity of a periodic magical renewal (Zulu) and of a final reckoning (Christian) ensures an accumulation rather than a mere concatenation of horrors, a regular teleology of the evil will. Each time Chaka is doctored, he becomes further involved with the diabolical sources of his strength. More and more ambitious deeds of violence are actually *required* of him until Chaka, sickened with visions of horror, is finally murdered by those who are nearest to him in blood.

The early pages of Mofolo's book are devoted to the effects of Chaka's first doctoring. To compensate for the ill-treatment meted out in the Ifenilenja village to herself and to her illegitimate son, Chaka's mother Nandi has medicine administered to him by an old witch-woman, who prophesies that if the boy will go regularly by himself to bathe in the great waters of the river, he will one day be visited by the exceptional. Certainly the medicine strengthens him, for Chaka heroically kills a lion before the terrified and envious eyes of the other boys. His father cannot resist sending the skin of this lion to Dingiswayo, chief of the Abatetwa, the most powerful people in the neighborhood, as a token of the prowess of his first-born.

"Chaka's time for going to the river had come again," the solemn voice of narration informs us—and indeed there is something eerily Zarathustrian about the whole affair. This time he is visited by the exceptional.

> When he had come out [of the river] a strange wind blew, the reeds on the banks quivered and tossed violently and then were suddenly still and stood straight again, as if no wind had ever blown. The water receded, the wind fell, and the deep, green pool rippled slightly to show some great thing passing through the midst of it.[12]

Chaka goes unhesitatingly back into the river, only to see a great serpent rise out of the waters.* The boy clutches the doctored lock of his hair and closes his eyes in stoic terror. When he finally musters enough presence to open them, the great snake is in the act of returning, disappointed, to its source. But the spirit deigns to come forward again, and this time grips the courageous boy in his embrace. Having pulled itself up by wrapping twin tongues about Chaka's neck, the snake thoroughly licks his face before receding into the waters again. The effect of this experience is instantaneous: Chaka manfully kills a hyena. But his father, rather than boast of the accomplishment to a neighboring chieftain, in a fit of jealous anger acquiesces in his legitimate son's plot to kill the boy. Since life seems filled with nothing but evil and terror, the abandoned son leaves the village determined to live from then on by force, and force alone.

As he rests for a while from his travels, like the young Buddha under a tree, Chaka the exile has his first fateful meeting with Isanusi ("one who sees into the future"):

> He awoke when the shadows were lengthening, and saw a witch doctor standing by his side, regarding him with a strange expression ... he saw a mocking look on his face; his mouth was drawn down in a grimace, and in the depth of

---

* Ancestral spirits of chiefs often appeared to Chaka's people in the form of snakes, but none ever so impressive as this one. See W. M. Eiselen and I. Schapera, "Religious Beliefs and Practices," *Bantu Speaking Tribes of South Africa*, I. Schapera, ed. (London: George Routledge & Sons, 1937), p. 252.

his eyes he could see unbounded malice and cruelty. He seemed to see a man far more evil than any sorcerer, more cruel by far than any murderer—the very father of malice, wickedness and treachery. Chaka's body shuddered and his eyes quivered. When he looked again he found the man's face full of pity and compassion and very sorrowful. And when he looked into the depths of his eyes he saw there perfect kindness, a sympathetic heart, and the truest love. The expression on his face which he had seen before had vanished entirely.[13]

Isanusi knows who Chaka is, and that he has been visited by the great spirit. Confirming Chaka's cynical and despairing view of existence, Isanusi gives him medicine appropriate to his desperate request for a great chieftainship—that is, all the available strengthening medicine except that promoting murder and bloodshed. Do you want that too? I didn't bring it with me. Isanusi tactfully stands back so that Chaka can think it over.

I desire it! says Chaka, and the die is cast. "Of his own free will Chaka had chosen death instead of life." Together they set off to fetch this most potent medicine from a magic tree, which grows somewhere on the veld by the sea. Isanusi anoints Chaka, his club, and his spear with juice from the bark, and reveals that Chaka now *must* spill blood or the powerful medicine will turn against him and destroy him too.

Chaka continues his journey to the Abatetwa, with whom he has determined, in the early days of his prowess, to live and fight. Once he had been an ordinary young man,

But after seeing his own father's sons trying to kill him without cause and his father himself taking their part, he had fled away and when he was in the desert his inner nature died, and this was the spirit with which he now returned: "I will kill without a cause him whom I wish to kill, be he guilty or be he innocent, for this is the law upon earth."[14]

The first person he kills in this mood and with this new strength is, ironically enough, a madman who has of late been wreaking havoc in the villages and in the bush.

As a warrior for Dingiswayo, Chaka continues to bathe secretly in the river at the appointed time. Returning one morning from the waters, he sees two strangers sitting on their haunches staring at him. One is surely a warrior from a distant land. The other, Ndlebe (Ears), is obviously not a warrior, but

> seemed flabby with droopy ears and a loose mouth. His ears were the largest ever seen, like caves to receive the wind, or rather, the tidings and talk of men. His eyes were watery, full of deceit and treachery. . . . His hair was curled, flopping over his eyes and down his neck in plaits, which increased his evil appearance and made him look like an idiot. [And yet] . . . the appearance of his legs and flanks showed that he was a wonderfully swift runner. The skin on his feet was parched, and chaps covered his heels and even the soles of his feet.[15]

These two characters, as unsavory as the henchmen in Victory, have been sent by Isanusi to help Chaka prepare the regiments with medicines in time of war, and in time of peace to smell out all tidings and secrets.

Eventually, despite his legitimate brothers, Chaka succeeds to his father's chiefdom, and finally, owing to his remarkable talents and the accident of war, to Dingiswayo's as well. Isanusi now tempts him with a chieftainship so big that were a man to begin walking to the bounds of the territory in his youth he would return, wearily, in old age—a chieftainship over warriers as numerous as the stars in the heavens. But for this Chaka must supply his own medicine. His warriors must march forth to battle with food which has been mixed with the blood of the one whom Chaka loves most dearly. "We witch doctors," Isanusi equivocally says, "do but give a man the medicine he desires, even if it brings his destruction. We are the purveyors, only, nothing more."[16] The one Chaka loves best is Dingiswayo's sister Noliwe. Isanusi having previously put into his head the idea that marriage would be unwise, lest sons one day seize or divide the kingdom, the sacrifice seems doubly inevitable and unfair.

Here, however, Mofolo interjects an interlude, a digression on Chaka's new behavior as chief, to provide fictional time for him to weigh Isanusi's words and the probable costs of alternatives. Chaka has, we now learn, renamed his expanding nation the Zulu ("people of heaven") because once, upon hearing thunder,

Chaka declared, "I am as great." He has also inaugurated a new royal salute—*Bayete!*—meaning "He that is between god and man." Were anyone temerarious enough to be tempted to use this greeting for anyone but Chaka, the following curse would apply:

> . . . lions will tear you to pieces, your cattle will fail to give birth ever again, your women will not conceive, your fields will not bring forth, rain will not fall, and your enemies will wax strong against you.[17]

The praising of Chaka is also described in this section, including praises by the very cattle, starved for the purpose, in their stalls. "All things," sings the herdboy, "living of the Mazulu praise thee, thee in praise of whom the cows have bellowed and even now are bellowing." In the end, Chaka decides to murder Noliwe.

As a result of this murder the chief of the Zulus undergoes a great change. His capacity to distinguish between war and murder is gone. He begins the great slaughtering of the cowards who have gone into battle "as empty sound only" and returned empty-handed, without any enemy spears as trophies. Those who weep at his excesses have their eyes plucked out; and those who murmur against him for this have their tongues plucked out. And those "who saw what happened on that day were delirious all night and wasted away, for it was the first time that men had seen such things." [18]

But they are to see more. Chaka even kills his own mother when he finds out that she has been shielding one of his illegitimate sons against the customary murder of such unfortunate creatures. (He himself, of course, according to his own canons, should have died at birth.) Then, in a complete *volte-face*, the remorseful Chaka hurls into a ditch all those who do not weep enough for mother Nandi. Corroded by doubts and insatiable desires, Chaka calls for feasts and festivals, and then murders all those who sing with poor voices, or who—afraid because of their poor voices—don't sing at all. Then his pain lessens and he becomes, temporarily, " a man again." When there are no more enemies to be fought, Chaka, growing suspicious of his stronger generals, maneuvers his own choice regiments into fighting against and exterminating each other. Finally, his own brothers kill him, and he lies where he falls, for not even the crows and hyenas will touch him. Isanusi comes forward at the very moment of Chaka's death to claim his promised reward—of cattle.

V.

Chaka has been resurrected and given a contemporary apotheosis by the distinguished Senegalese poet Léopold Sédar Senghor. In a dramatic poem on Chaka, composed just a few years before independence in West Africa, Senghor transforms the Zulu chieftain into a kind of black Prometheus, a suffering South African martyr whose sacrifice foretells the ultimate liberation of all mankind, throughout Africa. In a dialogue with a sententious white voice which invokes the superficial moral standards with which the exceptional man is judged, and is supposed to judge himself, Senghor's Chaka reveals the profound core of his apparently destructive intentions. In so doing he reveals his personal anguish, the unbearable intensity of the suffering that he has already caused as a self-conscious murderer of his people, and especially of the woman that he loved. Is this a complete vitiation of Mofolo's ethical point of view? Or does Senghor's interpretation, the product of a different stage of political development in Africa, of a sophisticated cultural awareness, support Mofolo's interpretation on a level that is not apparent to us at first?

I have set the ax to the dead wood, lit fire in the sterile bush
Like any careful farmer. When the rains came and the time
    for sowing, the ashes were ready. . . .
Each death was my death. There were coming harvests to
    prepare
And the millstones to grind the white white flour from the
    tenderness of black hearts.[19]

Informed of the coming of the white man, Chaka's powerful imagination at once grasped what this would mean. Mofolo's Chaka prophesies to his enemies that no rival but the white man will replace him. Senghor's Chaka describes the future scene in detail.

I saw in a dream all the lands to the far corners of the horizon
    set under the ruler, the set-square, the compass
Forests mowed down hills leveled, valleys and rivers in
    chains . . .

> Peoples of the South, in the shipyards, the ports and the
>   mines and the mills
> And at evening segregated in the kraals of misery. . . .
> Could I stay deaf to such suffering, such contempt? [20]

Because of what he foresaw, Chaka killed the poet in himself to
become the politician, the man of pure action, or in Senghor's
imagery, the knee in the tam-tam's flank, pestle, rod. Senghor
has, in effect, transposed Isanusi's words to Chaka about the witch
doctor's role as purveyor only and ascribed them to Chaka himself, as the deed that accompanies the word, as action which
elevates deeds into poetry. The deeds are clear, but what is the
gist of the word, the burden of poetry created out of destruction
and suffering, the quality of being to which the martyred Chaka
now in death returns?

The choral leader praises Chaka as strength and strengthening:
"You are the Zulu, by you we sprung up thick as corn, you are
the nostrils through which we draw strong life. You are the
broad-backed. You carry all the black-skinned peoples." [21] But
she also calls him "lover of the night" (to which he now returns),
"the creator of the words of life," and "the poet of the kingdom
of childhood." Love, night, poetry, and childhood are the resources of heroism in the individual soul. As variants of a sublime
passivity they impede heroic action, however, and must be
temporarily discarded when the deeds of the objective world are
to be done. For the black man these are the true negations by
which secret strengths—hidden because always denied by false
white premises—may be known.

Sophisticated, feeling interpretations of the heroic African past
cannot, in the final analysis, be understood without some refer-
ence to the concept of *négritude*. The poetic practice of expressing oneself in a black man's mode (deeper and wilder and more
vivid than indigo) has been cultivated by most French poets of
African ancestry ever since Césaire. The poetry of *négritude* is
based on the double assumption that there *is* such a thing as a
black man's style, and that the language of poetry is evocative in
a quasi-magical sense.*

---

* The coincidental similarity between various romantic European notions
of "the word"—be these symbolist, surrealist, or other—and various
West African notions of verbal "force" has had a significance for modern

This concept was first subjected to philosophical analysis about a decade and a half ago by the ubiquitous Jean-Paul Sartre. According to Sartre, there are two ways of establishing a racial identity. One can proceed from the outside in, by interiorizing certain objective characteristics discernible in the course of history—in this case, during the course of African history—and by claiming certain ways of conduct that appear to be typically African as one's own. Or one can establish one's racial identity from the inside out, by sounding the depths of one's consciousness, feelings, and personal store of images, and in some way objectifying these—as in a poem.[22]

According to Thomas Meloné of the Republic of Cameroun, a recent interpreter of *négritude*, the primary pathos of this second approach lies in a subjective return to sources of being that are no longer *there*, in seizing an emotional inheritance destroyed or corrupted by time. *Négritude* as a poetic, objectifying process, therefore, is a recreation of the absent and, as such, is closely linked to the methodology of the symbolist poet Mallarmé:

> The Negro wills himself son of Africa. This moment when the child discovers a father, when he finally realizes love, is clothed with an exceptional significance . . . the Kingdom of Childhood. By re-establishing contact with the Absent, the Negro has established a link with the past, for the African past is his own proper past. Prodigal son who recovers his father after centuries [hyperbole here] of wandering, he declares himself as one who has remained the child that he once was, this child, *royal* and *pure*, that the hostile world of western civilization has been unable to corrupt.[23]

This is *négritude's* romantic, passive side. The active aspect is an attack on colonialism (on whatever in Western civilization corrupted the pure, royal child), the political commitment (in existentialist terms, *l'engagement*) subsequent to that most important voyage of cultural self-discovery.

African literature and for European theories about that literature which cannot be underestimated. The sorcerer's *balafon* in *Soundjata* that receives and transmits the "strength" of the human word is like the famous aeolian harp of the European imagination. The vibratory devices used to evoke absence in Mallarmé are used to evoke ancestral presences in African poetry. The curse of the sorcerer or "doctor" is the devastating surrealist *mot injuste*.

The return to childhood, then, as part of the psychological process of *négritude*, may account in part for the insouciance, for the simplicity of *Soundjata*; it may account—whether or not the author at any conscious level intended it to do so—for affinities this book holds to French literature of *l'enfance perdu*. Soundjata's purity is not only that of the neophyte Moslem nation; the establishment of his kingdom out of his boyish dreams means the re-establishment of the author's personal paradise lost.

The alienated African sensibility may return to its childhood through folk tales as well as through heroic legends of the past. The proliferation of written folk tales in recent years is not only the result of a concerted effort to give African schoolchildren something of their own tradition to study in the classroom. Some of these traditional materials are "told" as art tales by highly sophisticated writers. This revival of the evensongs of an un- spoiled African childhod obviously has a complicated meaning for the African adults who read and write them. African folk tales are traditionally told at night. They are not appropriate to the workaday world, to the daily struggle for existence. The spirits abroad in the night somehow enter into the tales, either as a critical or sometimes criticized audience, or substantially in a fictive guise. The world of the folk fable is a world of pregnant symbols and silences, a world of talking animals, of spiritual advice. Absorbed, at any hour of the day or night, in the process of this passionate childish experience, the real world becomes what the German romantics called *fabelhaft*—transformed, ac- cording to the dictates of the poetic will, into a home for the yearning soul that has been bruised by the harshness of the workaday world, the grownup world, or specifically in this case, the colonial world.

In this context, Hazoumé's return to the parabolic village of the old storyteller in *Doguicimi* is not only a strategic retreat from the historical Dahomey whose bloodiness the Europeans always stressed, but it is a personal retreat as well. Just as Ghezo's assertion, when pressed by the Portuguese, of the legitimacy of blood sacrifice seems natural as a *prise de soi*, the preliminary gesture in the dance of *négritude*, so the folkloric sections at the end of the book are a poem to the uncorrupted, unlearned, un- documented, artistic, nuanced, free African self! Hazoumé might well be called a contemporary of Césaire; but he was a scholar, not a poet, and therefore but half "free." That he was free at all is remarkable; that his freedom should have taken the form that it did is not so surprising. That Hazoumé wrote before all the definitions and manifestos that have made *négritude* a public process is but a sign of the vitality of the phenomenon described by the logic. Sartre's thesis is given further documentation by Hazoumé.

What of Mofolo, then? In what way is *Chaka* an assertion of *his négritude?* Perhaps in the same way that Milton's Satan is an assertion of the poet's proud, rebellious will. Senghor, like the English romantics who later made Satan the hero of the piece, has temporarily abrogated the moral framework in which Mofolo wrote. The highest tribute Mofolo's imagination could pay to the bloody hero whom his mission teachers condemned was to put him in league with the Christian devil. The horror and atrocities of his career put the great Zulu forever on the map of Africa, and any honest person who had not been exposed to modern theories of the great Immoralist, of the romantic Scourge, would have left him to the vultures in the end. That the vultures would not have him is proof of his magical invulnerability in legend, of Mofolo's deepest desire to leave him so.

Thus, says Meloné, at the conclusion of his essay, in the full light of his conscience the Negro-African finds only a discontinuous collection of instants that were plenitude and perfection. He will never recover them completely.[24] Soundjata in his youth was perfection. Chaka in his pride was plenitude.

A dissenting note as postscriptum: In Wole Soyinka's play, *A Dance of the Forests,* given as a part of the Nigerian independence celebrations in 1960, the village orator Adenebi says to Rola the carver,

> The accumulated heritage—that is what we are celebrating. Mali. Chaka. Songai. Glory. Empires. But you cannot feel it, can you? . . . This is the era of greatness. Unfortunately it is to those who cannot bear too much of it to whom the understanding is given.[25]

The villagers in this play call back the ancestral spirits of themselves, the denizens of a supposedly glorious past, only to find a collection of rather unpleasant people, knit to the living by sordid and passionate behavior that has never been expiated. The mood and the situation are those of Pirandello, oddly cynical, perhaps, given the nature of the occasion, but typical in sophisticated Nigerian writing of English expression. No fabulous kingdom, but a slave-trading autocracy is uncovered, and the villagers (and the audience, presumably) wish that the whole thing would go away. Soyinka suggests that people are more important than empires, that ancestors might be better thought of as sins, and that until one has come to commonsense terms with oneself as an active human being, *négritude* is just tigritude (as Soyinka has said elsewhere)—and how ridiculous that one is!

Notes

1. Basil Davidson, *The Lost Cities of Africa* (Boston: Little, Brown and Company, 1959), p. 92.

2. Robert Pageard, "Soundjata Keita and the Oral Tradition," *Présence Africaine*, XXXVI (April–July, 1961), 61.

3. Djibril Tamsir Niane, *Soundjata, ou l'epopée mandingue* (Paris: Présence Africaine, 1960), p. 11.

4. *Ibid.*, p. 4.

5. *Ibid.*, p. 64.

6. *Ibid.*, p. 127.

7. Paul Hazoumé, *Doguicimi* (Paris: Larose, 1938), p. 29.

8. *Ibid.*, pp. 379–81.

9. *Ibid.*, p. 423.

10. E. A. Ritter, *Shaka Zulu* (London: Longmans, Green & Co., 1955), pp. 14–16.

11. S. D. and E. J. Krige, "The Louedu of the Transvaal," *African Worlds* (London: Oxford University Press, 1954), p. 61.

12. Thomas Mofolo, *Chaka*, F. H. Dutton, trans. (London: Oxford University Press, 1931), p. 26.

13. *Ibid.*, pp. 43–44.

14. *Ibid.*, p. 57.

15. *Ibid.*, p. 44.

16. *Ibid.*, p. 124.

17. *Ibid.*, p. 139.

18. *Ibid.*, p. 195.

19. Léopold Sédar Senghor, "Chaka," *Selected Poems*, John Reed and Clive Wake, trans. (New York: Atheneum Publishers, 1964), pp. 68, 72.

20. *Ibid.*, p. 71.

21. *Ibid.*, p. 75.

22. Jean-Paul Sartre, "Orphée noir," *Anthologie de la nouvelle poésie nègre et malgache* (Paris: Presses Universitaires de France, 1948), p. xv.

23. Thomas Meloné, *De la négritude dans la litterature negro-africaine* (Paris: Présence Africaine, 1962), p. 54.

24. *Ibid.*, p. 130.

25. Wole Soyinka, *A Dance of the Forests* (London: Oxford University Press, 1963), p. 8.

III VILLAGE LIFE

*"Come near me while I sing the
ancient ways . . ."*
—W. B. YEATS

To return to the common lot and the commonplace: Just as most African writers to date have been born and raised in modest villages, so their novels have been written for a variety of ordinary reasons that need not imply *négritude* as first or final cause. The average African writer of the later colonial period (Mofolo's free-wheeling genius excepted) did not demand imaginative auton-omy, any more than his leaders demanded political autonomy. He merely asked to be understood, to let his authentic experience prevail over the grosser European stereotypes of himself as a member of a "primitive" community. Thus a modestly talented Togolander of the 1950's wrote a European novel about genuine African village life simply because "Africa is often misunder-stood." Were it to be disclosed as it really is, from within, "with-out bias or disdain," white readers' scorn or indifference would turn to indulgence based on a recognition of "the humanity therein." [1] Apparently, then, the author will remain neutral. In writing about his people he will not be ostensibly writing about a unique self.

But from the very beginning he is involved in a certain contra-diction. The educated African who wants to tell Europe about communal Africa must write about a life that, in a sense, he no longer lives. The European anthropologist, having had a sustained experience as a participant, withdraws to recollect in tranquillity before organizing impressions of his chosen exotic society into the coherent familiarity of his art. But the indigenous author of a novel about his own village life does not recollect in tranquillity. *His* attachment to traditional ways, once suppressed, must now be self-consciously strengthened; and to go back over the experiences of lost youth must be a rather disturbing affair, no matter what one's cultural situation. This African writer is, after all, the man who once renounced in black and white that which he now seeks to recreate in polychrome. Thus even if the writer be consciously committed to social evolution and political change, such is the nature of his exercise that a sentimental or nostalgic strain is likely to enter into his reconstructions, making them far more personal than he intended at the outset for them to be. Because village novels are based on childhood reminiscences, and because in Africa they contain the memory of generations as well, to remove from these memories some of the terrors and anxieties of one's *present* existence is an understandable personal necessity and, under colonial conditions, a matter of racial pride as well.

There are always exceptions to be noted. Some African writers, usually strong converts to Christianity, have tended to stress the terrors of the *former* existence, to point out how bound by superstition and sloth the villagers, despite their humanity, are. Books with this tone, however, which have owed whatever modest publicity they may have had to mission presses, are now all but extinct. But another attitude, combining a truculent, or rather humorously insinuating, approach to the reader, a pious attachment to the old ways, and a kind of exasperated self-irony, is far from extinct. This line, although found in a controlled way in the pre-independence novel, is really more characteristic of the post-independence novel which attacks colonial residues while being at the same time dependent on a European readership, which ennobles traditional institutions while at the same time realizing the comic limitations of a "backward" existence.

An example of this ironic attitude in fiction may be taken from a novel (published in 1954) by the Congolese writer Jean Malonga. After giving an account of an African mother's thoughts on the overwhelming advantages of prepubescent marriage, the author interpolates the following: "Well satisfied by this reasoning, a rationale which is perhaps revolting to the reader, M'polo . . ." and so on.[2] In context this amounts to a gay provocation of the prudish Western reader. Malonga feels no need to apologize for or to justify the practice, nor on the other hand would he be likely to marry off his own daughter at the age of eight. These were our customs, he seems to be saying; outlandish weren't they, sensible too. Irony here is a double protection for the author: against the Europeans he hates but must court as his readers, and against his own past, which he has no intention of reviving in any literal sense.*

The novel about traditional life, with all its ambiguities, served African history very well in the years preceding independence. Suing, out of suffering, for the indulgence due the misunderstood was the African counterpart of the lenient "interested" attitude of the European public during the period of colonial disaffiliation. While making real people out of the phantom savages that traditionally danced in the minds of the European public, while preparing that public for the inevitable assumption of political responsibility by these newly humanized "natives" or *noirs*, such novels at the same time allowed Europeans to indulge in a few of their old preconceptions. These preconceptions had been engendered by Europeans who insisted (sometimes without even having been on the scene) on showing the more traditional, the more exotic (not to say erotic) sides of African life. An African who wrote of these things (even if he patently ignored the erotic, which had nothing to do with *his* fantasies) could not be gainsaid. The life, in a rather vague way, was familiar; but that the *noirs* were competent to write effectively about it in a European language—that was new. And that their approach in some cases was most sophisticated came as a real surprise.

The appeal to the conscience of Europe through its imaginative frontiers has, since independence, switched to an indemnification for psychic losses suffered during the colonial period. This last flatters the moral propensities of a Western audience that has become guilt-stricken about its role in the denigration of peoples

---

* For a superb example of this ironic ambivalence in the drama, see J. P. Clark's *The Song of a Goat* (Ibadan, Nigeria: Mbari, 1961). The tone of this ostensibly tragic play about the conflict between an individual's personal desire (and potency) and the traditional wisdom of the village community is disturbingly and yet somehow delightfully inconsistent. To the tragic strain is counterpointed a ribald τράγος ὀδη′ and a certain skittishness inevitably develops in the reader. Whether or not this Dionysian skittishness can, at the proper times, be squelched probably depends on the maturity of the players and the audience at any given production. But the unsettling hilarity is in the play—a projection in verse of a highly strung modern Nigerian personality who simply cannot go about things simply, who must outrageously emphasize the incongruities implied in playing African wisdom straight.

of color. But although African writers are still in large part dependent upon a European readership, the situation is changing and the writers' rhetoric is now largely directed inward—towards Africans for whom African men of letters would now like to be exemplary selves. While the author's historical situation as a spokesman is important for an understanding of certain restraints he places upon his own emotions, as upon the social behavior of clansmen depicted in his books (restraints which are often extremely difficult to distinguish from the natural decorum of traditional societies like those described), still the poignancy of the rhetorical situation cannot really account for any given African's choosing at some point to take up a Western pen and write. The writer is an offshoot of colonialism, a restless village boy become an exceptional African man. He writes first of all because, endowed with an artistic temperament, he has been twice born into a cosmopolitan world of written skills.

The conflicts created by the author's colonial condition appear in these deceptively simple "village" novels in a variety of ways. Sometimes, as suggested above, they appear in the tone, in the delicate *sehnsucht nach heimat* of the dispossessed, in the ambivalent anger of revulsion against certain tribal practices, or in the ironic stance of the man of two worlds. But they also enter more directly, through the protagonist, because of this person's special relation to the author. Since the man who writes the novel about village life is not by temperament or training the ordinary villager, neither will his protagonist be. The two may not be special in the same way, but innovative energy is present in both, an energy at odds with the social inertia and fixed beliefs of the group. Sometimes the author's life story is paralleled pretty exactly in the novel, and the hero leaves the village as a student or convert or money-maker in the end. But it may also happen that the story is cast in a more legendary vein, with the author transformed into a culture hero or innovator whose activities, significantly, are resisted by the elders; or the hero may even be persecuted by these elders and run out of town, even out of existence, on a rail. The opposite stance is also a possibility: The author's creative energy may focus, in his novel, on a poetic stalwart who resists the more degrading aspects of social change and is all but crucified by the new Philistines.

Ironically perhaps, given the ostensible nature of his task, it is only when a village writer is able to develop a hero with a personality strong enough to take the group on singlehanded, as it were, to act as antagonist against the collective hero (the village itself), that he succeeds artistically and the story comes alive. For the village way of life (the collectivity), in opposing the energetic, dissenting hero, declares itself and its values. Thus a dramatic confrontation succeeds in exposing the vitality of village institutions in a way that mere description never could. Evocation (as opposed to mere description) also succeeds in animating immemorial customs; but a passionate, poetical evocation is really part of a drama in the author's own mind.

II.

The desire to make African village life plausible to the European imagination was early felt by a French-speaking Negro from Martinique who served for many years as a political officer in French Equatorial Africa. In 1910, René Maran wrote the following decisive words in a letter to a friend in France:

> Now, with a French heart, I sense that I am on the soil of my ancestors, ancestors that I reprove because I share neither their primitive mentality nor their tastes, but who are none the less my ancestors for all that.[3]

It is the identification that is decisive. Whatever squeamishness there is about the statement dates Maran, sets him apart from the continental and even from the Caribbean Africans of a more recent time. The commitment of this islander to his African origins marks, in a very special sense, the beginning of authentic genre literature out of Africa. Unlike his fellow islander, Aimé Césaire, Maran was born too soon, and did not have the temperament to develop into an acknowledged neo-African literary pioneer. Nor was his work effective politically, in the way that he had hoped. He was a talented man who, in remaining true to himself despite his times, was destined to have events continually reinforce the temperamental morbidity and the supporting pessimistic philosophy he developed as a lonely black student, the son of a civil servant, in a boarding school in provincial France.

That Maran also faced the facts of his national origin, of his European education, tastes, and interests, the "French heart" exposed above should make clear. He had no desire to falsify history and make himself an African, but as a colonial officer of conscience and sensibility he had every reason to disown the brutally callous regime that he, in his manner, had to serve. So his French imagination went to work for an African cause which concerned him ethically, the way it concerned Felix Eboué, as a favored colonial subject of African descent. Because of his situation, Maran's "exoticism"—for it is a kind of exoticism in the French romantic tradition—has a moral urgency that other European exoticisms have lacked.* Although his style and vocabulary anticipate the free verse rhythms and the detailed, poetical genre painting of certain modern African passages praised for their *négritude*, Maran's work is much too pervaded with a kind of neoclassical (or Parnassian) French stoicism to be an endemic expression of the neo-African point of view. Nor is his moral urgency ever an excuse for sloppy writing. Maran, like many colonial persons since, was in love with the French language, a feeling which the French, with their own endogamous love of their language, have always been able to inspire.† And Maran thought, as others have thought, that the best way to show his love for the French language was to write it well.[4]

* More precisely, Maran's exoticism might be called "psychological exoticism"—the presentation of the aboriginal mind as a thinking mangrove, a doubting liana, an illiterate reed. For French examples of this school see Roland Lebel, "Tableau de l' Afrique occidentale dans la litterature française," *Afrique—occidentale française*, II (Paris: 1949), pp. 379–86 *passim*. A fascinating contemporary example of exoticism with a moral urgency like Maran's is Victor Stafford Reid's *The Leopard* (New York: The Viking Press, 1958). This recreation of the mau mau mind by a Jamaican who had never been to Kenya is not, of course, strictly speaking, an "African" novel. But it has a romantic vitality of its own and, as an essay in understanding, it should be allowed to wage a dialectical battle with Elspeth Huxley's essays in misunderstanding.
† Senegal's poet-politician Senghor, it may be remembered, was appointed official French grammarian at the constitutional convention for the Fourth Republic. Maran went further than most colonials in his fascination with the history of French words, rejoicing, for example, in the fact that *couleur* in the seventeenth and eighteenth centuries could be either masculine or feminine when immediately followed by qualitatives, with masculine being *"plus élégant."* See his letter to Léon Bosquet in Bosquet's introduction to Maran's *Le Petit roi de chimérie* (Paris: Editions Albin Michel, 1924), p. 38.

Maran spent seven years revising his first novel, *Batouala*, which catapulted him from an obscure post in Ubangi-Shari into the notoriety of the Goncourt Prize in 1921, and ultimately, because of the controversial nature of the book, out of the civil service altogether. The subject matter, unlike the prose, was inelegant: cruelty and drunkenness among whites and African villagers alike, violent passions that invest the poverty-stricken lives of the Africans with a certain dignity which the coarse, calculated inhumanity of the whites prevents them from understanding except in their own terms—as violence. The narrative at once plunges the reader into the freely associating consciousness of the leading character, Batouala, a consciousness which so reflects his equatorial surroundings that natural occurrences seem to be his very thoughts externalized. But Maran gave Batouala more than poetry. He dignified this man, one of colonialism's less consequential victims, with commonplace thoughts as well, with reactions to his dog's loyalty and his wife's infidelity that anybody could understand. And, in addition to this, *Batouala* effectively showed the Europeans what they seemed, at the time, rather surprised and outraged to learn: that "they" don't like us.[5]

Although Felix Eboué wrote Maran that the great satisfaction he felt at the award enabled him to "*supporter sans trop de dommage pour mon equilibre, la saleté de mon gouverneur général,*"[6] and although in 1925 a devoted teacher in Bambari was already reportedly giving passages from *Batouala* to African students for *dictée*, Maran's influence in Africa was isolated and personal, rather than pervasive and political. In France, the very origin that had temporarily intrigued the literati discredited him with the politicians. To the business interests he sought to combat, his literary nature made him additionally suspect. (Even his friend Gide, whose *Voyage au Congo* substantiated Maran's fiction, had a hard time getting the right people to take seriously what he had to say on the subject.) It was not until Maran's loyal colleague from Guiana, Felix Eboué himself, was made governor general of French Equatorial Africa (on December 31, 1940) in an unprecedented move by the French government that something positive could at last be done for that benighted territory of the concessionaires.

But *Batouala*, despite all the care given to its composition, all its virtues and its notoriety, is not Maran's best book. Nor did he think so.[7] His masterpiece, *Le Livre de la brousse*, published about fifteen years later, was never translated into English (as was, however badly, the Goncourt winner), and it remains almost unknown in this country, probably elsewhere as well. *Le Livre de la brousse* is similar in conception to *Batouala*, but, as a Frenchman might use the word, more *noble*. The world of the drunken whites has disappeared from the background and an increased importance is given to the animal world, the world of such personified natural forces as Doppelé, the vulture-with-the-bald-neck who hovers constantly above the scene, and Moumeu the crocodile, aging and wary, who finally gets the hero in the end. Archetypal animals such as these, exemplars of the grim struggle for existence around the equator (and farther north), became in their turn the real heroes of most of Maran's later books. But in adopting the animal characters of the traditional African folk tale, he used them to express his own neo-Darwinian and anti-colonial points of view.

To evoke nature's changing moods in *Le Livre de la brousse*, Maran uses a precise vocabulary which indicates the continual process of erosion, destruction, and putrefaction that underlies all proliferation in the tropics. This changing yet constantly repeated chorus of potent minutiae, expressive of Maran's own philosophical preoccupations, his stoical moodiness, may serve as an introduction to his version of the neo-African French style. It is evening:

> Soudain, blême, rouge, verte, une clarté extraordinaire l'enveloppa, l'aveugla,—et la foudre s'abima dans la Tomi. . . .
>
> On ne voit rien, mais on entend l'innombrable, le mystérieux gargouillement de l'eau que déglutissent les mille bouches et les mille pores de la terre.
>
> Encore un instant,—et le sibilement des chauves-souris vrillera d'appels discontinus le chant striduleux des grillons et le froufrou des termites grignotant le chaume des toîtures ou minant les secrets de la terre.
>
> L'espace appartient désormais aux troupes puantes que commande Taha 'mba, la fourmi-cadavre, aux coassements des crapauds, aux crissements des cigales, et aussi, et surtout au gémissement du vent lent sur la brousse, immense plainte humaine qui, depuis que le monde est monde, berce en tous lieux le sommeil des hommes.[8]

Against these forces and against the fearful villagers of Krébèdje who attempt to outwit them, or placate them, or—all else failing—merely suffer them, stands the passionate antisocial Kossi, the hero of *Le Livre de la brousse*. Kossi, extraordinarily unruly and destructive as a child, a calabash smasher, becomes in adult life the living legend of a hunter. He has rid the tribe of Mourou, the supposedly invincible panther, and—so his Banda people think—of Bamara the lion as well. He is, if the truth be known, no more responsible for Bamara's death than Falstaff for Hotspur's; a wild bull had got there first. But convinced that the imposition of victorious power on the imaginations of man and beast is the only way to live in a world dominated by fear and destruction, Kossi permits himself first to eat the heart of the lion and then to broadcast his spurious accomplishment to the village group.

If this were not enough to arouse their jealous hostility, Kossi again puts himself above the tribesmen by refusing to accept the elders' judgment on a man who had attacked Kossi's father with a knife and who is Kossi's own rival in love. Kossi does get the girl in the end, but his wounded father soon dies, and the rival is merely fined for the crime, according to the original judgment. So the outraged son picks up all his dissatisfactions with tribal justice and moves them, his new wife, and his old mother twenty spear-throws away from the offending village.

During a period of devastating rain, plague, and vermin, sensing that superstitious discontent is being diverted to the non-conformist, Kossi goes back the twenty spear-throws to Krébèdje to try to regain the favor of his suffering people before they have a chance to expiate their wrongs by sacrificing him. He finds them dancing out their sorrows, and he, the champion dancer, with one leap places himself in the center of the earthen circle. Drum, song, and clap increase in intensity as the others step back to watch the outcast perform.

> Kossi outdid himself. Never had he danced with such verve.
> . . . Arms floating, Kossi pretended to fly. This was delirious.
> The women cried "Doppelé! Doppelé!" [the vulture]. Dogs
> barked, children cried, the tam tams roared. The wind rolled
> cascades of thunder across the horizon but nobody paid any
> attention. Kossi was there.
> He danced. With him, thanks to him, the elephants
> danced, the ants, the python, the catfish, the anteater, doves,

Koukouroue-the-parakeet, the lizard, tortoise, shrimp, the waters of the rapids, the rain, spider, stars, the bush fire, the storm wind. He made to enter his dances the very infinite, even the trees, even the grass, even the stones.[9]

Kossi, the marvelous hunter, forces nature to do his bidding at the dance. All the animals he has understood and therefore been able to kill are reborn in gesture here. He seems able to incarnate the very elements. Can he then take the whole burden of nature upon himself? Will his dancing stop the storm, rid them of the plague, of the very vermin? The fearful villagers of Krébèdje never have a chance to find this out, for Kossi's wild dance is suddenly interrupted by the hidden spokesman of Ngakoura, god of gods. Kossi's irreverence to elders and ancients, says the voice, is responsible for devastations of nature which all the inspired dancing in the world will never prevent. The god also holds Kossi responsible for the predicted and now rumored arrival of the mysterious and apparently equally devastating white men from across the big sea. As punishment and prophylactic, Kossi must sacrifice his wife to the god. With this, the awesome voice suspends itself in a threatening silence and the rain, which actually *had* let up in mid-dance, again begins to fall.

Kossi will not obey the god's command, but his mother will. While her son is out hunting, she entices the young girl out of her hut so that the god may have at her. Kossi, returning from the hunt, finds his beautiful wife disemboweled somewhere along the way. For this deed nefarious members of a secret society are responsible—a society to which Kossi himself had once taken great pride in being initiated. Kossi flees to the open water to live among the itinerant river people whose adventurous cosmopolitan lives have always intrigued him. And there, pursued by the newly arrived Europeans, Kossi is at last devoured by his old "natural" rival, Moumeu the crocodile.

The plot pattern Maran established in *Le Livre de la brousse* has been followed by African "village" writers ever since. Whether or not they have consciously done so makes no difference; probably in most cases they have not.* The vehicle is, as

---

* This does not mean that Maran has not had his quota of direct imitators. The fanciful forest sections (the fleeing animals) of Hazoumé's *Doguicimi* are patently Maranesque in spirit, and a credit to both writ-

has been suggested, a natural one for the conveyance of a certain ambivalence towards the culture being described. The theme of the innovative youth at odds with the conservative community of elders is as inexhaustible as the social, as well as the psychic, realities it decries. The augmented energies of the culture hero— Soundjata or Chaka in a humbler guise—are both an expression of and a potential menace to the group.

One of the most interesting, because it's the most forward-looking, versions of this theme is Sembene Ousmane's *O pays, mon beau peuple!* published in Paris in 1957. This novel by the famous "black docker" of Senegal and Marseilles is about a man educated by experience abroad rather than by formal assimilationist schooling, a former soldier for France who returns to his conservative Moslem village in Casamance with half-formulated plans for singlehanded economic development and a very real white bride. His father, imam of the local Mosque, refuses to have anything to do with him unless he renounces his wife. But among the progressive ideas that Faye Oumar has brought back with him from Europe is the idyl of a separate ménage for husband and wife (which does not prevent him from establishing a secret liaison with a beautiful and disturbed mulatto girl in a different quarter). Faye and his wife Isabelle do build an idyllic house upriver, to which they gradually begin to invite those younger people of the village who are already beginning to wake up.

----

ers. Nazi Boni's (Upper Volta) recent novel, *Le Crepuscule des temps anciens* (Paris: Présence Africaine, 1962), is remarkable for being a diluted version of *Le Livre de la brousse*. Here again are the personified creatures of the bush, the exclamatory phrases pointing up the intensity of bush life, the exceptional hunter hero. But Maran's Bandas at intervals dance religiously in tragic exultation on a dancing floor wrested from an equatorial overgrowth which threatens at any moment to overwhelm them; Nazi Boni's Bwa people dance giddily in the midst of plenty at the slightest provocation. Whether this is a reflection of the temperament of the writer or of the easier society he describes is open to question. The Bwa hero's enemies have been reduced to two, the sinister old wizard Lowan and his terrorist son Kya, and the hero is ultimately destroyed by poison rather than by crocodile—a far less dramatic ending to a far milder career.

Although it was the ardent desire of all of them to live with no concern for tomorrow, the country—awakening from its lethargy—was dragging the youth along, like sludge in the river. Their personal future, and that of their people, exacted more of them each day. They began to aspire towards an Africa in which they would no longer have to live out a drama provoked by the conflict of two races on their soil.[10]

A member of a family of fishermen of long standing, Faye Oumar decides further to violate precedent by returning to the soil. He desires to redeem the land in two senses: to increase the productivity of the Casamance, which he sees as the potential rice basket of Senegal, and to wrest the profits of peasant labor from the European company which has comfortably installed itself in his village, setting the prices and exploiting indigenous need and strength.

In two years Faye Oumar is able to build up a rice seed bank, and a great deal of good will among the peasantry, by insuring them against famine from his own stock of dried fish. But his aggressive temperament and ready fists have made him anathema to the white community, and when he proposes the establishment of a rice cooperative and marketing board to his "progressive" friends, one of them betrays him to the Company and he is mysteriously and brutally murdered for his pains. His wife, meanwhile, has established real African roots through Faye's eccentric mother, who doctors the frail French girl incessantly so that she may be able to produce a child. Through the old pipe-smoking sorceress Isabelle is also initiated into the mysteries of African plants, into the redemptive aspects of a brute nature that the hard-working peasantry is constantly forced to combat. In the end, Isabelle promises to stay in the village with her mother-in-law, at least until Faye Oumar's child is born. As for Faye, he receives his romantic apotheosis in a Sholokhovian vein:

The criminal arms which beat him down were deceived. It was not in the tomb that he lay but in the hearts of all men and women. He was present in the evening when the fires were lit in the rice fields. . . . He preceded the sowing of the crops, he was present during the rainy season and he kept company with the young people at harvest time.[11]

III.

The theme of age, as opposed to the innovative energy of youth, is given a special poignancy in the Nigerian Chinua Achebe's first novel, *Things Fall Apart* (1958). Not only is this the purest and most precise village novel so far in English, but, equally surprising, the hero is an old man. Achebe's poised and stately prose is a perfect vehicle for his task. In this artistic recreation of his own grandfather's era, Achebe invests the old man Okonkwo—and with him an entire generation of village elders—with an immense classical dignity. The form and the subject are perfectly suited. Each detail of daily life, as performed with simple elegance, is described with noble restraint of style. The Umuofia villagers are at the mercy of an historical situation from which there can be no turning back. But Okonkwo alone defies the disintegrative effects of colonial occupation; his style and personality are therefore tragic. Since there are no comfortable, inherited hierarchical positions among these people, there is a great deal of personal anxiety which the new circumstances aggravate to the extreme. (Status in the community may be indicated by "titles," but these are taken after the fact, are bought as signs. As a man dances, say the Ibo, so the drums are beaten for him. There are also proverbs which indicate that changing rhythms require new dance steps.)

Since the Ibo people are renowned for the premium they place on successful enterprise, this book appropriately begins with a straightforward declaration of the hero's worth: "Okonkwo was well known throughout the nine villages and even beyond. His fame rested on solid personal achievements." [12] As a young man he had won fame by throwing the star wrestler Amalinze-the-cat. His middle years were characterized by economic prosperity—three wives and two barns full of yams—as well as by inter-tribal prowess (five enemy heads) and intra-tribal prestige (two "titles" taken already). Since Okonkwo's story is to be a tragic one, the hero's flaws are also made apparent from the beginning. He is quick to anger. Afraid of weakness in himself, he despises it in others. He has no patience with unsuccessful men like his father, who let him down.

Okonkwo's father, far from wishing to achieve prosperity and honor for himself and his family, was not even a good provider. Lazy and improvident out of a philosophical conviction that "all is vanity" (a legend he read in a dead man's mouth—which gapes but does not ask for food) and perhaps also out of a dreamy unwillingness to grow up and put away the pleasing, ineffectual instruments of music for those of toil, Okonkwo's father died leaving the family heavily in debt and the disgrace of an ambitious "materialistic" society. To his young son he bequeathed, in addition, a fear and a rage that were to last a lifetime (and, as bequests to his unborn grandson, even beyond).

But hard work and ingenuity, always respected among these villagers, eventually brought wealth and fame to the vigorous Okonkwo. And—such is the relentless logic of the generations—the very qualities which enabled Okonkwo to become a self-made man reduced *his* eldest son Nwoye to a cringing inadequacy, linked in Okonkwo's mind with the poetical irresponsibility of the father he so despised. Okonkwo knew, without in his son's case realizing how well he knew, "how to kill a man's spirit."

> Okonkwo ruled his household with a heavy hand. His wives, especially the youngest, lived in perpetual fear of his own fiery temper, and so did his little children. Perhaps down in his heart Okonkwo was not a cruel man. But his whole life was dominated by fear, the fear of failure and weakness. It was deeper and more intimate than the fear of the forest, and of the forces of nature . . . .[13]

Such a destructive primacy of personal anxiety does more than merely ruin a son; in this case it leads to impiety. Achebe translates Okonkwo's sickness into action by simply showing, without making a great to-do over it, how he thrice offends against the Earth Goddess—She who should have been at the roots of any wise man's fear:

First, justifiable anger against his youngest wife, who had left the compound one afternoon to plait her hair at a friend's house and did not return in time to serve him his customary third dish in the evening, leads Okonkwo to an unjustifiable breaking of the Sacred Week of Peace. This is a time between harvesting and planting when the Earth Goddess, without whose blessing crops will never grow, is traditionally honored by absence of acrimony among the human community. Okonkwo beats his wife. He must, and does, pay one goat, one hen, a length of cloth, and a fine of a hundred cowries for the violation. His neighbors call him the little bird *nza*, who so far forgot himself after a heavy meal that he challenged his own *chi* (soul, tutelary spirit, or the divine in him) to a fight. "Even the oldest men could only remember one or two other occasions somewhere in the dim past" when someone had dared to break the Week of Peace.

The second offense against the Earth Goddess has far more serious consequences. Because of Okonkwo's prestige, a young hostage from a neighboring tribe—a mere child called Ikemefuna —is put in his personal charge. For three years Ikemefuna lives in Okonkwo's household, endearing himself to all, especially to Okonkwo's eldest son who, with the example and affectionate companionship of this hardy young enemy, has actually begun to grow more manly himself. At the end of this time the Oracle of the Hills and Caves suddenly announces that the hostage must be killed. Ezeudu, the oldest man in the neighborhood, a noble warrior in his prime and now a man of three titles, comes to Okonkwo to warn him: "That boy calls you father. Do not bear a hand in his death." As the village elders march out into the forest with their unsuspecting victim, Okonkwo remorsefully retreats to the end of the file. But when Ikemefuna, struck by the first of the sacrificial matchets, turns, beginning to run in terror towards his beloved protector, Okonkwo—always afraid of betraying any weakness—in cold blood cuts him down. "What you have done," says his best friend, Obierika, who had stayed away from the sacrifice, "will not please the Earth. It is the kind of action for which the goddess wipes out whole families."

The final offense is really the beginning of the retribution. Okonkwo, seemingly no longer in control of his own actions, fires wildly into the night at the funeral rites for Ezeudu, the very elder who had warned him not to lay a hand on Ikemefuna. While it is the custom to fire at funerals, Okonkwo inadvertently kills the honored dead man's sixteen-year-old son, and for this he is banished from his clan for seven years.

While Okonkwo is living in exile with his immediate family, as guests of his mother's clan, the missionaries arrive in the forest. The villagers give them the haunted part, where abominations like twins are abandoned. Surprisingly enough the Christians prosper, despite the fact that the majority of the villagers, including Okonkwo, thinks that they are surely mad. But Okonkwo's miserable son Nwoye is captivated by them, at first in secret and later as an active convert back in the paternal village where only he, of Okonkwo's family, is allowed to return. Under the name of Isaac, he attends a mission school.

> It was not the mad logic of the Trinity. . . . He did not understand it. It was the poetry of the new religion, something felt in the marrow. The hymn about brothers who sat in darkness and fear seemed to answer a vague and persistent question that haunted his young soul—the question of the twins crying in the bush and the question of Ikemefuna who was killed. He felt a relief within as the hymn poured into his parched soul. The words of the hymn were like the drops of frozen rain melting on the dry palate of the panting earth.[14]

Okonkwo, shamed to the marrow by this turn of events, wonders how he could possibly have produced such a degenerate, effeminate son. He thinks, in his blindness, that he has the answer: "Living fire begets cold, impotent ash."

His own eventual return to Umuofia is a disappointment. Life, like the forest, has overgrown his reputation. The old virtues, which he once stood for and now hopes, his penance done, to embody once more in Umuofia, are becoming superfluous. Not only the lowborn, the weaklings, the outcasts have recently been joining the new church, but an occasional man of pride as well. Not only a lunatic religion but a government has appeared from abroad; and—most important for the enterprising Ibo villager— a trading store (as well as high prices for palm oil and kernel) has been set up by an equally enterprising white man. Destroying loyalties of family, clan, and soil, this white man, so Okonkwo's best friend Obierika now tells him, "has put a knife on the things that held us together and we have fallen apart." What the elders do not see is that the white man has been fortunate, from the British point of view, in being able to capitalize on the commercial imaginations of the younger generation, on an individualism that has traditionally been encouraged along with the other loyalties.

There is a saying in Ibo which recalls that when Eneke the bird was asked why he was always on the wing, he replied that since men have learned to shoot without missing their mark, so he has learned how to fly without perching. The opportunistic villagers are now busily proving the truth of the old adage. But Okonkwo gives another interpretation to the words; he thinks they mean that power must be met with power. An opportunity for organized violence—give the heroic Umuofians this and they will drive the white men out.

The provocation, at least, is not long in arising. Enoch, the overzealous convert son of the village snake priest, to spite his own father has with impunity—or so it seems—killed and eaten the sacred python. Thus emboldened, Enoch goes on to further impiety. During the memorial festival dedicated to Mother Earth as custodian of the dead, he goes so far as to unmask one of the sacred spirits of the ancestors. The next day *egwugwo*, masked spirits, from all quarters of the clan and even from neighboring villages converge upon Enoch's compound, burn it to the ground, and then proceed to destroy the white man's proud little adobe church as the breeding ground of all new profanities and abominations. The district commissioner reciprocates by imprisoning six village leaders, among them Okonkwo, who has managed to reinstate himself to that degree. The old man's first reaction to these events is exhilaration. He is sure that the villagers, inspired by the fierce audacity of the *egwugwo*, will now as a group turn upon the alien authorities in revenge for the indignity done their respected elders. But instead Umuofia capitulates before the ultimatum of a mere fine. The villagers pay the cowries and Okonkwo, having been brutally treated in the prison, is released a sullen and a bitter man.

The village crier announces another meeting of the clan in the morning, but Okonkwo knows by this time that nothing effective will be done. Nevertheless, he doggedly makes his own private preparations for that grand battle his spirit cries for and that the spirit of the times will never permit. Alone in his hut, he takes down from the rafters his old smoked raffia war dress and examines headgear and shield. These he finds satisfactory, and with quiet dignity he places them aside for the morning. "Worthy men are no more," he soliloquizes from his bamboo cot. "Isike will never forget how we slaughtered them in that war." Like Ajax eulogizing the old virtues implicit in Hector's guest-friend sword and decrying the stubborn fact that winter's stern and hard-packed snow must yield to the summer's thaw of compliant and reasonable men, Okonkwo realizes to the depths his own anachronism and silently vows a dramatic revenge upon the times.

The next day, Okonkwo's matchet cuts down one of the white

policemen sent to break up the village meeting. Struck dumb with an impotent rage against the entire system, Okonkwo runs to hang himself in the bush. Self-destruction is perhaps the ultimate violation of the Earth Goddess, and his own men are forbidden by custom to cut him down.

> "Will you bury him like any other man?" asked the Commissioner. "We cannot bury him. Only strangers can. We shall pay your men to do it. When he has been buried we will then do our duty by him. We shall make sacrifices to cleanse the desecrated land." [15]

That man, says Okonkwo's closest friend, Obierika, was "one of the greatest men in Umuofia. You drove him to kill himself; and now he will be buried like a dog."

Things Fall Apart was criticized by a European scholar and critic in residence in Nigeria for showing a lack of understanding of the religious organization of the Ibo. In his third novel, *Arrow of God* (1964), Achebe returns to an era slightly later than that depicted in his first, and here he does give a rather full account of the religious institutions of his grandfather's people. He does not, however, present these institutions in a scholarly manner, but rather as dimensions of the soul and complications in the lives of Nigerian villagers between the two world wars that still, in different ways, both plague and enrich educated Nigerian sensibilities.

In a recent interview, Achebe said that having "learned a lot more about these particular people, you know, my ancestors," [16] he had himself come to think of his first book as no longer adequate. Such a writer as he does not have to do research. As he himself admits, when he was born in 1930 things had not changed that much, and as he grew up he was able to talk freely with those whom he now remotely refers to as "ancestors"; ceremonies were still celebrated, with less intensity perhaps than in the old days, but their original meaning could be inferred by a mind mature enough to grasp the significance of their forms. But this is the point: As the author's own imaginative life has thickened with awareness, so the society he writes about—Umuofia in another guise—has also become more complicated, the forces and characters surrounding the central consciousness of the hero standing out in sharper, more radical relief.

Ezeulu, the hero of Achebe's *Arrow of God*, bears a certain resemblance to Okonkwo of *Things Fall Apart*. Again we are confronted with an old man's personal struggle with the undeniable facts of Christianity and colonialism, a struggle exacerbated by tensions and loyalties within the self, and within the clan as related to the self. But here we have the further complication of a god, Ulu, whose agent, or "arrow," this grand old Ezeulu effectively is. And in making Ezeulu the vehicle of a god, Achebe begins to ask a series of psychological and moral questions, questions which we Westerners usually discuss in connection with the exceptional, the fanatical (like Luther or Joan of Arc), but which in the Nigerian context are associated with the deepest common proprieties. What is it like being in a society where *all* men act in the company of the unseen as a real presence, as a plurality of presences whose influences are immediately felt, exploited, and perhaps misinterpreted or dangerously gainsaid?

Since, like Okonkwo, Ezeulu is a man deeply concerned with personal strength and weakness, the book begins with his own drum beat—a soliloquy in which he muses on the realities of his power as the spokesman of the god. The occasion is the priest's official observation of the new moon which inaugurates the planting season. From the threshold of his sanctuary, Ezeulu proclaims the moon to his people with a gong.

> Whenever Ezeulu considered the immensity of his power over the year and the crops and, therefore, over the people, he wondered if it was real. It was true he named the day for the feast of the Pumpkin Leaves and for the New Yam feast; but he did not choose the day. He was merely a watchman. His power was no more than the power of a child over a goat that was said to be his. As long as the goat was alive it was his; he would find it food and take care of it. But the day it was slaughtered he would know who the real owner was. No! The Chief Priest of Ulu was more than that, must be more than that. If he should refuse to name the day there would be no festival—no planting and no reaping. But could he refuse? No Chief Priest had ever refused. So it could not be done. He would not dare.[17]

Ezeulu's controlled urge to put his priestly power to the test has its harmless social counterpart in his irrepressible urge to prove to young men that they are no longer what they used to be by suddenly outgripping them when they shake hands. This restless will of his is linked to a series of anxieties that go deep into his family's history, deep into the history of his clan. We gradually learn something about that family. His father was an all-powerful figure, combining the offices of Chief Priest and medicine man all in one. Ezeulu's brother inherited his father's magical gifts, while Ezeulu succeeded to the priesthood alone. This divided spiritual inheritance continues to disturb the aging priest, and when a medicine man is wanted, Ezeulu typically refuses to call his brother in.

His own sons seem to represent further waterings down of the stock. The handsome one, Obika, the son who resembles Ezeulu the most, is athletic and spirited enough, but addicted to bad company and palm wine. His eldest son, Edoka, seems slow and cloddish, and Ezeulu refuses to recognize his aspiring talents as a carver of masks. This profession, to such as Ezeulu, is obviously déclassé. The third son, Oduche, has become a Christian at his father's insistence, so that the power appertaining to those who can write will someday be his. The fourth, the spoiled son Nwafo, for the moment is his only hope, although it is not for Ulu's priest to pick his successor, but rather for the god to manifest his choice through divination.

Ezeulu's mother, we learn, was subject to attacks of madness, and this is another one of his fears. Even Ezeulu's god Ulu's position must be considered somewhat tenuous. Ulu is not an immemorial custodian of a particular clan; rather he was founded by dignitaries of six villages who at one time decided to band together the better to resist the slave raids of a powerful but unrelated neighboring group. Ulu was created to preside over this new confederacy, an image was carved for him to inhabit at festivals, and a member of the weakest village, the village of Ezeulu's ancestors, was chosen to be his priest. Ezeulu's anxiety about his god's legitimacy, about man's and god's combined strengths, is exploited by the priest of Idemili, the sacred python, tutelary spirit of the most martial of the six villages. And leagued with the jealous priest of a jealous god is Ezeulu's strongest personal enemy, Nwaka, a man of such riches as to enable him to take the highest title. Nwaka is an aggressive braggart whose considerable popularity is a continual affront to Ezeulu's kind of manly, aristocratic virtue.

Between the planting moon and the harvesting moon, Ezeulu's downfall almost casually unfolds. Rivalry between Ezeulu and Nwaka, the men, and Ulu and Idemili, the gods, is intensified by Ezeulu's Christian son Oduche, who dares to imprison a representative of the heathen python in his footlocker! Ezeulu is again accused of collaboration with the white man, a crime of which he was once not altogether innocent, and when a supervisor of a road-building project whips his handsome son, Obika, Ezeulu does not report the brutality to district headquarters, but rather blames his son for lateness and insubordination as the wages of palm wine. Yet when Ezeulu is called to district headquarters to be appointed warrant chief over the six villages, he is insulted by the patronage; he then realizes the white man as a communal enemy, refuses to cooperate with the colonial authorities, and spends thirty-two days in the district jail for his pains.

According to tradition, the exile of a powerful presence, of a leader like Ezeulu, should prove devastating to the king and kingdom lodging the inimical foreign element. And Winterbottom, the district officer, does fall mysteriously ill. Naturally Ezeulu is credited with having had something to do with this. (But, ironically, the British administration is actually strengthened through the unwilling agency of Ezeulu, and in the end it is the high priest, his god, and ultimately his people who suffer the most from his enforced exile. All are drained of their traditional spiritual potency; Christianity and the Union Jack, rather than Ulu and Ibo democracy, triumph in the end.)

Suspicious that the villagers are giving him no moral support in his heroism, and that his enemies and Ulu's are taking advantage of his Babylonian captivity to complete the disorganization of the six villages, Ezeulu returns home only to find a heartwarming welcome—fifty-seven visitors in one day! Why then, when the Chief Priest was the white man's captive, did the people of Ulu's villages sit on their hands? Tempted by thoughts of reconciliation, Ezeulu is suddenly visited by the god:

"Ta! Nwanu!" barked Ulu in his ear, as a spirit would in the ear of an impertinent human child. "Who told you that this was your own fight?"

Ezeulu trembled and said nothing. "I say who told you that

this was your own fight which you could arrange to suit you? You want to save your friends who brought you palm wine. He-he-he-he-he!" laughed the deity the way spirits do—a dry, skeletal laugh. "Beware you do not come between me and my victim or you may receive blows not meant for you! Do you not know what happens when two elephants fight? Go home and sleep and leave me to settle my quarrel with Idemili, who wants to destroy me so that his python may come to power. Now you tell me how it concerns you. I say go home and sleep. As for me and Idemili we shall fight to the finish; and whoever throws the other down will strip him of his anklet!"

After that there was no more to be said. Who was Ezeulu to tell his deity how to fight the jealous cult of the sacred python? It was a fight of the gods. He was no more than an arrow in the bow of his god. This thought intoxicated Ezeulu like palm wine.[18]

At important religious moments, half of Ezeulu's body is painted over with white chalk. This visitation reminds him that half of the things that he *ever* does, on or off the job, as it were, are to be attributed to *mmo*, the Chief Priest's spirit side.

The Feast of the New Yam marks the end and the beginning of each year. No man can taste new yam, that is to say, harvest his crop, until the proper ceremonies take place. At every New Yam feast, the original coming together of the six villages is re-enacted, a census taken, and Ulu either thanked or appeased, depending on whether or not his people have increased or declined. The Chief Priest customarily announces the beginning of each new month from the door of his sanctuary; but since Ezeulu's time in jail has encompassed two new moons, these months have gone by unproclaimed. In Ulu's mind, and therefore in his priest Ezeulu's mind, they have not occurred. And while two of the thirteen sacred lunar yams remain uneaten, the celebration of the festival lags two months behind the time of natural ripening. The ground hardens, imprisoning the stillborn yams. The villagers hunger, and still Ezeulu continues to reckon by his own private, spiritual time. Only his closest friend, Akuebue, knows of the old priest's compassionate anguish for the Umuaro clan who have chosen Ezeulu's ancestor "to carry their deity and go before them challenging every obstacle and confronting every danger on their behalf." Only Akuebue knows that the Chief Priest has been obedient rather than self-willed.

Ezeulu's entire family suffocates in the silence surrounding the obdurate, god-ridden old man, and when Obika the handsome son, a fabulous runner, is asked by grieving villagers to run as Ogbazulobodo, the night spirit who chases out evil, the proudest of Ezeulu's sons cannot refuse, even though he has been suffering from a troublesome fever and should not go out at all. "If I say no," Obika told himself, "they will say that Ezeulu and his family have sworn to wreck the second burial of their village man who did no harm to them." Also, it is clearly the case that Obika is Ogbazulobodo's natural vehicle; nobody else can carry him so well. So the young man dons the rope skirt with the rattling attachments, seizes the iron staff, allows the heavy jangling necklace to be put upon him, and then, as Ogbazulobodo, he vanishes like the wind through the village paths, "leaving potent words in the air behind." Although fire rages in Obika's chest, as Ogbazulobodo he feels it distantly, as if it belonged to someone else. He completes his rounds with miraculous energy and returns to the ceremonial hut—no longer an avenging spirit, but a dead man.

At any other time, Ezeulu would have been equal to his grief. But the thought that Ulu, whose will he had divined and obeyed, should thus strike back at him crazes Ezeulu with humiliation. It is as if Job had not only been tried, but forsaken as well.

What could it point to but the collapse and ruin of all things? Then a god, finding himself powerless, might take to his heels and in one final, backward glance at his abandoned worshippers cry: If the rat cannot flee fast enough, let him make way for the tortoise.[19]

Ezeulu is allowed by his retreating god to live out his last days "in the haughty splendor of a demented high priest." A few days after Obika's death the Christians hold their harvest feast. They had promised, during the long weeks of Ezeulu's intransigency, that any villager who made an offering of thanks to their God would be automatically immune from the wrath of Ulu, and could harvest his crop in peace. As things turn out, this Christian offer meets with a most gratifying, almost total, response.

This is the fall of Umuaro, but there is also the Homeric Shield of Ezeulu. Achebe has beaten into the texture of his story a myriad of intricate domestic details—shafts of sunlight like Ezeulu's irrepressible little daughter Obiageli, who mocks, licks the spoon, sings and tells stories, and carries her baby nephew around on her back. There are scenes of squalor and hardship too—like the dreadful dysentery of Ezeulu's grandson, a green slime on a mud floor which the dog licks up. It would be a mistake to say that Achebe idealizes his village past; rather, in true Homeric fashion, he makes the life of Ezeulu's compound seem intricate and ordered, disputatious and real.

Now that the passionate battles between the spiritual forces have been silenced, a latter-day Nigerian imagination like Achebe's cannot, perhaps, do better than to return to the life of the villages in art. Some of our generation, writers of our Western tradition, are fond of quoting the German poet Hölderlin, himself obsessed by the retreat of the gods—the eponymous poet of a dry time, the perennial romantic who feels he has been born too late. Just as Hölderlin was fond of celebrating the feasts of the ancients to which the Greek gods were invited, occasions which seemed to him to produce states of being equivalent to the most joyous pinnacles of his own inner life, so Achebe and others of his generation celebrate their theophanies. The Feast of the New Yam in the six villages, the feast which did not take place that fatal year of Ezeulu's madness, was not only a celebration of Ulu, but a celebration of all the minor deities as well.

> This was the one public appearance these smaller gods were allowed in the year. They rode into the market place on the heads or shoulders of their custodians, danced round and then stood side by side at the entrance to the shrine of Ulu. Some of them would be very old, nearing the time when their power would be transferred to new carvings and they would be cast aside; and some would have been made only the other day. The very old ones carried face masks like the men who made them, in the days before Umuaro abandoned the custom. At last year's festival only three of these ancients were left. Perhaps this year one or two more would disappear, following the men who made them in their own image and departed long ago.
> The festival thus brought gods and men together in one

crowd. It was the only assembly in Umuaro in which a man might look to his right and find his neighbor and look to his left and see a god standing there—perhaps Agwu whose mother also gave birth to madness or Ngene, owner of a stream.[20]

The festivals have lost their power, but not their meaning. The ancient scarified faces of the gods have been superseded; the carvings that were their vehicles have been replaced by others, and again by others. Most recently they have been carved out of the irony of words.

IV.

Perhaps someday Achebe will turn his attention to Christian religious institutions as vehicles for the exploration of his father Isaac's psychology. Here and there Achebe has already hinted at the inner anatomy of the sort of youth who out of a rebellious sense of insufficiency flees to Christianity as a refuge from a sterner, more exacting way of life, a youth who as a man tries to crush out the new ways of feeling among a pious, if promiscuous, generation of the future which equates Western Christianity with colonialism and seeks a sophisticated dialectical return to African forms of belief. In the meantime, there is one village novel written from the convert's point of view—the village seen as a jungle of terrors, guilts, and quasi-paternal tabus.

Kavwanga (undated—1954?), by G. Bolomba of the former Belgian Congo, explores the meaning of conversion for the sensitive young nephew of a strong, traditional, indeed rather sinister *lemba*, or maternal uncle, a far more consequential figure than the father in Kavwanga's social frame. Kavwanga's village is small, consisting of only thirty-five dwellings, or one hundred and fifty souls. Times are hard; the colonial administration is well ensconced in the area. Although relations between Belgians and villagers are hostile, at the time the story takes place revolt has been limited to mere imprecations by members of a league of secret societies from several neighboring villages.

The action begins with a minor, although unprecedented, act of civil disobedience in the village. Kavwanga's *lemba*, apparently heeding an ancestral dream warning, refuses to pay his family's head taxes. He is dragged off to a work camp for this, and the family debt is assumed by Kavwanga's eighteen-year-old brother, who grudgingly goes off to work temporarily for the nearby European "Company." The brother's move, under conditions requiring a cash payment of the head tax by members of a subsistence economy, was not at all extraordinary in these times. But the injustice of the whole proceeding, of the tax itself, of the uncle's incarceration, of the privileged lives of the Europeans viewed for the first time at close range at the "Company" installation—these rankled. About this same time the town's first catechist, Sitefani, arrives to tell Bible stories and teach reading to the children. Kavwanga, an apt and sensitive pupil, is at eleven or so willing to give up the glorious freedom of the forest for this new school. He is well aware of his father's stolid and his *lemba's* angry opposition. He is, in addition, precociously aware of the universality of hostile forces, both within the adult human heart and without, and in the spiritually potent forest as well.

> He knew that here on earth man is surrounded by a host of powerful spirits: some watching over him and protecting him while others, far more numerous, willed his destruction. The older he grew the more Kavwanga realized and already began to share the feelings which frequently overcame the souls of his parents: prolonged anguish, unending jealousy, the idea of vengence, criminal wishes and incantations—with the perpetual fear of always imminent reprisals.[21]

This being his view of the world, the refuge and distraction provided by the catechist's school seem worth fighting his elders for.

The African catechist has *pris de l'ésprit* at the mission and seems to thrive undaunted by secret, nefarious rites practiced against him. But Kavwanga's apprehensions are far from being stilled by alphabetism, and the promised "added force" from the Christian god seems all too slow in arriving. Away at a regional school, to which Kavwanga has been in due course considered fit to advance, the boy learns that his father has been killed by poison trial, an ordeal administered following the mysterious death of an elder too friendly to the European authorities. Kavwanga's anxieties are hardly diminished by these events; his father was a scapegoat, might he not also be?

His widowed mother, though favorable in principle to the idea of a Christian education, now contrives to keep Kavwanga at home with her in the village by providing him with opportunities to indulge (and, unknown to her, to feel guilty about) his awakening interest in the opposite sex. It is too late. Other pressures on him have been stronger. The village catechist has always encouraged Kavwanga; the Father Superior himself has shown great interest; and a devoted younger priest, whose mother is dying of cancer in Belgium, has made a special project of the youth—a sort of vow to heaven on his mother's behalf. Kavwanga, in short, has all but decided to become a priest when a strange crisis of the spirit befalls him on the school playing field.

What actually happens to him, within him, is rather mysterious. Perhaps it cannot really be explained. The physical events are easily told: Kavwanga rushes aggressively into the fray (a sort of free-for-all football game without rules) and collides with a smaller boy, knocking the fellow out and stunning himself. He is, in the process, rendered strangely insensible to the kind attentions of his spiritual guide and benefactor, the young Belgian priest. He refuses to go to the infirmary; he is not physically ill, he says. He had, apparently, the previous night suffered from a nightmarish threat by the incarnate spirit of his (most important) maternal grandmother. He still suffers from this visitation, so far as anyone can tell, as well as from feelings of guilt over his strange involuntary behavior on the field. Was this a sign of worse things to follow, the beginnings of retribution? When Kavwanga later tries to apologize to the boy he hit, the boy mocks him and Kavwanga walks away, consumed by a strange anger that has no sufficient cause and is permitted no "Christian" expression.

Kavwanga continues to give vent to this anger in a diffuse and clumsy sort of way. The perfect student becomes a truant at school. But this is just a beginning. Sometimes he turns this strange new anger against himself, rising in the process to sublime spiritual heights. Turned against others, his rage disgraces him and, in such a community, makes him naught.

> Jean [his Christian name] no longer recognizes himself . . . .
> Certain days he prays really well, he is joyous, he submits
> easily, he even deprives himself of meat for others. He is as
> if lifted up and carried towards his ideal . . . . Bruskly, every-
> thing changes . . . . He is distracted in his prayers, is coldly
> disobedient, gets into rages, insults his companions, and
> senses himself close to committing some real folly. Could

he not be possessed by some evil spirit? Or cursed by . . . .
by whom? His mother? His grandmother? Mustikère [his
elder brother]? [22]

Desperately, Kavwanga asks a young teacher from his own
people if the Fathers really understand the occult forces besetting
those who turn away from tribal ways. No, says the honest convert, even the Father Superior does not fully understand our
world of forces: "We alone feel in our hearts many things that
we cannot possibly express." But the Christian *god*, he continues,
does see into our hearts. He alone understands these things. And
the menacing dream from the ancestral spirit? asks Kavwanga.
Don't give it a thought, the young Christian teacher strategically
replies.

The road is long, but Kavwanga gradually succeeds in disciplin-
ing himself to ignore the reproofs of his furious progenitors—
lashes of conscience that he takes to be the true sources of all
that recalcitrant rage. Painfully following the path the missionaries
have cleared for him out of the forests of harm, Kavwanga returns
(in an epilogue) from the city, fourteen years later, to his own
village as L'Abbé Jean, resplendent in the white robes of his
office.

Kavwanga is a minor novel; one could easily point out the
gaps and deficiencies in plot and motivation. But the facts and
sequences that are given are extremely suggestive. Whatever the
author's conscious intentions might have been, the incidents
make their own connections. Take the brother, for example, who
went to work for the tax money and who came back embittered
by firsthand acquaintance with the Europeans, a constant threat
to Kavwanga's peace of mind: Was this brother suddenly represented in Kavwanga's consciousness by the random school boy on
the playing field that Kavwanga unaccountably knocked down?
Or was it a transposed image of the "devoted" Belgian priest,
whom Kavwanga must inwardly have resented terribly, with
whom he fortuitously collided there?

The author never discusses the secret societies' activities at any
length. However, these desperate and outraged last resorts to
superstitious terror and violence seem like counterparts to the
rebellious unconscious of the young convert Kavwanga before he
finally submits to the discipline of Christian authority. The tortures

of Kavwanga's conversion are a tribute to the strength of the old ties. He cannot break them simply by becoming "educated." Only when a stunning place for Kavwanga in another world is all but assured can he finally feel free of that uncle, of the ghost of that maternal grandmother, of that whole set of oppressive fears and beliefs. The white robes of the priest are a constant reminder to himself and others that his body defies his own tradition; his mind, one imagines, will never be entirely at ease.

Although Kavwanga the convert's angry, dream-ridden mind runs parallel to the murderous machinations of the secret societies, Bolomba shows no sympathy at all for the cults. He writes his book entirely from the Christian point of view. But the communal expression of rage over the restraints of the colonial condition, the use of magic and terror to fortify the spirits of the group against that which is destroying their way of life are treated with critical understanding by the author of a very different sort of "village" book. The case for reversion is far more difficult to make than the case for submission or for forced conversion, although one wonders why this must inevitably be so. A maimed body is more difficult to look at than a maimed spirit. But is an account of the excesses of various recidivistic organizations really more frightening than accounts of "lonely Africans" maimed by excesses of missionary zeal?

Turn to the Dark (1956) by Mopeli-Paulus, written in collaboration with Miriam Basner, tells the story of a Basuto Christian student's *return* to "tribalism." The heroic enthusiasm of this student, however, renders him particularly vulnerable to cynical behavior on the part of elders of all persuasions. Since darkness and light turn out to have equally disastrous personal consequences for him, the young maverick in the village context is left with no alternative to depression and despair. For like the village he is ultimately forced to leave, he has a religious disposition that is not easily altered along with the times. The times—outside the village, barely impinging upon the consciousness of the inhabitants—require a secular philosophy based on an understanding of economic needs.

The texture of this novel is interesting, given the extraordinary geographical differences between African villages west and south.* Like Chinua Achebe's *Things Fall Apart, Turn to the Dark* is a carefully worded book. A consistent tone is maintained throughout, a tone strangely suited to the environment. In the case of the novel from Basutoland, there is an exuberance of feeling for a dry, deprived, and blighted landscape. In the West African novel, by contrast, all emotion tends to be muted, as if a burgeoning vegetation demanded restraint from the human community. Exclamations, encomia, and an inflated rhetoric fill up the vast wastes of hill and veld, of what we in the United States call "the frontier." Praise of the land and of cattle, traditional poetic utterance among various tribesmen south of the Zambezi, are woven into the texture of the book from Basutoland, just as the wise economies of the proverb filter through the pages of Achebe's novel—like sunlight, one imagines—into the earthen compounds of West African villages that have been with humility cleared of the jungle by man.

In the village novels generally, no matter how competently done, one is usually made well aware of how social institutions, special social situations, and human emotions are related to the more permanent aspects of the environment, as well as to such changes as plenty and dearth. What we might see as metaphorical relationships seem completely natural in these books. Here is an example of the "feel" of a high, desolate village in Basutoland, an example of what one might call the ecology of the emotions in *Turn to the Dark.*

The social situation is crucial. A ritual murder has just been committed but not yet found out. A marriage is about to be celebrated, but the bride does not yet know that her husband and parents have had a hand in the awful affair. The meteorological situation is crucial too. The famous Year of the Red Wind-storms has arrived to plague the land of the Basotho, although the fearful villagers of Makong, Majoaneng, and Bonoheng don't

* James Ngugi's recent novel from Kenya, *Weep Not Child* (London: Heinemann, 1964), shows a remarkable similarity of texture. Whether this is to be accounted for by the climates and topographies of the villages described, which certainly are similar, or by similarities in mental climate among the authors' respective peoples—peoples linguistically and agronomically allied—who can say. But that verbal texture and scene are related in the African novel, or perhaps in any novel, is indisputable!

know this yet, of course. They are still unaware of just how long the rising winds will blow.

> The wind is sweeping the yards of the huts outside, but the doctor and his apprentice speak in low voices. There is a metal can and an old sack beside Mafa, and on the floor, beside him and about him, are horns—horns filled and empty; horns stuffed with old fatty medicines, or so dry with age that nothing remains inside them save a pinch of powder; twisted horns of springbok and long horns of great oxen slaughtered for meat by the great chiefs of olden days when they reigned and the rocks at khotla shone with the marrow of the bones and the fat of the meat of feasts. The chiefs of today do not kill for their subjects . . . .
>
> Men stood on high ground and watched sand like a blanket blowing in folds right over the countryside; sand like strong smoke from a veld fire stirring the empty air with whirlwinds; sand like winnowing grain in a basket heaping against the walls of huts, shifting and increasing and shifting again . . . .
>
> Thursday came, the day of the slaughter of the ox to seal the marriage of Lineo, and still the sky was dark, and still the wind blew, but the feast could not be postponed because the air was full of sand, or because the hearts of the bride- groom and parents of the bride were full of fear and misery . . . .
>
> Ma Lira [the mother of the bride] had insisted on remain- ing at the vlei where the women were toiling, coated in dust that turned to mud and joined the mud of the reed bed as the day went on; blinking their eyes to see their work, rub- bing their faces with their hands; seeming, when evening came, to be like women fashioned out of clay.[23]

The exaggerated agitation of the environment seems like a com- mentary on the "medicine" revival in which some of the villagers are concurrently engaged. Both phenomena are of the same quality—frantic and dry.

As the story begins. Lesiba, the hero, is returning to the village. The disillusioned leader of a student strike against unpalatable mission food, he arrives "determined to leave the world of the white man alone." But this will not be easy. Lesiba's father is the village *moruti* (preacher) who, terrified of offending the white missionaries who are his superiors, is always at pains to put up a good Christian front. The *moruti* purifies his returning son with the bile of a black sheep, according to the old custom—in secret, lest the members of his scattered congregation (men who would, under the same circumstances, probably do exactly the same thing) see.

Phofu, the village headman, is also much concerned with the world of the white man, but for different reasons. Phofu is anxious lest this young man, Lesiba, to whom he takes an immediate fancy, persist in his false romantic vision of the changing world to which he has in fact returned from school. In undertaking to set the boy straight, Phofu exposes the following unpopular opinions in a rather foolhardy way: The whites are avaricious. But it is equally clear that the chief is a superstitious fool who listens to the advice of his dagga-sodden counselor, Khanya, as well as to the dangerous imprecations of Mafa, the crazed and cruel witch doctor from the heights of Bonoheng. The chief does not understand that the men of Basutoland (in Phofu's opinion) must awaken politically, cast off undesirable guardians such as these, sharpen their tactics against the British, and attempt to form, in short, a contemporary nation state.

But Lesiba, reluctant to see poverty and servitude rather than plenty and freedom in the lax and degenerate chiefdom of his early years, turns against this modern, realistic elder headman to become a member of the chief's reactionary entourage. To do so in full standing requires his attendance at the *mophato* or initiation school—a radical departure for a Christian-nurtured boy of nineteen. On the pretext that his new fiancée and her family wish him to be truly "a man," Lesiba sounds his father out. The apprehensive old *moruti*, although he had once been circumcised himself, forbids this pagan practice in Lesiba's case—again with an eye to the parishioners. Lesiba, now indeed a prodigal son, must go it alone. He does attend the *mophato* in defiance of his father, and returns according to custom, triumphantly praising himself, at the head of the line of newly virile boys. The weary old chief is prepared under the circumstances to accept Lesiba as a kind of adopted son; but this alliance will prove far more compromising than Lesiba ever dreamed. For the chief's advisors have finally persuaded him that the medicine horn must be refilled and Lesiba, as proof of his new loyalty, must participate in the affair.

> He looked at the Chief, and saw with new eyes the Great One, the Calf of the Beast, who had promised him great things. He saw a sick man pleading for help in his sickness . . . . He had turned his face from his father and church; how could he now turn against the blessings of the fat of the earth? . . . Like a hare that must choose between the flames and the spears of men all about it and leap again towards the scorching fire; Lesiba knew that he would choose murder rather than be rejected by the Chief.[24]

Actually, these murders were scandalously common in the High Commission Territory during the late 1940's. For the most part they were apparently the result of another misapplication of the doctrine of indirect rule. Having initially given "the sons of Moshesh"—chiefly descendants of the great warrior-politician—comprehensive authority over their own people, the British became suddenly aware, about fifty years later, of quite a proliferation of chiefs and their most profitable tribunals. Nervously, the British immediately instituted reforms: The chiefs became subject to appointment by the high commissioner in consultation with the paramount chief. When the paramount persisted in appointing his numerous relatives, further reforms were made: Tax profits were reduced, native courts were drastically cut in number, and the national council was made more representative. Chiefs and headmen, "anxious to recover by recourse to magic the position they had lost or feared to lose as a result of these reforms,"[25] turned to communal complicity in murder as the best "political" stratagem now.

Chief Johannes of the villages about Makong, however, is too fearful and guilt-ridden to initiate such a project himself. Rather like Henry IV in his later years, he helplessly plans his own equivalent of pilgrimages to Jerusalem—tribal schools in the bush, a pious return to the old ways. Quick-witted, if degenerate, counselors plan "evidences" of attacks on his life, encourage rumors of sedition on the part of the more modern elements in the community, incite his superstitious fancy by hints of the coming of the *baloi* (witchwomen of the night winds), and finally, by careful interpretations of the bones of augury, lead him to believe that medicine murder alone will restore strength and honor to himself and his people. Any outlander's heart can be used to prepare the strengthening medicine, and a Zulu woman who happens to be visiting Lesiba's future in-laws presents herself as the perfect victim. Her hosts can do nothing but cooperate and keep silent. Although Lesiba refuses, at the last moment, actually to cut out the innocent victim's heart, he is hopelessly compromised. When the district police discover the body (why was it not more carefully hidden?), Lesiba flees to the mountains.

His companion in exile is none other than the liberal headman Phofu, also officially suspected. Phofu, in no way accessory to the crime, as the chief's most outspoken and important critic is a most convenient red herring. Rather than count on the eventuality of the white man's justice, Phofu flees incarceration in the white man's prison, reputedly a brutal experience. He dies, eventually, of exposure on the remote cattle post that he and Lesiba have chosen as their place of exile, but not before the youth has finally paid tribute to this old man's courage and sense. Lesiba returns alone, determined to preserve his *honor* at least by keeping quiet. His false Christian father rejects him in full view of the parishioners. (The terrified chief had played him false immediately after the discovery of the murder.) Without any parental or communal support whatsoever, Lesiba gives himself up to the territorial authorities whom he hopes, although brutal, will prove just.

Eventually the real murderers are discovered and Lesiba returns after three years in jail, only to find his fiancée living in his parents' house, pregnant by his pious brother Joseph. "Shhh, not so loud," says his father the *moruti*. "Not a word must blow through the rafters. This must be the secret of the home." His mother nervously commends him to new fields of gold in the Free State, by that telling him she has had to sell his prize black ox in his absence. Money, money is always needed—for taxes, for school fees, because of the drought, and so on. Lesiba has no choice but to leave the village. It is not absolutely certain where he will go. The book ends with an ironic praise of the prodigal's beloved countryside, to which in the beginning, with such high hopes, he had returned.

Majoaneng! That folds itself in a corner of the hills! Majoaneng, that basks in the early morning sun when it rises above
the shoulder of Pulumo in the east! Majoaneng, where the
rabbits wait for the first light and tempt the hunter to chase
them up the rocks to the plateau .... Khotso!! Peace!
Peace! [26]

V.

The exceptional person is a problem to himself and to his
community anywhere in the world. In a dry time, spirit will
expend itself lavishly in an attempt to find or to create conditions
more hospitable to spirit. The African in these novels who aspires
to the supposed spiritual riches that a Westernized life will bring,
or who tries, conversely, to plunge his roots deeper into his
own spiritual soil than that eroding soil in this day and age will
warrant, such an African declares a hope and in most cases
admits a defeat that any of us can recognize immediately. These
aspirations and exasperations, and the situations they engender,
are precisely what make even the poorer of these novels literature, rather than something that ill-natured critics persist in
calling anthropological or sociological data in fictional form.
What sort of difference, then, does the African setting really
make? How does it qualify these hopes for a finer, more reward-
ing personal life?

We are not, it must be made plain, dealing here with hopes
involving social, educational, or vocational advancement. These
are the complicated concerns of another set of African novels, to
be discussed later. The village novels are far more simple and yet
more subtle than that. They seem to have been written by the
"last romantics" among the Africans, by men whose hidden concern has been ontological in the extreme, by men far more
preoccupied with the *quality* of life than with the rules of the
social game. However, there are always social conditions necessary for and appropriate to these dreams of a finer personal
reality. The middle-class African goes back to the "village" where
the kind of aristocratic yet selfless harmony he desires could
once, fate permitting, or in rare cases, can still be found. Religious conversion and reversion are types of escape from the
pressures of the African situation under colonialism that any
romantic European can understand. But to those of us trained
to feel society or culture as restrictive, to consider communal

responsibility at best as a duty or at worst as a bore, how remark-able must the African enthusiast seem who seeks beatitude by imaginatively putting himself in tune with the requirements of others, both the living and the dead.

The African *paradis perdu* is not a lonesome, grassy place for unaccommodated souls hard by a stream where infantile lovers hold hands; it is a social community—in the thick of things. Nowhere are the lineaments of the African paradise sketched with more patient candor than in David Ananou's *Le Fils du fétiche* (1955). This novel from Togoland, the one written ostensibly because "L'Afrique est souvent mal connu," uncomplicated by passionate attachments to religious or political causes, is a gradual uncovering of the subtle human pieties and precautions govern-ing village life. The paradox implied in the village novel as a form is found here too, all the more poignantly because of the hero's great good will. Having done his best to understand and to defer to both commonsense and supernatural sources of that sublime politeness practiced in such an idyllic African community, the hero finds that once it is achieved he cannot abide his own paradise. This does not mean that the hero is disillusioned; far from it. True to his vision of social harmony, he considers him-self merely a fortuitous exception to the rule.

Le Fils du fétiche conveys the feelings of the superior average man in an unexceptional agricultural community, the village of "Seva." It is a humorous study of the interplay of personality, community, and the occult. It is a happy book, which is not to say that it is idyllic; rather it is work-a-day, strenuous, and problem-atical. The story begins with a preliminary statement of the theme of reconciliation, as the unborn hero's father is return-ing from a year's retreat at a fetishist convent consecrated to thunder, where he went to recover from a severe mental depres-sion. There, bit by bit, this young man, Sodji, has been able to "rid himself of the morbid sentiments which had made life and work in the fields too painful to bear." Able now, at twenty-two, to accept the thankless necessity of work in an unproductive land, he returns to find his two quarrelsome wives as distressing to him as ever. He attempts to solve this problem by courting a third, the winsome Avelssi. Fortunately the two shrews, in a rare fit of cooperative jealousy, conspire without success to poison him. Thus Sodji can legitimately send them back to their respective families and set up housekeeping with Avelssi alone. Sodji is really happy now, "but nothing gave his state of soul away." Having already learned from experience how prolonged and variable are the events that weave the fabric of human life, Sodji is convinced that to tell or show his joy would be imprudent.

Nevertheless, the worst of all fates for an African villager strikes him: He has no children. After three sterile years, the thunder priest having apparently failed him, Sodji in desperation consults the priest of a rival cult in neighboring Vogan, promising to consecrate his future first-born to his tutelary spirit Dan (the serpent). After two more sterile years, despite Dan and all the drugs, baths, and supplications available, a cousin of Avelssi's finally takes her to the white man's hospital at Lomé for a successful series of injections. Sodji, unwilling to court the displeasure of any of the forces around him, names his newborn Dansou (son of Dan) just in case.

The boy grows up irrepressible, despite various illnesses and an unaccountably bad fall. The young hero comes back from a visit to a maternal uncle in Vogan (where he has managed to get himself into a great deal of mischief) full of new ways of doing things. These he at once begins to demonstrate to his fellow villagers of Seva. He initiates a new mode of roof building, a sort of staircase in thatch; he teaches his friends how to make relief designs on their walls; he excels at basket weaving and rope making; he introduces collective fishing, with dazzling results. And finally, the songs improvised by this young culture hero, songs permeated with his father's stoical philosophy, achieve a true *succès d'estime*. "The pot now used for frying chickens will serve in the future for boiling meagre greens" is an example, in adage form, of the philosophy. Here is an excerpt from one of Dansou's popular funeral dirges, an example of the philosophy in song:

"To weep one whole night (or a day)
Without one drop taken
Is inadmissible at funerals.
So bring on the drinks, slaughter the animals!
So much the worse for the deceased,
The living have got to live."
These words they pronounce in houses that mourn

Have always filled me with pity for the dead.
May those who still can enjoy life, enjoy it;
For there's no more of it when you cease to live.[27]

But the man of exceptional talents, as Maran's Kossi learned to his despair, can never dazzle others with impunity. Perhaps Sodji's natural pride in his adolescent son's accomplishments prevented him, at first, from exercising in Dansou's behalf the caution that came so naturally to himself.

"Horrible" Afiavi, a teen-aged girl friend of Dansou's sister, out of a passionate if unrequited love for the young hero, one day comes running with the news of a plot against Dansou's life. Father and son hasten to consult a neighborhood sorcerer whom Afiavi believes to be implicated in the affair. From this sorcerer the ingratiating Sodji is able to extract the truth and a promise to cancel all outstanding magical debts against Dansou upon payment of 5,000 francs. The conspirators had given him only 3,000, but after all, as the witch doctor says, echoing the theme, "It's more difficult to repair than to destroy."

Three men, it turns out, are against Dansou: The first complains in general of his arrogant vanity; the second, Tetévi, fears him as a rival in love; the third claims to have been slandered in one of Dansou's more humorous songs. But before the counter-medicine has had a chance to work, Dansou has softened up his enemies in a natural, good-humored way by inviting each separately to his hut for a drink. He is able by this means to exact a confession and pledges of friendship from their leader, Tetévi; but he does so with a confidence he certainly would not have without the visit to the witch doctor and the payment of the 5,000 francs. Dansou now decides, in a flurry of contrition, that he might as well marry "Horrible" Afiavi. After all, she is devotedly loyal, and he doesn't think there are any rivals for her hand.

After the month of meditation and repose prescribed for all newly married couples, Dansou begins with a good heart "the practical life, with all that it entails—of liberty and servitude, of rights and duties, of independence and responsibilities." But good intentions are not enough. This couple also proves to be childless. Dansou's well-meaning mother-in-law finally brings them her own private remedy against sterility; but Dansou, suspicious out of much misfortune, perhaps, and stubbornly independent of mothers-in-law in any case, sends her angrily back to her own hut. His tactful father protests that he could merely have accepted the potion without feeding it to his wife. And enjoining his son to be "more supple in his neighborly relations," Sodji hastens to make a blood pact with the in-laws before it is too late. In a short time, conception! Can the relaxation of familial tensions always achieve such spectacular results?

In due course, as predicted, the calabash planned for chickens boils greens. Sodji dies "the friend of all," and Dansou listens to one of the funeral dirges of his own composition with the aculeate chagrin that comes of having one's gloomy juvenile philosophies all too hastily verified by life. The irrepressible joy Dansou once felt at having finally fathered twins (highly prized rather than abandoned in this region) turns in the months following Sodji's death to weary sorrow over their dangerous illnesses, to exasperation over his wife's commercial failures and their mounting debts. Nor is this all: There is trouble with the in-laws again. Afiavi's truly horrible father, never in favor of a marriage not to his own commercial advantage, finally decamps, cursing his daughter and her sentimentally compliant mother, to try factory work in Lomé. Once established there, he kidnaps Afiavi and tries to force a more suitable marriage upon her. It is up to Dansou, according to the best priestly advice available, to attempt a reconciliation in his father's tactful mode. With the help of the president of the C.O.S. (Club des Originaires de Séva) in Lomé, Dansou succeeds in holding a reconciliation ceremony.

> In South Togo, the ceremony of reconciliation, one of the most important [the author by now scarcely need say this], takes place when two or several persons consent to live again on good terms after a quarrel or after they have sworn never to love each other again. The mere fact of consent does not suffice . . . . It is absolutely necessary to concretize this desire to be in harmony again and to solicit the intervention of the gods.[28]

The father-in-law having decided to return in good standing to his natal village of Seva, Dansou prudently removes to Sekondi, Gold Coast, whence his family originally came. Note that his decision has a familial base. He does not go off to Sekondi primarily to seek his fortune. Statistically, however, here is one more exceptional villager in the city. It is the painful paradox of this book that however faithfully he follows his father's modes of adjustment, however strong his personal beliefs, Dansou never really gets along at home. He is obviously too much for the village. Here in Sekondi lives Dansou's beloved cousin from Vogan; here Dansou can earn a good living as a cooperative fisherman; here also he and Afiavi are easily converted to Christianity by an aged catechist who happens to be living upstairs. As a convert, Dansou is again an enthusiastic success. "Fervent as he had been in his pagan practices, just as flame like he now became in responding to the call of the Redeemer." One has come to expect something very like this of Dansou.

Since *Le Fils du fétiche* is a novel of reconciliation rather than of revolt, the hero's conversion to Christianity at the end does not at all imply a real break with tribal ways, despite certain pious ejaculations to the contrary which the author felt compelled to make for the benefit of his Western readers at this point. Conversion in this book comes by chance, and yet opportunely and, considering the circumstances, wisely—after all of the other lessons had been learned. The gospel provides the hero with a bonus, a sort of spiritual vacation without pay after long, tense years of atonement in another context. Dansou has entered a new, partly Westernized community and will, with his remarkable father's ancestral blessing, learn prudently to listen for the right signals from all sources. He will, as a modest culture hero in his own right, continue to improvise his own ways in those areas considered safely open to innovation—the technical and artistic sides of life. This son of the serpent will not, however, suffer the bruised heel.

<h2 style="text-align:center">VI.</h2>

Western cultural interference with the traditional life of the average villager in all of these novels is, for various reasons, at a minimum. A freedom to return to past beliefs and practices, in thought at least, is one of the advantages of having been born in a British protectorate, a British colony in West Africa, in a French mandated territory, or in the Belgian Congo. The educated writer's spiritual return to his village in such territories may be ambivalent, but there is little anguish in it.

It remains now to contrast the foregoing with two village novels written by Africans who have felt all the exacerbations of the "assimilated." Not many novelists from French West Africa have chosen to use the village as setting, and it should be obvious why this is so. Their novels are usually concerned more with the human personality in isolation than with the configurations of being-in-a-scene. Nevertheless, the two village novels that have been written by men who were forced to pass through a stage of physical isolation (as foreign students in France) and radical cultural alienation are the most beautifully written (with the exception, perhaps, of Achebe's) of them all. They sound the well of *négritude* in a poetic mode. Their works, like Hopkins' poem, are composed of a leaden question and a golden reply.

Camara Laye's *L'Enfant noir* (1954) and Cheikh Hamidou Kane's *L'Aventure ambiguë* (1961) are reflections on the quality of life lived in the old days before Westernization; and they both show the old communities beginning to undergo social change. These books are also reflections on the authors' childhood days, and as such are permeated with a sense of personal loss. The authors have certain key things in common. They both grew up in Moslem communities and both were born into aristocratic castes. Camara Laye's "village," Kouroussa, in Guinea was, at the time of his childhood, more town than village, bordered by the immemorial Niger and a modern railroad track; but he spent a good deal of time in a nearby agricultural community, Tindican, where his maternal relations lived. His father, head of the family in Kouroussa, was the most important forger in five cantons, whose skill with gold was proverbial; his mother also was born into the blacksmith caste, from which soothsayers and circumcisers are usually drawn. The unusual psychic powers proper to the members of this ancient fellowship had fortunately been passed down on both sides of the family, so that both father and mother were gifted and well born. Kane's Samba Diallo, the hero of the ambiguous adventure, is a member of the proud elite of the venerable Tukulor people, the first of the Negro tribes to be Islamized and great spiritual leaders throughout the region still. He is the nephew of the princess of the Diallobé, popularly known as La Grande Royale, and the favored disciple of the Grand Master of the faith, Thierno, the ascetic Moslem sage. Kane himself is also heir on his mother's side to the wisdom and lyricism of the Peul (Fulani) cultural tradition, dating back into the middle ages.

Both authors received privileged French educations, although Camara Laye's was in large part technical, in accordance with his practical uncle's advice. He excelled as a youth, however, in French language and literature rather than in mathematics, and when dwindling financial resources forced him to work in a Simca factory outside Paris, he wrote *L'Enfant noir*, his first novel, during the long, lonely nights. Laye is now a member of Guinea's diplomatic corps. Kane's Samba Diallo studies philosophy in Paris. Kane was, in his student days, associated with l'Abbé Pierre, and with Mounier and *Esprit*. Having been at one time head of economic planning in Senegal, he now works for UNESCO.

These authors have another thing in common: Their books have been subject to attack in Africa from various quarters. Camara Laye's has been criticized by the leftist press for its failure to take an anticolonial stand; and the sinuous rhythms and symbolisms of the innocent life he depicts, deemed "evasionist" by the *engagé*, have been commended *ad nauseam* by African as well as by European amateurs of *négritude*. Kane's book, because it ends with a suicide, has been called "un-African" by *négritude's* champion from Cameroun, Mr. Thomas Meloné; and yet it is obviously the author's principal endeavor to define and convey a sort of Koranic *négritude*. Furthermore, suicide under stress is not alien to the African experience, as Okonkwo's behavior and the mournful logs of the slaving ships, for example, show. Both books are of profound interest to the European mentality they reject. Their concerns are too universal to be the sole property of Africa, which is probably the chief reason why they are attacked.

What is unique about Camara Laye's book, in comparison with other novels with ostensibly the same theme, is not the ritual of gold smelting in his father's forge or the joyous harvest at Tindican. Laye simply evokes the music and symbolism of daily life with more sensitivity and power than anybody else. It is his aching sense of the passage of time and his continual feeling of separation, as a boy, from the full and deeply poetic life of the adults around him that make *L'Enfant noir* a very special book about the African scene. Each time an African mystery comes up, in the story, it is immediately qualified by regret. For example, Camara's father, the smith, reveals to his son his special intuitive and communicative relationship to the snake, "the guiding spirit of our race."

"I have told you all these things, little one, because you are my son, the eldest of my sons, and because I have nothing to hide from you. There is a certain form of behavior to observe, and certain ways of acting in order that the guiding spirit of our race may approach you also.... If you desire to inherit it in your turn, you will have to conduct yourself in the selfsame manner; from now on, it will be necessary for you to be more and more in my company."

He gazed at me with burning eyes, then suddenly he heaved a sigh.

"I fear, I very much fear, little one, that you are not often enough in my company. You are all day at school and one day you shall depart from that school for a greater one. You will leave me, little one ...."[29]

And later the boy muses to himself:

"Yet I should have liked, I should have liked so much to place my hand, my own hand, on the snake, and to understand and listen to that tremor too; but I did not know how the snake would have taken my hand, and I felt now that he would have nothing to tell me; I was afraid that he would never have anything to tell me"[30]

And when Camara describes his mother's special powers, particularly those associated with the crocodile, he concludes: "Yes, the world rolls on and changes. I, too, had my totem, but I no longer remember what it was." When he describes the ceremony of circumcision which permitted him and those of his age group to "attain that second life that is our true existence," he does account for many of the "mysteries" that had so astonished and terrified him as an uninitiated boy. The roaring of the great Konden Diara is easily explained—a trick of whirling boards. But the long white threads binding the great bombax tree in the sacred clearing to principal trees and houses of the town—how did these get there? Up over sixty feet of thorns?

I never succeeded in obtaining an explanation: at the time I might have obtained it, that is, when I should have taken my place among the older boys who conducted the ceremony, I was no longer living at Kouroussa.[31]

And he ends this chapter: ".... is there any part of the rite that still remains? The secret ... do we still have secrets?"

Finally, at the grand harvest scene which incorporates so many of the communal harmonies of village life, Camara, like Levin among the Russian peasants, admits to being "a mere spectator." Camara's uncle sets him to trimming stalks, "Now it isn't your job to cut rice, I shouldn't think it ever will be." Camara muses that farming was a dream for him. Even his own immediate family was part of a town; and yet corporate craftsmanship seemed to be a direction in which he would never be able to fulfill himself. "School ... Did I like school all that much?" This is the apotheosis of the country existence, the harvest:

> They were bound to one another, united by the same soul: each and every one was tasting the delight, savouring the common pleasure of accomplishing a common task.
>
> Was it this delight, this pleasure, even more than the fight against weariness and against the burden of the heat, that urged them on, that filled them to overflowing with rapturous song? Such was obviously the case: and this is what filled their eyes with so much tenderness, that wonderful serenity that used to strike me with such delighted and rather regretful astonishment; for though I was among them, with them, surrounded by these waves of tenderness, I was not one of them: I was only a schoolboy on a visit—and how I longed to forget that fact.[32]

Camara Laye is a born writer whose distance, even *in* childhood, from that childhood's remembered scenes, from that remembered promise of depth and joy, is the precondition of an inner and compensatory poetic life. His special status as a scholar-exile in a time of change reinforced the notion of transience which, as a Moslem, he accepted as a matter of faith.

In *L'Aventure ambiguë*, Kane's alter ego, Samba Diallo, is raised in a different sort of Moslem community altogether. Here Islam is not mitigated by the heightened reality, the humanity of an indigenous African religious life. Here there is no redeeming work. The luxurious nobility of a northern court is pitted against the austerity of a life-denying faith. Samba Diallo, whose birth entitles him to the former and whose temperament and brilliance commend him to the Grand Master as a protégé, chooses the religious style as a matter of course. The book begins with one sort of punishment: "That day Thierno had beaten him again. However, Samba Diallo had memorized his verse." Such gratuitous mortification of the flesh releases a more authentic suffering in him, that of the spirit which experiences existence as death. Outside of this bony negation there is only The Word, which Thierno's pupils have to memorize and recite exactly as it pleased god to fashion it—without, in their early years, even knowing its Arabic sense. The main part of the book is taken up with punishment of quite a different sort, the intellectual torture of "la connaissance de l'occident."

The hero's great-grandfather had gone forth with his trained elite, and this elite only, to fall to the arrogant fusillade of the French. La Grande Royale, Samba Diallo's aunt, although she detests the idea of a European education, nevertheless insists that the young elite of her day go forth to meet the modern age. In becoming masters of European technology they may again become the masters of themselves. "The word may be suspended, but life, life suffers no interruption." [33]

Therefore, just as one prepares the fields for a new harvest by burning them and plowing them under, so the natural leaders of the Western Sudan will have to risk a temporary suspension of the word and the old customs so that the youth may reemerge great. The aunt thus insists that her nephew be among the first to go to the French school. A European education for Samba Diallo, however, turns out to be a flagellation of the mind.

This is the real ambiguity of the adventure. Samba Diallo, always intrigued by the absolute, studies Western philosophy and is particularly depressed by the reduction and the arrogance he finds. Descartes and those to follow ask an increasingly narrow set of questions and come up with increasingly certain answers about less, and less, and less. (The idea that God can be known, or brought near, is anathema to a true believer.) The broadly educated Samba Diallo finds Rilke a suitable companion in his loneliness, for like Malte Laurids Brigge he sees but absence and vacuum in the proliferation of Western "things"; he sees Paris as devoid of personal encounters, of nature too. (The religious fanatic back home, a "fool" and a close friend of the Master, was particularly depressed by the pavements of the European city he once visited, in the sense in which an English poet once phrased that Rilkian feeling: "Can the foot feel, being shod?") What Samba Diallo really regrets, even more than the loss of his homeland, as he confesses to one of his few friends, is that "*ce soit mon enfance.*"

So, summoned by his anxious father, Samba Diallo returns home, having lost the faith, having refused to adopt any Western philosophy in its stead, but having retained and reinforced the stern *memento mori* with which he began. The Master, in the meantime, has died and although Samba Diallo was once to have been his successor, another of ordinary lineage has taken his place. The fanatical fool, however, even more crazed by despair following the old man's death, persists in seeing Samba Diallo as the true Master and, in a lonely graveyard encounter, insists that the young man enter a mosque and pray. Samba Diallo refuses. Either the old Master reenter your heart then, cries the fool, or you die for his glory. The young man is silent. Cornered, in impotent incredulity, he assents to annihilation; the fool, patently "the killer" now, in Ionesco's sense, fires his gun. In an epilogue, Samba Diallo's spirit accepts a timeless paradise where all the apparent things of this world are fulfilled.

L'Aventure ambiguë is the most aristocratic and the most intellectual of the returns to traditional life. But it too has certain things in common with *Le Fils du fétiche*, the most mundane. The process of reconciliation observed in Ananou's book becomes submission to the discipline of another world in Kane's; controlling one's temper becomes self-flagellation. A full enjoyment of familial and communal life is the son of the serpent's plausible goal; a mystical participation in the plenitude of being is the rather desperate hope of the son of Diallobé.

Is Islam south of the Sahara, then, but animism turned inside out, structurally the same somehow, but transcendent rather than immanent—human sweat and sinew swathed in the mummy cloth of a burnous? In any case, the double estrangement of Kane's hero is appropriate to the privileged nature of his education and his caste. The writing of a novel about village life is anyone's ambiguous adventure. The isolated consciousness of the narrator weaves in and out of the compact community he is describing, interpreting, projecting as his past and future choice.

Notes

1. David Ananou, *Le Fils du fétiche* (Paris: Nouvelles Editions Latines, 1955), p. 7.

2. Jean Malonga, *La Legende de M'pfoumou Ma Mazono* (Paris: Editions Africaines, 1954), p. 14.

3. This letter is quoted by Léon Bosquet in his introduction to René Maran's *Le Petit roi de chimérie* (Paris: Editions Albin Michel, 1924), p. 15.

4. Letter to Léon Bosquet, *ibid.*, p. 41.

5. See, for example, René Trautman, *Au pays de Batouala* (Paris: Payot & Cie., 1922).

6. Albert Maurice, *Felix Eboué, sa vie et oeuvre* (Bruxelles: Institut Royal Colonial Belge, Tome 37, 1954), p. 16.

7. Mercer Cook, *Five French Negro Authors* (Washington, D.C.: The Associated Negro Publishers, Inc., 1943), p. 139.

8. René Maran, *Le Livre de la brousse* (Paris: Editions Albin Michel, 1934), pp. 32–33.

9. *Ibid.*, pp. 242–43.

10. Sembene Ousmane, *O pays, mon beau peuple* (Paris: Le Livre Contemporain, Amiot-Dumont, 1957), p. 46.

11. *Ibid.*, p. 234.

12. Chinua Achebe, *Things Fall Apart* (New York: McDowell, Obolensky, 1959), p. 3.

13. *Ibid.*, p. 14.

14. *Ibid.*, pp. 151–52.

15. *Ibid.*, p. 214.

16. "Conversation with Chinua Achebe," *Africa Report*, Vol. 9, No. 7 (July, 1964), p. 20.

17. Chinua Achebe, *Arrow of God* (London: Heinemann, 1964), pp. 3–4.

18. *Ibid.*, pp. 240–41.

19. *Ibid.*, p. 286.

20. *Ibid.*, pp. 253–54.

21. G. Bolomba, *Kavwanga* (Namur: Collection Lavigerie, (n.d. 1954?), pp. 11–12.

22. *Ibid.*, p. 145.

23. A. S. Mopeli-Paulus and Miriam Basner, *Turn to the Dark* (London: Jonathan Cape, Ltd., 1956), pp. 150–52.

24. *Ibid.*, p. 123.

25. Lord Hailey, *An African Survey* (London: Oxford University Press, 1957), p. 507.

26. Mopeli-Paulus and Basner, *op. cit.*, p. 284.

27. David Ananou, *op. cit.*, p. 68.

28. *Ibid.*, pp. 186–87.

29. Camara Laye, *The Dark Child*, James Kirkup, trans. (London: Collins, 1955), p. 21.

30. *Ibid.*, pp. 23–24.

31. *Ibid.*, p. 108.

32. *Ibid.*, p. 61.

33. Cheikh Hamidou Kane, *L'Aventure ambiguë* (Paris: Julliard, 1961), p. 62.

IV CITY LIFE

Go down angels to the flood,
Blow out the sun, turn the moon
    into blood!
Come back angels, bolt the door,
The time that's been will be no more.
    —AMERICAN NEGRO SPIRITUAL

The glorification of the African past and the dignifying of a traditional way of life are, as we have seen, not only the political gestures they claim to be, but also modes of self-disclosure and fantasy. The ostensible theme of another group of novels is Africa present. These serve our contemporary sense of the African situation by stressing African modernity, the sophisticated African style, and the kind of Africa to which a Western vote of confidence must be given if development is to proceed. The scene of these novels is the real scene in which the author lives, the city, although the hero may be shown setting forth from the village in the beginning or returning to it for a visit, to confront a family crisis, to take stock of the old ways or, disillusioned, to resume some kind of romantic residence there for good. These city novels are exemplary. Like European heroes of novels before, these special African heroes act as pioneers in coming to terms with a new environment with which others of their mobile class are expected to cope.

The superficial delights and real terrors of the city have been known ever since Aesop, who was in all probability an African too. Expanding African cities like Lagos, Accra, and Dakar impress those who visit them with their vivacity and their incongruities— fine public buildings and sprawling, corrugated slum dwellings, elegant discourse and incredible journalese, ambitious, intelligent economic planning and egregious personal self-improvement schemes. As in all cities, the appearances govern the realities. Citizens display their wares in the market. They dress in peg trousers, in three piece,* in colorful printed or embroidered cloths—to catch the eye, to be emancipated, or to be all African. To walk on the street is to cut a self-conscious figure. A man's very gesture, the most delightful gratuitous improvisation, indicates an estimated time of social arrival.† There is always the temptation to enter public life for superficial reasons—to attract a following, to be able to afford a splendid personal style. Bribery and delinquency—the one to get in, the other because one is hopelessly out—are acute social problems.

It is possible for the foreign visitor to see and hear too much of the new, the flashy, the tawdry, and not enough of the old, although it is certainly true that the reverse has usually been the case in Africa, for tom-toms, baobabs, and mangroves still flourish in the popular European mind. But by an African, however, these glittering and fractured modern phenomena may be seen and— if the African is an artist— used as signs. They stand as material counterparts to that complicated set of pragmatic attitudes and ironic subterfuges which any sensitive person must use on the way to the establishment of a sound moral stance in a society where nothing seems stable, where there is little to get a grip on. An unequivocal "traditional" stand is impossible; an unequivocal Christian or "Western" stand is likewise impossible. Changing social and political conditions have, in the urbanized African, produced a new breed of cat.

II.

The first substantial West African novel in French, *Karim* (1935), by Ousmane Socé Diop, is at the same time the first portrait of

* "The smart professionals in three piece ... / Those who want to be seen in the best company / Have abjured the magic of being themselves." George Awoonor Williams, *Rediscovery and Other Poems* (Ibadan: Mbari, 1964), p. 10.
† "He brought his wrist up to eye-level and frowned at it, the very picture of a man kept waiting, a man who had expected no less. His arm dropped, elbow flexed stiff, hand at mid-thigh level, palm downwards, fingers splayed. There the hand made a light movement, balanced from the wrist, as if sketching an arpeggio, or saying good-bye to the pavement, or greeting it? An elegant little gesture, full of charm, given out of an abundant sense of style to a waiting world." Doris Lessing, "Outside the Ministry," in *The Classic* (Johannesburg), Vol. I, No. 2 (1963), 15.

the provincial African come to the city. Nineteen years later—
and the cultural lag is significant—Cyprian Ekwensi produced
the first real West African novel of English expression on a similar
theme, *People of the City* (1954). As treated in these novels, new
urban groupings, a cash economy, and a new literate African,
unbound by traditional ties, are obviously problems created by
colonialism. But such consequences of Western occupation could
be discussed without committing the author to an outright
anticolonial position which, temperamentally and at the time of
writing, he probably didn't feel anyway. Direct attacks on the
system and a flagellation of the self which has profited from the
new sophisticated life at the expense of the old integrities are
themes to be taken up later by different temperaments and most
suitably in French.* The milder ambiguities shown in the city
novel proper center about the excitement felt in the mores
deplored.

Ousmane Socé Diop and Cyprian Ekwensi are Senegalese and
Nigerian, respectively. The professional careers of these two
writers are themselves indices of culture. Diop has been ambassador to the United States since 1960. He has been active in politics
since 1937, and has been in public office for years. He belongs
to the tradition of French-speaking diplomats of literary distinction, as exemplified in Africa by his own countryman, Senghor.
Ekwensi is now director of information for the Federal Ministry
of Information. He was formerly head of features for the Nigerian

---

* It might be parenthetically noted that cultural conquest works this way
too, from the outside in. The material aspects of a civilization penetrate
first, superficialities to be easily and creatively absorbed. An ingenious use
can always be found for new materials, vulgarly seen in the mind's eye as
top hats, alarm clocks, and guns, without really altering the manners and
values of the group. But new possessions in time create new power structures, an acquiring and dispensing class of men who must seek their
spiritual *raison d'être* in terms of the system with the material goods of
which they have to deal. A foreign way of life which has produced these
advantages is to be envied, then emulated, and finally defended against
one's own. And once this foreign ethos has taken root, a new political
authority can be imposed without relying upon brute force alone—the
trader, the missionary, and the commandant being three stages along
the colonial way. The urban novel, the psychological novel, and the
political novel are three logical stages of revolutionary response to the
colonial situation.

Broadcasting Corporation, before that a pharmacist, and before that a forester. He has always been a popular writer, whether for schoolboys, for the mass market in Africa and abroad, or, under an assumed name, for the Onitsha market where he got his start.* The first novels of Cyprian Ekwensi and Ousmane Socé Diop, however different in tone and approach to life, have a similar setting, a common theme, and—remarkably—a similar plot as well. Both deal with young men who explore the complexities of modern urban life, primarily through a succession of experiences with women of varied status and various charms—a series of Ariadnes to guide the simple heroes through "the swirling context of local sights and sounds." [1] As a labyrinth, however, the Lagos of ten years ago is significantly different from the Dakar between the two wars.

The hero of *Karim* is twenty-two years old when we meet him. "Well dressed and correctly behaved in the streets, he passed for 'serious' in the opinion of his elders." But, despite his *certificat d'études* and his job in a French commercial house, he is more *bon vivant* than *sérieux*. He is, in addition, the victim of a myth of noble prodigality among the Wolof people, his ancestors. It was easy for these warrior heroes of former times, astride splendid steeds, to pillage their enemies, sell them into slavery, and return with more than ample means for maintaining beautiful women,

* The lively popular literature sold in the bookstalls of the Onitsha market in the Eastern region of Nigeria should not be confused with the "new African literature" as practiced and preached, for example, at Ibadan, a university community. (Some well-meaning articles scattered here and there in English periodical literature tend to foster such confusion.) But the Onitsha literature reflects the same sort of high life that is treated, at least *en passant,* in much serious literature, and the sons and daughters of many of the newly literate market stall readers will doubtless provide the sensitive general readership of the future, upon which Nigerian poets and novelists are fortunate in being able to count. For a full description of this popular literature, full of incongruous superlatives and felicitous malapropisms used to describe the charms and the wiles of the new "painted" women, their ostentatious boyfriends, their villainous traditional fathers, and their wealthy "arranged" husbands, threepenny opera with enticing titles like "Saturday Night Disappointment," "Why Harlots Hate Married Men and Love Bachelors," and "Rosemary and the Taxi Driver," see Ulli Beier, "Public Opinion on Lovers," *Black Orpheus,* No. 14 (February, 1964), 4–16.

as well as liberal friendships among their peers. In St. Louis, the "old" French city where Karim lives, the sumptuous Wolof customs are more or less observed despite the fact that opportunities for modern commercial pillage are limited. It is not easy for a modern clerk to keep up with the Wolofs, but when Karim does fall in love with a beautiful girl, he tries to court her in the traditional style.

The traditional "intended" lady was a heavy financial burden without any tangible benefits. The suitor was supposed to supply her with cloths for special occasions, especially for Moslem fêtes, pay griots to sing her praises at tam-tams, and was even responsible for such minor expenses as having her earrings repaired. A loyal friend is willing to speculate on rice futures in hopes of forestalling Karim's creditors, and a friendly jeweler is willing to fix his lady's earrings for nothing. But with a wealthy rival for her hand, Karim simply cannot cope. For his Marième, who hennas her feet in the oriental manner and powders her face in the European, who is as accomplished in the Charleston as she is in the traditional steps, goaded on by her avaricious and unsentimental mother, has no choice but to insist that her impecunious favorite suitor engage in the traditional diamelé (spending duel) with his unfavored rival of means.

Finding himself actually participating in a diamelé Karim stalls for time in an ingenious Chaplinesque manner: When the rich rival presents a 1,000 franc note to the presiding griot, Karim passes five franc notes rapidly all around the room, to all of the servants, hoping that in the general confusion no tabulation will be made. He hopes right. For the moment he is a great success. But a 1,000 franc note and a coffer full of gold, presented directly to Marième, cannot be gainsaid, and Karim is forced to retire in defeat. The diamelé may not be a subtle way of impressing one's future mother-in-law, but it does have the virtue of being brief and sure. Now Karim is free to go to Dakar, the "new" French city, to try to make—and quickly—the necessary fortune that he has lacked all along. But before leaving he gets in touch with a wise old marabout who gives him, on credit, a gris-gris (charm), which cannot really insure that Marième will marry him in the end, but which will act as a kind of fortified prayer.

Once in Dakar, Karim lodges with his uncle and is able, with the uncle's help, to get a rather dull job translating invoices. He meets, for the first time, those educated young men to whom his cousin Ibrahim—like Karim dressed in fez and *boubou*—contemptuously refers as "black Europeans." Had he not been told they were such, the toothbrushes and books in their rooms would have given them away at once. (Karim, of course, uses a dental stick, and, although he has completed an "education," never thinks of reading or of improving himself in any way during his leisure hours.) While the black Europeans are out on the town, Karim stays piously at home to hear Tante Aminata tell traditional folktales in a quiet courtyard amidst all the cosmopolitan bustle of Dakar.

For two months Karim leads this impeccable life. Then, to change the pace a little, with a friend he rents a Renault to go to a *sabit** in nearby Rufisque. Here the young hero meets another woman, a delightful widow, who almost ruins him. His rival this time is poorer than he is, and Karim jumps at the chance to spend his clerk's salary in exchange, this time, for the realities as opposed to the promises of passion. When the next *sabit* is held at Rufisque, Karim hires a Chrysler and goes alone.

The "black European" teacher who shares his rooms lends Karim money when, as must have been expected, he runs out, but warns him in the future to stay away from women like the widow of Rufisque. Improve your mind, the teacher urges, forget the noble prodigality of the Wolofs. We can no longer act in the framework of an indigenous society that doesn't exist any more, a society that really is in a state of decomposition, or of evolution —who can say which? So Karim gives up the widow and takes to reading books. First he reads *Batouala*, which delights him, but since there aren't any more African novels he reads Dumas, the next best thing, then Hugo, then Corneille—all of which, in ascending degrees of difficulty, continue the appeal to his heroic Wolof soul.

Karim now dresses in a Western suit and colonial casque, and buys flashy ties to go with them, for one who is *evolué* wishes to

* The *sabit* is the sophisticated urban equivalent of the *tam-tam* which he had so very much enjoyed in Marième's courtyard back home. Metallic instruments are used at the *sabit*, partly, the author explains, because Europeans claimed that real drums disturbed their sleep and so prohibited them, and partly because "evolved" Africans themselves felt drums too retrograde. Anxious nonetheless for "ancestral distractions," the black denizens of Dakar hit upon this compromise, to the delight of the neophyte Karim.

"single himself out." With new costumes go new customs, to which he quickly adapts: ballroom dancing, swimming, movies, and café-sitting along the corniche. There are also discussions in the rented rooms of the educated, discussions of the very cultural changes they are all undergoing, held, as the author says, by those whose deepest feelings argue for the old traditions but whose interests vociferously declare for Europeanization in all things. "But beyond their talk, in spite of their talk, year after year a hybrid civilization was forming which was obedient only to the laws of the struggle for existence."[2]

Finally Karim meets an evolved girl, Marie, whose fiancé is conveniently abroad. She too requires a new dress, this time for a Catholic fête in Gorée. Karim obliges and escorts her to the ball in his own new singular style: "He sported a three piece suit with a flannel vest, shiny black shoes, white shirt, silk tie, topping all with a sombrero—which gave him quite an air." They dance until morning to music which becomes increasingly African—beginning with waltzes into which a barely perceptible African rhythm is inserted, passing through fox trots with a South American beat, and finally to the goumbé, a sort of African rumba. The words to the last goumbé, an homage to two young people, now dead, who had danced at the fête last year, recall the high life of medieval Paris, as anatomized by Villon:

> Le monde n'est que vanité,
> L'on meurt et tout s'en va;
> Songez à Papa Thialis,
> Songez à Mery Goomis.[3]

The next day Karim oversleeps, and when his boss bellows at him: "You're like all negroes, lazy and good-for-nothing," the proud young Wolof quits. His uncle (most distressed because jobs aside from manual labor, which naturally everyone shuns, are so scarce) tells him that Europeans are always like that. They let off steam. They don't really mean it, he says.

Now a period of real suffering ensues. Karim does get a temporary job, helping with a European company's inventories in the bush, but he comes back to Dakar, with no future prospects, only to find Marie enceinte. He honorably promises to support the child, but will not marry her because, as the author says, religious differences really do mean a great deal to both parties. Luckily,

Marie is able to miscarry with the aid of traditional herbs and concoctions; but now Karim himself is sick, the inevitable paludism. In the hospital he dreams of St. Louis and takes to reading the Koran.

Cured of the fever, and of the city, Karim returns home only to discover his wealthy rival jailed for an indebtedness of over 50,000 francs! He sees Marième dancing again—like the Niger descending the rocks. For this Karim easily forswears the singularity of his European dress, and the book ends with an account of a traditional Senegalese wedding. When the signs of Marième's virginity are published à l'arabe, Karim gives a lavish tam-tam in her honor and prepares to settle down. The experimental period of his boyhood is over, and with it whatever charms la civilisation métisse in Dakar ever had. "Farewell," says the author in conclusion, "farewell to the mobile life of fantasy, the heedless, the devil-may-care."

This first novel about an African urban experience conveys two distinct concerns of the author, delicately intermeshed. The first of these is to write a novel of manners, in the classical European sense: social behavior described first of all for its own sake, the author delighting in isolating all the significant details of civilized existence in the community he knows best, and beyond this, social behavior as revelatory of group values and individual frames of mind. African "city" novels generally tend to resemble European novels in this regard. West African "village" novels and South African "location" autobiographies—given the primacy of the "social field" in traditional African life—are really novels of manners in Lionel Trilling's profounder, extended sense. States of soul, by African standards, cannot be indicated, nor can metaphysical preoccupations be expressed, except through active personal relationships within the community (the living and the dead), art itself traditionally being such a relationship.*

* It is worth noting that The Liberal Imagination is read and often quoted by African critics. The most remarkable novel of manners in Mr. Trilling's sense is Noni Jabavu's The Ochre People (New York: St. Martin's Press, 1963). This is not a novel, strictly speaking, but rather a personal essay written upon the occasion of the author's return to her family on a visit, after marriage to an Englishman and a protracted residence abroad. Family tensions and affections, along with communal expectations, are revealed most ingeniously by Miss Jabavu's rendering the flexibilities of everyday Xosa utterance (constructions which contain the relationships

Novels of manners, in the restrictive sense, are of immense importance in times of social change. In Dakar in the twenties, for instance, precise distinctions of dress as indices of character —the Chrysler the second time rather than the Renault, the hennaed feet and the powdered cheek—all are intriguing as signs of where one thinks he is going, of what one thinks he is. For, despite the fact that in the end Karim rejects Dakar for St. Louis, one feels Westernization like some fog from the Atlantic gently creeping in, permeating everything, even traditional St. Louis. And when real thoughts and allegiances are hidden, perhaps not even formulated, what is there to cling to but the outward signs? The social critic in such a time is, like the *arriviste* he writes about, committed to being an accurate eye. Unsure of his ground, he must have his shoes down pat. In addition to being this kind of a novel of manners, *Karim* is a novel of good manners, which is not—schoolteachers to the contrary—to be confused with the former. Tasteful without ever being priggish, elegantly succinct, *Karim* is eminently civilized.

But *Karim* does not accomplish, for it does not even attempt, the final purpose of the unrelenting novels of manners—to show the dust heap upon which the niceties of social illusion are built, the sordid facts behind the hastily built facade, the wrinkles behind the make-up. The *métisse* civilization which the young *evolués* discuss in the evenings, that which develops in accordance with the laws of the struggle for existence under colonial conditions, is, we are told, hard-headed—opposed to the truer traditional instincts of the heart. The young men who obey these laws are, we would assume, first of all made hypocritical and then their hearts wear out from lack of use and these young men become entirely what they seem to be. We do not see this, we merely follow Karim's vision, which remains singularly innocent. Although *Karim* is about social changes, then, these have no real evil in them for him, nor for us. For Karim the city is a heart's intermittence, a fantasy. He has his *wanderjahre* and returns to St. Louis, where reality and responsibility lie.

This leads us to the second concern of the author. *Karim*, like Camara Laye's *L'Enfant noir*, is an elegy for lost youth, a poetic

and the expectations) into English equivalents. She expresses her own complex attitudes through her situation (as it unfolds, with little extra analysis) among relatives, her seniors mainly, with whom she must get along.

evocation of the moods and images proper to a vanished scene. But the object of such tender fancies is not the traditional town of Ousmane Socé Diop's book. It is the city. That Karim should have emerged from his city experiences psychologically unscathed should not be cause for wonder, perhaps. The novelist plays up the dichotomy between traditional and "hybrid" modern urban life. Smooth transitions from one to the other are possible for certain temperaments. Karim, whatever the misfortunes that befell him in Dakar, is constitutionally an aristocratic person at his ease.*

Ekwensi's *People of the City* is a novel of urban manners in what one might call the analytic, as opposed to the synthetic, sense. Like Balzac or Dickens, Ekwensi is intrigued by the relentless potential honesty of "the facts." But he does not at the same time weave a coherent veil of illusion, he does not organize the appearances into a coherent expression of current social values beneath which the realities starkly lie. *People of the City*, in its form, is a novel of bad manners, a rogue's tale, really, despite its superimposed plot which is designed to show to a susceptible popular audience the moral evolution of the hero, "exemplary" in the Onitsha market sense.

Amusa Sango, the hero, is a dapper young man about Lagos who was born in the "Eastern Greens." He has a job with the *West African Sensation* as a crime reporter, and in his spare time he leads a dance band. He also has time for women, which the book presents in a series, as fleshly counterparts of his developing moral sense.

He begins amusing himself with Aina, a really beguiling girl from the slums who is unfortunately arrested (and subsequently jailed) on suspicion of stealing a cloth in front of Sango's apartment at 20 Molomo Street. Sango refuses to be compromised in the affair. (But later, frightened by her powerful mother and by her need, he pays her off, using his band's salaries to do so.) At

* One is here reminded of an example of Senegalese flexibility, of diplomacy in the "double" sense of the word which once made one from a less pliable tradition fairly gasp. Senghor, one morning, was able to welcome a congregation of African leaders by giving them fighting talk on the necessity of a strong stand against Portuguese colonialism and that very afternoon get on a plane himself and fly off to his farm in France for the duration of Dakar's apparently "intolerable" rainy season.

the modern, integrated All Language Club where the band is playing, Sango then meets the fascinating if emaciated Beatrice, also a former provincial. She is now the common-law wife of an English engineer and mother of three of his children, whom, of course, the engineer doesn't recognize. She is also now (and always) the cool object of the touching and most genuine affections of a grizzled old timber dealer and lorry driver from the Gold Coast. She likes "high life and drinks and music," and her dissipation is nothing to her.

A reportorial venture to a coal strike in the hinterlands and the murder of a close friend by a Lebanese merchant make Sango for the first time actively aware of the reality of social problems. His dispatches from the mine, although anti-European, gain him a promotion, but his too controversial exposé of the Syrian and Lebanese "menace" gets him fired forthwith. He is now in a sufficiently sublime moral state to meet a really good girl. He does. She is wearing a white dress and her name, by an odd coincidence that has confused the critics, is also Beatrice. Probably the author meant to suggest a preliminary, or false, Beatrice, to be followed by the real thing.

Beatrice II has a fiancé studying in England who later in the story conveniently, if tragically, gases himself upon receiving bad grades. But more important than this unfortunate young man is Beatrice II's father, a man of great birth and deportment who at one time had left Dahomey during a struggle over a chieftain-ship, and who now leads a dignified middle-class life in Lagos. Here for the first time Sango is made actively aware of domestic reality—of "a real home." The father, however, proud that his other daughters have married well-educated professional men, considers Amusa Sango beneath his daughter's consideration. But when the respectable fiancé dies in his efforts to succeed, the chiefly father is modern enough to let his daughter marry whom she will. The book ends as Sango, having sent a homely, "arranged" fiancée of his back to her convent in the bush, having seen the slum girl Aina through a dangerous abortion, having learned of the inevitable death of Beatrice I in the arms of her faithful lorry driver, prepares to set forth for the Gold Coast with Beatrice II at his side to accomplish something worthy of his strangely charismatic father-in-law.

Their wedding is a quiet one, "not even the sound of a drum to liven things up." The tableau of Beatrice II receiving her few decorous well-wishers would *seem* to be an all-too-human shadowing forth of the bourgeois boredom to come.

> Sewing-machine in hand, idly sewing a dress while around her sat her friends, sipping lime-juice and eating chicken. A mixture of bashfulness, joy and sorrow.[4]

But where the lively author of all of this stands is almost impossible to determine. (He certainly never tried to entertain guests at the sewing machine.) The brute facts, the injustices of life under colonial conditions in this city, are perhaps intended to speak for themselves—above the pious hum of the sewing machine. Nevertheless, since the real vitality of the book lies elsewhere than on the antimacassars of its rather Victorian morality, it is elsewhere, to give the author intellectual credit, that one must now turn.

The book is not named for its amusable hero. One assumes, therefore, what one in fact finds, that it is the "people of the city" that really count.

> Sango caught a brief glimpse of Bayo. Always in the right place at the right time. In his flash tie, knee-length velvet jacket, heavy-soled shoes and sun goggles, he waved. He was riding a bicycle—probably borrowed.[5]

The dandy, Bayo, on somebody else's bike or seducing a teen-aged "city girl" in Sango's room, is a social problem of great concern in Lagos, as is so in Accra and other West African cities. He resembles his more violent brothers, the *tsotsis* of South Africa, in that the system, *mutatis mutandis*, is keeping him out. Young men of Bayo's stamp have either dropped out of school too early, failed a crucial exam, or cannot afford the bribe that would place their deficient applications for white collar jobs before the appropriate personnel directors. But, money being essential to the delinquent who would aspire to the high life in society's despite, the next time we glimpse Bayo he is involved in a modest penicillin racket (from which he is luckily able to extricate himself before any action is taken against him or his ignorant "patient"). Still later, we learn that Bayo has decided to "become a serious man and move with the times." At this point he falls desperately in love with a Lebanese girl, and here a whole new world of social tension in Lagos is opened up. The love affair itself closes tragically when the pistol of the cloth merchant Zamil puts an end to Bayo, the African city boy.

The most fully drawn Lebanese character in the book is Lajide, the landlord of 20 Molomo Street, an unscrupulous dealer in a variety of things, the well-liquored and surfeited custodian of eight wives. We glimpse him buying bolts of sumptuous velvet (a fraction of which poor Aina wishes she could afford) for all eight wives at one blow; and later, when his eldest wife dies, we are with him when he receives her ghost. We see his remaining seven wives—in a scene of remarkable vigor and clownish brutality—loyally beat up Beatrice I, who has betrayed *them* by playing up to Lajide and *Lajide* by exposing one of his crooked business deals. The Lebanese in this book are a powerful minority, and not only in a financial sense. The violence and oriental extravagance of their lives obviously appeal to the author's imagination. To passionate exotics such as these, many urban fantasies in all nations cling.

And finally, among the many telling portraits of city people, Ekwensi's brief sketch of a teacher turned politician is irresistible and should be noted here. Although he is on the moderate side of things (the Realization Party to which Sango's respectable father-in-law belongs), his enthusiasm for his new calling knows no moderation. "Politics is life," he says, "with every election things change. . . . I like it." When Sango thanks this enthusiast, at one point, for offering him a free room to live in, the politician disarmingly replies: Don't mention it. "It is my plan to devote the rest of my life to self-sacrifice." Although we do hear that the Realization Party has lost the election, we are given, unfortunately, no further news of this charming fellow. Dickens would have devoted twenty pages to his affairs.

The dandy, the politician, and the Lebanese landlord are excellent candid shots of modern Nigerian life. But there is another strain to be heard in this book besides those improvised by the modern combo or the brass band, an eerie, rather sinister strain from the tribal past. Immemorial drums are heard in the story only intermittently, yet their elusive sound evokes a kind of horror that the author himself does not seem to be too emancipated to feel. Sango, as journalist, is sent to cover a mysterious *apala* dance, during the course of which an hysterical participant suddenly dies. And then there is the matter of an unsolved murder in a deserted spot with which Sango's memory involuntarily associates the frightful story of the Ufemfe Society's part in the suicide of one Buraimah Ajikatu, aged thirty five.

This unfortunate father of four had worked for years in a department store with no hope of promotion. He suddenly decided to join the Ufemfe Society (whose exact nature is never gone into in this book), and from then on things began to pick up. He was promoted and was earning a good salary until one day the Society came to demand his first-born son. Much later Sango notices, among other signs of conservative respectability, that a certificate of membership in this clandestine society is hanging on his future father-in-law's wall. Could this be one reason for the old man's rather frightening appeal? This Ufemfe Society, apparently combining the virtues of a businessmen's fraternal association with the vices of a racketeer's protection syndicate and a recidivistic cult from the bush, is the most provocative of the telltale hearts hidden beneath the thin floorboards of this book.

People of the City gives a tantalizing sense of the extraordinary possibilities of hybrid city life in West Africa as material for fabrication and scrutiny in the novel. Those two basic and complementary drives, the hectic pursuit of pleasure and the equally hectic flight from poverty and fear, which lie right at the social foundations of all modern city life, are here and there disclosed and in all of the complexity of their new-old African setting. But Ekwensi cannot sustain and develop these insights, and it is too bad that, so far, his first is also his most exciting book. He draws people well, as a sidewalk artist with a keen sense of the bizarre might sketch the passing crowd; and in looking over his shoulder one is always at the mercy of random impressions, some more telling than others, but all of them alive.

III.

A second pair of novels, Chinua Achebe's *No Longer at Ease* (1960) and the late Abdoulaye Sadji's *Maïmouna* (1958), probe the problem of life in the city with more urgency, each from its characteristic Nigerian or Senegalese point of view. Karim and Amusa Sango both tasted of the delights and the dangers of the city, but they did not really try themselves out. They left before they could become substantially corrupted or hurt, the one to

return to a stable life of tradition, the other, again characteristically, to venture forth to the Gold Coast where professional
opportunities and political conditions for Africans were at that
time more advanced. The hero and the heroine of this second
pair of novels are ruined by the city, disgraced and excluded in
the midst of youth from the very society which once tempted
them to enter into it with enthusiasm and good will.

Both authors are alert to new singularities of style as signs of
a hybrid culture. Achebe most effectively shows how tribal institutions are in the city adapted to competitive economic ends,
how the social solidarity of the village group continues in association form to support the now isolated individual of the city as
he jockeys for position in the game. He also shows how strong
tribal ties, both African and British, prevent the evolved individual from becoming a free, independent citizen in his own
right. Sadji's urban situation is at the same time simpler and more
complex. Between the village communities of the hinterland and
the French bureaucracy stands a well-established elite indigenous
to the city, and it is with this group that Sadji primarily deals.
The attitude of this elite to the French is, simply put, hypocritical.
For the purposes of a lucrative, prestige job in the French system,
one wears a European hat. To impress those of one's own society,
one shows a few evidences of French culture. The attitude of
this group to those of the hinterland is one of scorn. But the real
foundations of this urban aristocracy, in the course of years under
colonialism, have changed. It has become, in effect, a black
bourgeoisie, despite the old myths and manners that have been
ostentatiously retained.

The Nigerian's primary emphasis is on morality—right conduct
under stress in a competitive society, amid all the confusions of
allegiance in a modern African situation. Like Ekwensi's, Achebe's
city book shows an acute awareness of cold, hard social fact; but
Achebe extends this awareness into a realistic analysis of behavior
and motivation. Sadji, the Senegalese writer, is more philosophical, interested in social institutions and environment generally as reflections and determinations of human character in
the abstract. It is the *esthétique de la morale* that intrigues him,
gradations of reality and illusion, of good and evil, rather than
the "decision-making" process, as we say.

Achebe's Lagos is an underground map, a network of moral
complications, of channels of social influence through which

the modern southern Nigerian must learn to find his way. And he does, for the most remarkable thing about this subterranean life of favors, loans, and bribes is, paradoxically, its very obviousness, stability, and ease. The alert villager need have no trouble at all adapting to the ways of the metropolis, provided that he is ready to accept the fact that in a certain sense he has not really left home. Most likely his fellow countrymen will have preceded him there and set up a local association whose members are bound and prepared to lend him money, find him jobs, get him out of trouble, and, generally, afford him a kind of diplomatic immunity from the terrors of competition, complexity, and the law.

We have seen, in Achebe's first novel, how easily the villagers of Umuofia, with the heroic exception of Okonkwo, adapt to Christianity and the local store. In *No Longer at Ease*, Achebe takes a hypothetical grandson of old Okonkwo and shows how he too fails to thrive in the moral climate created for him by his provincial society's by now quite cynical adaptation to the colonial bureaucracy of a later day. But Okonkwo's stock, as he had feared, has become weakened, and among Umuofians generally, Christianity and commercialism have taken their toll. The shift from a Yeats to an Eliot quotation as the title of the second book is the author's own sophisticated acknowledgement of a debilitation that the elder Okonkwo foresaw. For *Things Fall Apart* comes from the world of Yeats' cataclysmic vision, and how the Irish poet would have appreciated the wild old Nigerian! *No Longer at Ease* comes from the anticlimactic world to which Eliot's magi return. The career of the grandson Okonkwo ends not with a matchet's swing but with a gavel's tap.

The story begins with the public humiliation of young Obi Okonkwo, as a British judge is in the act of sentencing him for having accepted a paltry twenty-pound bribe. Everyone is curious as to how and why this happened. The opinions of Europeans and Africans on this both reflect an orthodox, "tribal" point of view. The judge, passing judgment on Obi, says paternally, "I cannot comprehend how a young man of your education and brilliant promise could have done this." But he means, surely, what Obi's cynical boss, Mr. Green, has the courage openly to say: "The African is corrupt through and through . . . sapped mentally and physically." A member of the Umuofia Progressive Union, on the other hand, wonders himself why Obi accepted the money. "What others do is to tell you to go and hand it to their houseboy. Obi tried to do what everyone does without finding out how it was done." Merely twenty pounds! The president of the Union can't get over this: The Ibo have a saying that if you want to eat a toad you should look for a fat and juicy one. The main part of the novel, an extended flashback, attempts to get at the heart of Obi's case.

The moral climate of the "new Nigeria" is established at the very beginning. We are told, in passing, that some civil servants have paid as much as two shillings (sic) to obtain a doctor's certificate of illness so that they might attend this significant session of the court. Obi himself has been long aware of the sort of thing that goes on. The first, and so far the only, Umuofian to be sent to study in Britain on scholarship funds contributed by his own villagers, Obi has hopes that as an educated Nigerian he may one day come back to set his corrupted countrymen straight. But on his way home from Britain to notorious Lagos, the well-established custom of bribery catches up with Obi halfway off shore. A young customs official offers, for a consideration, to reduce the duty on the radiogram sent in announcement of his return. More amused than horrified, Obi dismisses the young man at once. The next incident strikes home more closely. Interviewed for a job by the Public Service Commission, Obi is bluntly asked: "Why do you want a job in the civil service? So that you can take bribes?" If he does, Obi pertly answers, he would hardly admit it before the board. A lorry driver (while Obi is on the way home from Lagos to Umuofia for a visit) gives the police a bribe as collateral for his certificate of "road wordiness." "What an Augean stable," mutters Obi. What was he to Hercules? is the question Achebe wants to ask.

As a senior service man in the government scholarships office (for despite his pertness he does get the job), Obi is understandably besieged by relatives of desperate applicants—indeed, by a young female applicant herself in his rooms. But he crisply wards off all these. Meanwhile, however, his new life of status becomes hopelessly entangled in present debts and past commitments: repayment of the Umuofia Progressive Union's loan for his expenses abroad, the mounting costs of the "required" new car, his brother's school fees, his parents' poverty (after thirty years as a catechist his father has retired on a pension of two pounds a month).

All these might in the natural course of things harass him, but, in addition, Obi has bad luck, partly as the result of the worst aspects of contemporary city life and partly because of the most unenlightened elements of his "tribal" past. First, a sizable amount of money is stolen from his car. Then his "educated" fiancée suddenly proves to be *osu* (a member of a forbidden caste whose distant progenitor was once dedicated to the service of a god). His parents, despite their Christianity, will not countenance her origin, nor will the Umuofia Progressive Union, which goes so far as to forbid him to marry her, nor can the guilt-ridden girl herself. She has an abortion at his expense, and after a serious illness she goes away, refusing to have anything more to do with him or with any man. And as if all this were not enough to leave him on the verge of emotional and financial collapse, more bad luck overtakes him: His mother dies, and he is left with none of the warmth and all of the bitterness of his inescapable village past, with all of the anxieties but none of the rewards of his untenable city life.

Obi's mother is the sort of person who would have told folk tales instead of Bible stories had her husband left her alone. The description of Obi's parents' rooms as keys to their characters is a masterpiece of social analysis in miniature. The rooms, his mother's representing the old and his father's the new, together show the uncomprehending poverty and pitiful optimism of backwater life under the new dispensation. Here is the heartbreak of the hodgepodge:

Mr. Okonkwo believed utterly and completely in the things of the white man. And the symbol of the white man's power was the written word. . . . The result of Okonkwo's mystic regard for the written word was that his room was full of old books and papers—from Blackie's arithmetic which he used in 1908 to Obi's Durrell, from obsolete cockroach-eaten translations of the Bible into the Onitsha dialect to yellowed scripture union cards of 1920 and earlier. Okonkwo never destroyed a piece of paper. He had two boxes full of them. The rest were preserved on top of his enormous cupboard, on tables, on boxes and on one corner of the floor.

Mother's room, on the other hand, was full of mundane things. She had her box of clothes on a stool. On the other side of the room were pots of solid palm oil with which she made black soap. The palm oil was separated from the clothes by the whole length of the room, because as she always said, clothes and oil were not kinsmen, and just as it was the duty of clothes to try and avoid oil, it was also the duty of the oil to do everything to avoid clothes.

Apart from these two, Mother's room also had such things as last year's coco yams, kola nuts preserved in an old cylindrical vessel which, as the older children told Obi, had once contained biscuits. In the second stage of its life it had served as a water vessel until it sprang about five leaks which had to be carefully covered with paper before it got its present job.[6]

The effort to change and yet at the same time to preserve what one has, find a new use for it, and patch up the leaks with borrowed glue becomes too great when all affective ties to the world are broken. Paradoxically, Obi dispenses with his new "European" morality the moment his virtuous African mother dies. He becomes a man of the moment, a modern Ibo who takes a bribe and then a series of bribes, always carefully maintaining his own proud, if private, distinction between candidates who are qualified to be in the running and those that are not.

One might with some justice complain that Achebe's second novel about the city does not come up to his first and third novels about traditional life. Closing the book on Okonkwo's grandson, one is left with a clear sense of the pattern without much feel of the cloth. Obi's most human inconsequence dilutes everything. When Achebe attempts in this book to thicken the tinned soup of modernity with homemade Ibo proverbs, they have an ironic effect. Like T. S. Eliot's references to cultural summits in "The Wasteland," they but reinforce our notions of the poverty and the tedium of the present. The proverb-studded palavers held by the Umuofia Progressive Union in Lagos sound as tedious as the conversations held in London by the women coming and going and talking of Michelangelo. As far removed from the age of wisdom that produced them as from the economical and dignified tradition that passed them on, Achebe's proverbs in this book come to seem like cultural epitaphs. Did he really mean them so?

The past, with all its hardships and injustices, the village, with all its deficiencies—for the two are the same—become the inevitable yardsticks against which the dubious enlightenment and moral confusion of modern times is sternly measured. The village past, be it only a few kilometers and a bare personal decade away, is the stuff of poetry, as we have already seen, and it often enters a novel about evolving or arriving in the city as poetry. If Achebe's antiphonal use of the past and present—through vividly remembered images from boyhood, through traditional tags in modern settings—is occasionally reminiscent of the "long poem" in English, so Sadji's praise of the unremitting reality of the village has the quality of modern French poetry of plenitude.

Abdoulaye Sadji was born in Rufisque and graduated from the William Ponty normal school in Gorée in 1929. Thereafter he taught in various Senegalese cities, eventually becoming a principal in Dakar and later an inspector. He married a *métisse* and died (rather recently) the father of many children. Although he also wrote a short novel (*Nini*) about a young *métisse*, the heroine of his most important work, *Maïmouna*, like Karim traces her line back to noble African ancestors. But unlike Karim, Maïmouna leads a deprived life. She lives in a small village called Louga, *en pleine brousse*. We first meet her as she comes to physical maturity in an environment where her beauty seems superfluous. She cannot, like Emma Bovary, read novels, but rather, half-child that she still is, she re-enacts with her doll scenes of Senegalese courtesy that the local *griots* and her mother have kept alive for her. This brave and affectionate widowed mother keeps a market stall to which Maïmouna every day takes the simple midday meal that she has prepared herself. Otherwise Maïmouna has little to do except keep the house, care for her hair, oil her skin, henna her feet, play with her doll, and dream.

Her elder sister, Rihanna, by a stroke of luck had seven years before attracted the attentions of an accountant in the department of public works in Dakar who had happened to pass through Louga on a rare pleasure jaunt. Because the sister's traditional beauty, as well as her obscurity and inexperience, suited the needs and relatively limited resources of this discriminating young *arriviste*, "she was able to marry into a milieu perfectly suited to her instinctive delicacy—a distant heredity which revealed itself even in the fineness of her features." Maïmouna, upon whom this distant heredity was equally if not more operative, dreams of joining her sister's by now well-established bourgeois household in Dakar. Rihanna has always urged their mother to send Maïmouna to her, partly out of guilt over her good fortune, partly because she is childless and bored, and partly out of a sincere desire to "educate" her younger sister. When adolescent tensions stiffen relations between the solitary mother and daughter—to such an extent that Maïmouna goes through a debilitating attack of malaria—the proud and disappointed market woman lets her go.*

The milieu in which Maïmouna comes to live in Dakar is formal, leisurely, ostentatious in some respects, and in others rather severe. The women, well-chaperoned, lead restricted lives. Rihanna's husband has worked himself up from the position of a minor clerk to that of an accountant by assiduity rather than by genius. He has advanced from a rather modest social origin to take his place in the aristocracy *"du milieu indigène"* by circumspection and thrift. Because of his position in the European administration, he is regarded even more as a leader than as a peer. The maintenance of his social position requires a judicious, if occasionally lavish, expenditure of funds on all sorts of hangers-on and for strategic intermittent fêtes. He takes his wife, resplendent in clothes and ornaments, to the movies twice a month. He dresses for work in a three-piece suit, with soft hat and cane. He dresses at home in the latest Senegalese style, even if his feet hurt in the new turned-up shoes. The furnishings of his salon are part European (especially the photographs), part Arab (some sketches of Mecca). His life is an implacably successful compromise.

For Rihanna's sister, such a husband is pleased to arrange an advantageous marriage with a well-to-do merchant of a certain age. But Maïmouna, immediately and happily successful as a well-chaperoned beauty, feels that her numerous suitors who worship, as the author puts it, "new dynasties of the golden calf," might well satisfy her notions of wealth and position but never those of romantic love, of intimacy. But with downcast eyes Maïmouna accepts her brother-in-law's choice of fiancé, and then goes off on her own, with the connivance of a jealous maid-

---

* The connection between mental suffering and susceptibility to disease is presented, without explanation, as a matter of course by Sadji both here and toward the end of the book. Disease is a part of the climate of Louga. Personal unhappiness cooperates with chance.

servant, to become pregnant by a slim young *evolué* who has no intention of ever marrying a "traditional" girl. Although the brother-in-law manfully, and with the good manners he expects of himself and others, tries to cope with this distasteful situation (he really abhors young Westernized Senegalese), Maïmouna's snobbish sister, humiliated and fearful for her own reputation, sends her packing. (She behaves outrageously—confiscates Maïmouna's jewels and even her new sewing machine.)

At this time a smallpox epidemic is rampant in the village of Louga, and the susceptible Maïmouna contracts the disease almost as soon as she arrives. Her baby is stillborn and she herself barely recovers, to be disfigured for the rest of her life.

> And time went on, indifferent to the calculations of men, insensible to their joys and distresses. . . . The men themselves, tenacious and valiant, put themselves to harvesting the millet, to cultivating the groundnut fields. Hardy ones! All the reality of existence was there, the rest but insensate dreams. Maïmouna wept her misfortune out for a week. Then she dried her tears and boldly faced life again.[7]

She decides to set up her own stall in the market, and rapidly discovers a profound charm in the crowds, the odors, and, in the sight of the wares themselves, the things of this life renewed every day. "With the rush of days, of life—real life without tenderness or illusion—Maïmouna began at last to discover it, to love it with her brave mother's love." One day she recognizes a passer-by from Dakar. It is Diabelé Gueyè, a landlord and entrepreneur, one of her many former suitors. She calls. He turns, barely managing to recognize her even when she gives him her name. Astonished, he slowly passes by, shaking his head; and the book ends.

But it doesn't really end. Obedient to some fatalistic impulse from between the lines, one turns again to the beginning of the book: "The terrors of the night vanished with the first crowing of the cocks." Now Sadji's meaning dawns as well, as, in a bizarre image, the east bares its pale gums to the sleep-haunted villagers of Louga.

The early pages of *Maïmouna* are given over to evocations of significant times of day in the bush. Morning: As individual hovels take root, particularize themselves out of the shadowy chaos of night, so men and women are dragged from nightmare and sterile dreams to their individual occupations, and the pounding of pestles succeeds in bringing the day forth by fits and starts. Midday: Anonymity again appears and with it a loss of purpose; men and beasts ply their tasks with no emotion, mechanically—"They have forgotten the thousand hopes which burst forth with the dawn, the enthusiasms of the morning's freshness, and the evening seemed a long time in coming, the evening which brings fear and long reveries." [8] Night brings fantasy, stories of ill-treated orphans who succeed in becoming rich, of malicious animals outwitted by simple ones. And then, relived in sleep, these stories turn phantasmagoric, harass the sleepers with patterns of fear and frustration, until day, unpromising and tediously grey as it may appear, puts a temporary end to all the dangerous unrealities of existence.

These passages are a brilliant example of how French cultural forms have been used to express African cultural norms. Sadji, it must be remembered, was not born in the bush. His evocations of the moods of the bush are like Baudelaire's urban crépuscules. Spleen and ideal meet in Sadji's interpretation of Louga.

With Sadji's diurnal philosophy in mind, Maïmouna's adolescent dreams, followed by her sojourn in the big city, might be considered lunacies acted out, and her market days under the sun a kind of everlasting cure. But dawn comes to Dakar too, although few there watch it come, few are aware of it. The speciousness of urban life is not here brusquely pitted against the sureness of a village routine. Modern Dakar is simply shown to be a place for the acting out of illusions which all men, in fancy, share. Sadji's view then is close to that of Ousmane Socé Diop's. But unlike the comfortable St. Louis to which Karim returns, Louga, with all of its joyous communal rhythms, is a distressing place. Its poverty and disease are never minimized. Sadji does not idealize Louga; rather he accepts it—as an adversative subordinate clause with the apodosis truth. He maintains, despite all odds, that there is more reality in the destitution there than in the privileged courtyards of Dakar. And though all the terrors of existence hang over her, Maïmouna does accept life.

One could say that, like Obi Okonkwo and unlike Karim, Maïmouna is a victim of social change. True, a typical young aristocrat from St. Louis might well, between the two wars, have hazarded his fortunes in Dakar. But a beautiful, ignorant young girl from the back country would not have dreamed of such a venture. She was ill-prepared to meet the *evolué*. One could say she was a victim of the machinations of others: of Rihanna and her husband's insensitive conventionality, of the young man's selfishness, of the go-between maid's spite. But Maïmouna, Sadji makes clear, is a tragic figure. A throw of the cowries can never abolish chance, and Maïmouna was particularly fond of games of divination, as if she knew somehow that, more than other people's, her life was subject to chance. She happened to be peculiarly susceptible to disaster, but more generally,

> ... being a child of man she had been placed under the control of an enormous heredity of sadness without cause and frailty without reason.[9]

> ... destinies fulfill themselves, some projects fail and others succeed. Fatalists or merely resigned, the Blacks drink from the bitter cup of life.[10]

This is the tragic view of life which Sadji and Chinua Achebe share. In *No Longer at Ease*, Obi discusses *The Heart of the Matter* with his cynical boss, Mr. Green. Obi cannot agree with Mr. Green's estimation of Mr. Greene:

> The police officer is torn between his love of a woman and his love of God, and he commits suicide. It's much too simple. Tragedy isn't like that at all. I remember a man in my village, a Christian convert, who suffered one calamity after another. He said life was like a bowl of wormwood which one sips a little at a time, world without end. He understood the nature of tragedy.[11]

The tragic protagonist in Africa is a reticent figure, not acclaimed in our grand style. His misfortunes do not come singly, nor do they have much to do, in our sense, with the kind of person he is. He is a person with his power withdrawn, gradually worn away by fate, by nature, as well as by the deeds and opinions of his fellow men. Such a person is accursed. Like the termite-ridden faces, breasts, and haunches of the Dogon carvings, dug up to grace many an elegant private collection in the Western world today, the African who has suffered cries to be left alone where he is. He is obscure, like a tragic figure out of Hardy, despised like Philoctetes until Ulysses butted in. His bitterness, like Hardy's, is a provincial bitterness, a bitterness appropriate to the stern vicissitudes of climate and born of a deep sense of isolation from other men.

Our critics claim that we can no more have tragedy for various reasons: because of Christianity with its redemptive features; because, romantics that we are, we attach too little importance to this world's goods and honors, and thus underestimate the real loss that a hero's fall means (delighting rather too much in the intensity of his sufferings); or because we are no longer a community. It would seem this last is most relevant to the notion of African tragedy. Are not both Achebe and Sadji in effect saying that tragedy is impossible in the city, that Maïmouna is tragic, that the old Okonkwo was tragic, but that someone like Obi is patently not? And not only is tragedy impossible, but so is affirmation after or in spite of tragedy, according to the African view. The intensive bad fortune of the individual both involves the whole group by depleting it and isolates the individual who suffers as one accursed in his own and in others' sight. The only chance for affirmation is in the hope of the generations—a faith in life's continuity, in the perpetual presence of the spirits of the dead and the unborn. When this continuity is broken, there can be no common lot.

Notes

1. Melvin J. Lasky, *Africa for Beginners* (Philadelphia: J. B. Lippincott, 1962), p. 17.

2. Ousmane Socé Diop, *Karim*, first published in 1935 (Paris: Bibliothèque de l'Union Française, Nouvelles éditions latines, 1948), p. 105.

3. *Ibid.*, p. 117.

4. Cyprian Ekwensi, *People of the City* (London: Andrew Dakars, Ltd., 1954), p. 235.

5. *Ibid.*, p. 21.

6. Chinua Achebe, *No Longer at Ease* (New York: Ivan Obolensky, Inc., 1961), pp. 126–27.

7. Abdoulaye Sadji, *Maïmouna* (Paris: Présence Africaine, 1958), p. 249.

8. *Ibid.*, p. 55.

9. *Ibid.*, p. 44.

10. *Ibid.*, p. 154.

11. Achebe, *op. cit.*, p. 39.

V THE INNER LIFE

When at break of day at a riverside
I hear jungle drums . . .
Then I hear a wailing piano
Solo speaking of complex ways . . .
—GABRIEL OKARA

It is obvious that for a sophisticated, modern African there can be no literal "return" to the old ways of the village, except as a wholly different sort of man with a different role to play; there can be no walking again, except in memory, the "simple paths" of childhood. For the self-conscious African writer, coming to terms with colonialism and its aftermath has meant coming to terms with himself. To say that this is similar to the process that any honest man has to go through in any fluid society, that it is allied to coming to terms with one's parents and one's "background" and then going on from there, is not to underestimate the African aspects of this self-revelation and acceptance. To say that African writers have used poems and novels as means of understanding themselves as Africans, and that this is similar to what writers from other traditions have done when they have used writing as a means of establishing personal and ethnic identity, is not to underestimate the pangs of re-establishing personal and racial dignity while the memories of condescension and oppression are still fresh. And yet, wherever the Africans' claim to their Africa is unchallenged and complete, this is a joyous as well as an arduous task. Things are far graver where the demand for justice is met with deaf ears, or with force. Furthermore, the exhilaration produced by free Africa's recognition that at last our cultural (as opposed to our technological) verve is played out, that it is now the dark peoples' turn to speak, is more to be envied than pitied in Paris, London, or New York!

Suddenly, with the approach of independence, young men

in what is now free Africa felt it incumbent upon themselves to be historical, if not professional, Africans. Literary men, although often by nature and education apolitical, have not been exempt from this tendency. Although public utterance by Africans is often irritating because based on an irrefragable sense of moral superiority, in their novels and poems literary men have been honest and nuanced. They have given us the exasperation, the real anguish, often the incongruous humor of their situation as historical Africans. The famous Dialogue between East and West or between Black and White may accomplish something, but it is in literature (or, perhaps, personal conversation in any form) that real communication takes place. For writers this whole question of how to go about being An African has been a tremendously stimulating affair. Ezekiel Mphahlele phrases the problem this way: "For the African Negro the problem lies in the struggle to express the larger irony which is the meeting point between acceptance and rejection, once he has felt the impact of Western civilization." [1] This struggle has unearthed untold treasures of the imagination and tightened the intellect as well. Forcing ingenuousness into irony, it has made African literature exciting because complex.*

In the late 1950's, as the time for devolution of political authority drew near, African writers began to attack colonialism directly. It could be argued that almost *all* African novels to date, whether they deal with the heroic past, with traditional village life

---

* Had he not, for political reasons, left his native South Africa, Mphahlele would probably not now think in the elaborate, objective way he does. In Nigeria he taught students who had always been more or less allowed to be as African as they pleased. They depressed him because they were not as serious as his former students. In Paris and at numerous conferences, Mphahlele discovered the personal meaning, to French Africans, of that which he still tends publically to dismiss as a mere slogan, négritude. However, his own creative writing often expresses qualities of social solidarity and exuberance which could be put under this rubric, and he has even made general statements about African cultural traits that contradict his particularist and modernist point of view. Mphahlele, now in Kenya in charge of the Chemchemi Cultural Center (an East African Mbari), has taken on the extremely difficult and terribly ironic role of being an African-at-large, the representative of a multiracial society that does not exist. His freedom from parochialism, however, gives him immense authority as a cultural catalyst.

enigmatically revalorized, with the struggle for moral balance in the city, or with the problem of the establishment of personal identity, are, by implication at least, attacks on the colonial system. But the most introspective of the authors, those most absorbed by the problem of identity, tend to be the most overtly polemical. It is as if a recognition of the damage done to the self by the adoption of Western values freed the self to strike out directly at the colonial system which demanded that such a choice, with all its concomitant humiliations despite all its concomitant advantages, should be made. These introspective satirical novels are characteristically French.

A French rage for economy and clarity of expression may be seen in the satirical elegance and fastidious annotation of emotional facts in the West African novels which protest against the rigidities of colonial administration, cultural snobbery, and a set educational program calculated to "raise" talented Africans to rational French standards. The premium placed on intellect by the French governors has inspired intense critical activity as antidote to the colonial order suffered by the ambitious African elite. The relationship of the intellectually assimilated African to France, as expressed in literature, is like the love affair in French novels which fulfills and at the same time destroys itself by an abrasive scrutiny of the motives and intensities of the passions on both sides. Camara Laye's *L'Enfant noir* and Kane's *L'Aventure ambiguë* may be seen not only as novels in love with traditional village life, but as novels in love with France. The first love is pure. The second love is a tortuous mature affair.

If it is not difficult to understand why the subversive critical tendencies of the French novel took root in West Africa, why these tendencies were so long suppressed should not be cause for wonder.* Politically, British West Africans always had a clear goal; French Africans, until the end of the colonial era, had to express their hopes in ambiguous language—even to themselves. *Négritude* may be seen as having been originally a political

---

* For the French there is a time for poetry and a time for prose. An innocent American come to study French poetry in France shortly after the war was told by a professor who had fought in the Resistance that he never read poetry any more (although he was supposed to teach it). Just wait until you have lived what I have lived, he said, and you will recognize the value of novels over all, of prose.

gesture permitted by the system—powerful rhetoric but innoc-
uous politics. As a psychological manifestation it is tied to the
colonial condition of the assimilated African. The poetry of
négritude allowed the expression in an unconscious vein of a
romantic passion for origin which the highly Frenchified consciousness of the elite denied itself. The direct attack on colonialism has, in former French territories, coincided with the inevitable political reappraisal of this elite; and the elite themselves
will more and more be forced to scrutinize the motives and
qualities of their own rather abstract, first love of Africa, their
négritude.

The fluidity and inefficiency of the British system created a
whole set of anxieties, incongruities, and vitalities markedly
different from those associated with careers open to talent, with
assimiliation, and direct rule. For the writer of English expression
who has attempted to define himself, the problem has been far
more difficult, psychically and stylistically. If his conquerors
warped him less, they gave him fewer tools. In theory, the British
colonial subject in Africa was, culturally, left to his own devices,
and with what results? Literature in the vernacular was encouraged, and this encouragement may be of great future consequence; but the choice of whether or not to express oneself in
English is still a complicated and a confusing one in this part of
West Africa. The preindependence literature from West Africa
in English was rather meager, and often reflected the neo-
Victorian tastes of uninspired schoolmasters. The British patronage of Tutuola's "woodnotes wild" created acrimony as well as
confusion in Africa. The current sophisticated use of the best of
both traditions—Igbo and Ijaw turns of phrase translated into
English metrical patterns, Ibo proverbs imbedded in a cosmopolitan story line—is a reflection of the British attitude toward
their own language as an organic history of foreign influences
which, paradoxically, may keep Nigerians writing English long
after the Senegalese have turned away from French!

The tribal identity that the British Africans were supposed to
have was at first shrugged off as colonial prejudice. African
writers in English have always been eloquent critics of the color
bar. Generally, as we see him in literature, an African who grew
up under British domination is rather confounded by the claims
of his tribal past. The claims are real, but how to realize them?
In the writings of certain personalities they appear as a sinister

strain. It might happen that an English-speaking African in fiction has thought himself through the whole process of modernization, quite smoothly, but then it might prove, under stress, that his personality was not so well-made as he thought. He might then become anxious, his behavior unstable; he might seem no longer to know where he is. Then elements from the past could surge up in a rather nightmarish way and seem incongruous, inconsistent with the urban stance. Or the tribal claims might be felt in a different way, more in the urbane French way, as elected "sources," romantic origins. But in English these will not be evoked nostalgically. Traditional elements may be presented in a bizarre collage along with the latest thing. Or in reconstructing scenes from traditional life rather in the manner of the British anthropologist, the West African writer in English may release his venom towards those social forces which have made him ironic or quasi-agnostic about his own culture by attacking them, in-the-past, as stereotyped red knees in khaki shorts, sweating vacuities beneath safari hats or mosquito netting that anybody can roundly hate.

The legacy of British institutions has produced a variant, or a second phase of Africanness. *Négritude's* second phase is particularistic, tribalistic—an attempt to establish a singular ethnic identity before going on to broader pan-African identifications again. The Nigerian writers came into contact with the philosophy of *négritude* at the historical point at which independence was about to be celebrated, and in disclaiming the French version they were in fact simply giving it what one might call a common-law orientation. But the tendency was implicit already in French West Africa. The West Indian writers of *négritude* could establish no particular roots; they had no literal memories. But as Senghor's Senegalese poetry deepened, his Serer identity became a kind of parable of his Africanness. Like Faulkner's southernness it had a local habitation and a name, it was spelled out. In West African fiction, Achebe's reconstruction of Umuofia is unique. It is tending towards the chronicle. Umuofia is *négritude* through an objective correlative, however. The writer writes behind a particular tribal mask; he has not yet shown his face.

Novels of rebellion are difficult to write when the paternal rules have been vaguely (or often brutally) and at the same time inconsistently laid down. The pattern of self-definition traced in West African novels generally follows that of the most basic family fight. Since the most intensive European indoctrination has taken place in the schoolroom, fighting out of a colonial condition has meant, in most African fictions, a fighting out of a youthful condition in a political, or more broadly a cultural, context. The coming to self-consciousness of a person is seen in colonial terms. And the declaration of young African independence is described in language appropriate to the primary group.

The behavior of the "kind" European boss or teacher was, by his own culture's definition, "paternal," and this role was reinforced later, for purposes of rebellion, by the young colonial subject himself. But it often happens in literature that throwing off the authority of Father Europe means throwing oneself back into the arms of Mother Africa, an emotional return to childhood with no particular desire, at least for a while, to give it up. The image of the real African mother is strong in African novels of revolt. She is *the* traditional element in the story. Like those earthy goddesses of ancient Greece, she seeks only to perpetuate the tribe. She wills the hero's marriage to a traditional girl. The stronger the assertion by the proxy colonial parent that the patronized child be what he, the parent, is, the stronger becomes the young rebel's desire to keep the loving maternal element alive. Yet he cannot simply return to the village, and often he does not marry at all.

The final stage in the process of rebellion, at least so far, is the assertion of the modern ego whose characteristics may not be conclusively defined but whose energies are effectively felt, as they satirize both the Western element and the village element, or in a soberer mode, make a balanced evaluation of the two. The African personality thus evolved now becomes active and strives to reunite itself with the past by helping to realize the future through creative work. The European novel of analysis has entered the African tradition, becoming open-ended towards life.

II.

No African novels are more incisive than those from that complex territory now known as the Republic of Cameroun. The works of two highly gifted satirists, Mongo Beti (alias Alexandre Biyidi) and Ferdinand Oyono, have had such an impact on writers and critics from other French-speaking territories (and translations of Mongo Beti on African writers in English) that they are justly taken to constitute a school of letters. These two writers are usually referred to as the new "realists" although this term ought to be more qualified than it usually is. This is to say that their *technique* is expressionistic, oddly enough in the German sense of the word—an ironic and probably coincidental legacy of German occupation before the first world war.

The Camerounian sense of social reality is acute, the standard colonial condition probably having been somewhat exacerbated by the Camerounians' unique status first as mandated and then as entrusted people, upon whom French pride of empire did not operate to improve their circumstances, and whose complaints were theoretically given an international hearing. These are people whose critical sense would certainly have been kept alive as long as German colonial practices (remembered) and neighboring British colonial practices (heard about) could be played off against those of the French. The education of the Camerounians was almost entirely abandoned to the missionaries —again a chance to weigh church against state, good will against hypocritical colonial agency, and so on. Although, thanks to the tremendous efforts of the clergy, preindependent Cameroun had more scholarship students working for advanced degrees in France than any other French-speaking territory, these students had not been assimilated in the usual French sense, and as grown men they have tended to disaffiliate themselves from the European-oriented regime. Since the radical opposition to the present republic was put down with violence, intellectuals like Mongo Beti have underscored the urgency of *their* dissenting role.

The Camerounian writers are, finally, psychological realists, realistic about African personalities who have fallen afoul of the West. The construction of a typical novel from Cameroun places an African "victim" in the center of a net of colonial injustice, hypocrisy, and indigenous complacency, degeneracy, or ill-will. Such a victim can escape the net only by bursting forth with a vigorous and painfully acquired sense of self.

Mongo Beti's first novel, *Ville cruelle* (1954), was written while he was still a student at Aix and published in his twenty-second year under the pseudonym Eza Boto, a name he subsequently abandoned because of what he must have felt to have been a juvenile awkwardness about the book. This novel is primarily an attack on economic institutions as established in Africa by the

West. The source of the young hero's misfortunes—his ill-treatment under the colonial regime—is money, and money is also the grounds of his fantasy of escape from the adverse circumstances in the backwater communities he has come to hate.

The plot is easily summarized. The young hero is first observed casting off the loose town girl of whom his dying village mother disapproves. He then attempts to market his cocoa crop only to have it peremptorily confiscated as improperly dried. Having first been beaten by one governmental authority for objecting to this and then quietly sent on his way by a higher authority, he wanders off to get drunk in a kind of bar where he meets the doleful sister of a factory protest leader who is wanted by the police. The hero helps the two of them to escape, but the brother is accidentally killed en route to freedom. The hero fortuitously finds a large sum of money lost by a Greek trader, collects the substantial reward, and decides with his dying mother's approval to marry this nice new girl. The two of them then determine, not without regret, to forsake both village and town and seek their fortune in the big coastal city "of the future."

Here the approach is established which this author was to handle with far more depth and virtuosity in subsequent books. But it is worth pausing at the town of Tanga that the hero leaves, not only because the place and the inhabitants are brilliantly satirized, but also because here is the yardstick, the Africa in miniature, to which Beti returns again and again. But note that it is from a partially corrupted if vigorous backwater community that this Camerounian's not so simple path of childhood leads. The external picture is sharply drawn. Here are the corrugated roofs, the white walls, the red gravel streets of the new Africa. Tanga is a double city, built on a hill, separated from the powerful forest which encroaches no further than the river on the south side. Logs are carried down this river to busy, satanic sawmills which the Europeans have built to defy the old forest. This side of the hill is, therefore, devoted to commerce; here are the factories and the shops. At the top of the hill stand the administrative buildings, woefully indiscreet amidst the poverty exposed by the sun's stark glare. These buildings make the further mistake of turning their backs to the north slope of the hill, a quarter devoted to the expiring innocence of the aborigines.

This second town, the real town, at which the administrative buildings refuse to look, is emptied every morning, to come alive again at night when its inhabitants return from work on the south slope, only to find their places crowded by new recruits from the forest who have streamed in during the day. This north town has a fiery quality all its own which burns or melts and recasts all who live there. To be sure, the author says, the inhabitants, be they temporary or permanent, share certain qualities with their kin in the bush. Like them, the denizens of Tanga are *too* weak, *too* vain, *too* gay, and *too* sensitive.

> But beyond this there was something original about them now: a certain tendency for shabby dealing, for nervous disorder, for alcoholism and for everything that inspires scorn of human life—as is the case in all countries where big material interests dispute among themselves; this is our town that holds the record for murders—and suicides!
> They ran, walked, shoved each other about, fell from their bicycles—all of this not without a certain spontaneity, sole residue of their lost purity . . . .
> [Every night was a fête] as if they wanted to steep themselves in something they were in the process of losing, perhaps forever, joy without any cosmetics, naked joy, Original Joy.[2]

In Mongo Beti's subsequent books, the hero and the narrator-observer are fused, producing a highly charged protagonist who both is and is not a part of the events he describes. The characteristics that the protagonist as isolated observer will continue to share with his people is this "lost purity" of which bumptious vitality is only a residue. The protagonist as narrator also retains this quality, in the refined form of bumptious intelligence and wit. But Mongo Beti's *persona*, unlike the backwater townsmen, is aware of his loss, is continually searching for this purity in a more substantial and abiding form. As the focus of Mongo Beti's critical (anti-colonial) intention changes, and as the time of the author's residence in Europe lengthens (until he is a well-established professor of literature near Paris), the range changes too and the protagonist becomes increasingly detached. His ultimate stance is that of emotional paralysis, in which both indigenous villagers (or townsmen) and the colonial agents who play *their* part in the scene can be scrutinized with the same critical instrument. Although the type of European who goes out to the bush, whatever his professional reasons for being there, changes in Mongo Beti's books according to the times, the nervous, hilarious, calculating Tanga men remain exasperatingly the same; and the reader can no longer spare them the amused contempt the author once intended for their oppressors only.

Mongo Beti early attended mission schools. The "detached observer" of his second book is a little village acolyte in the entourage of an idealistic priest. The use of the precocious little Denis as narrator of the story of Le Pauvre Christ de Bomba (1956) is a fine comic device. For a naïve child, rendered the more naïve by a mission upbringing, has the task of disclosing to the sophisticated reader a naïve adult, the Reverend Father Drumont, who is himself in the process of discovering corruption in the world about him that he has been unaware of all along. Both child narrator and childlike priest become increasingly "experienced" in their appropriate ways as the story moves along. The situation—always hilariously evident to the reader—as it gradually dawns in both consciousnesses is this:

Reverend Father Superior Drumont, the "poor Christ" of the Catholic mission at Bomba, has spent twenty years in Africa only to discover, first, that when he fails to make the rounds for a while the forest is given over to opportunistic backsliders who see to it that the susceptible backwater elements misbehave; and, second, that his own mission in Bomba is actually full of venery and corruption. The sequence of these discoveries is important. Sallying forth on a tour of a particularly tough area, Tala, Drumont becomes disillusioned enough to see, back home in Bomba, what in fact has been going on under his nose all along.

It is on tour that Drumont also learns for the first time about the colonial game from the administration's point of view: When a road is to be built and labor forced to build it, the villagers flee for protection to the church. The church, then, by its conversions inadvertently softens up the population so that further political controls can be imposed. These then are imposed; the road gets built; and with prosperity and bicycles careening along the road a strong economic tie to the state is sufficient, and there is no longer any need for the church. Horrified at this discovery of the part that he really plays in Africa, and further horrified when a cynical secular authority tells him not to worry about Tala—that a road is to be built through there soon—Father Drumont turns in his ticket and decides to sail for Europe.

Back at Bomba, Drumont is also made to realize, by the outraged wife of his cook, that his *sixa* (a school for indigenous
Christian engaged girls) is little more than a bordello, and that
his African staff are all either procurors, perverts, or adulterers.
Even little Denis proves guilty of a brief sexual frolic, and at
last Father Drumont in his own way falls victim to the excitement
of the flesh. Wildly alarmed by the original allegation that his
trusted cook has been perfidious in a sexual way, Drumont
relentlessly interrogates each girl from the *sixa* on her sexual
adventures. His perverted assistant-cook is then ordered to beat
each compromised and diseased girl in his presence.

A medical officer is summoned to pronounce final judgment
on the place, and girls and staff disperse. Drumont in due course
returns to Europe, leaving his disconsolate acolyte to wander
aimlessly about the deserted mission buildings. Hearing reports
of road building and forced labor, Denis finally decides to flee
to the city and hire himself out as "boy" to a Greek merchant.
The Father has run out on his only true convert, his counterpart,
his friend. For Denis is a true innocent of both worlds. While he
refuses, despite Drumont's teaching, to feel guilty about his sexual
initiation, he does have a pure Christian heart. He alone is capable
of the kind of devotion which such a misguided saint as Drumont
deserves. Drumont's motives are of the best, but he succeeds in
wreaking havoc on an already susceptible crowd. As a "boy,"
Denis moves one stage closer to the corrupt.

At the heart of Mongo Beti's originality is his exploitation of
the comedy implied in the colonial situation. The behavior of
his indigenous characters is almost as exaggeratedly solipsistic as
that of his foolish religious characters and his single-minded
secular characters. Yet each element, despite its psychic isolation, knows the other, in some sense exploits the other, and
when it can seizes the day. If consent be the "primary material"[3]
of social and political life, then the possibility of irony in all
social and political situations is implicit from the start. The
dance of obligation and deception as described among the Pygmies and villagers of the Ituri Forest by Colin Turnbull is a model
case.* This game, *mutatis mutandis*, has its equivalent in that

* The Bantu villagers colonized this region as refugees from the east.
Unable to subdue the indigenous Pygmies by force, they invented a
myth of a long-standing master-servant relationship between the two
peoples. The Pygmies accept this assumption of Bantu superiority because

village-church-state cycle described by Mongo Beti. The French administration claims to understand both villagers and missionaries, attempting to play one off against the other. But as victims of colonial circumstance the villagers come off the best. All participating parties are appropriately corrupted by the game, but the villagers in this case retain their irrepressible high spirits to the end.

In *Mission terminée* (1957), translated as *Mission to Kala* by Peter Green, Mongo Beti's focus shifts in order to bear down on the institution of the Western schoolroom as reflected in the tormented soul of colonialism's prize creation, the student *evolué*. This too is a colonial game, with the rules of which the indigenous fathers comply.

> Do you remember that period? Fathers used to take their children to school as they might lead sheep to a slaughterhouse. Tiny tots would turn up from backwood villages thirty or forty miles up country, shepherded by their parents, to be put on the books of some school, it didn't matter which. They formed a miserable floating population, these kids: lodged with distant relations who happened to live near the school, underfed, scrawny, bullied all day by ignorant monitors. The books in front of them presented a universe which had nothing in common with the one they knew: they battled endlessly with the unknown, astonished and desperate and terrified. We were those children—it is not easy to forget—and it was our parents who forced this torment upon us. Why did they do it? [4]

An African child is accustomed to feel at home with a far wider range of relations than, to proceed to the other extreme for an example, an average American child. But boarding with

---

it pays, in cultivated foods; and although the Pygmies act the part in the village, even going so far as to become initiated (a counterpart of being saved) according to village ritual, the ritual really has no meaning for them and they behave in a completely different, free way on their own home ground, the forest, whose "terrors" they magnify to the fearful villagers in order to keep the latter grateful to them for animal food. Colin M. Turnbull, *The Forest People* (New York: The Natural History Library, Anchor Books, Doubleday and Co., Inc., 1962).

strangers is another matter; this is the consequence of the introduction of low-budget schools in rural areas. Although a precocious independence must inevitably develop in the hardy
child under such circumstances, a severe price must be paid
for these in the nervous demoralization of the more delicately
balanced. The virtual transference of real parental authority to
colonial authorities, secular or religious, further confuses the
kids. An unsentimental textbook might someday properly recall
that "in the former French territories a highly centralized school
system speeded up assimilation and the dislocation of familial
ties."

In *Mission to Kala*, Mongo Beti shows us how the damage is
done. If the father has, in effect, sacrificed his son to the Europeans, either to satisfy his own ambitions or to do what he
thinks at the time is good for his son under a colonial regime,
he will never be able to get the son's allegiance back. Subsequent attempts to assert parental authority over a son who has
been too long away being educated by the "others" will both
seem and *be* despotic. The prodigal will refuse to return to be
in any way a village type. But the son's acute filial hostility at
some point will begin to conflict with a mounting sense of
rebellion against hostile colonial authorities who educated him
to be like *them* rather than like his real father. With two fathers
to fight, with two ways of life to reject, what wonder if such
a student has trouble distinguishing himself.

Mission to Kala is cast in the allegorical mold, at once a moral
journey with overtones of the fairytale. A young student, Medza,
who has just failed his examinations, returns home on vacation
to the village relieved to find that his father is not there. He is then
sent, ironically because of his intellectual achievement, to bring
back his cousin Niam's wife, a loose woman who has run off with
her current lover to the extremely backwater village of Kala.

Like the Tala of the preceding book, "Kala gave me," says
the hero-narrator, "a simultaneous impression of savagery and
security." Arriving at this fount of boisterous back-country behavior, the hero is told that there is really nothing to do but wait
there for his errant relative to show up. In waiting—and this
comes as quite a surprise to him—Medza finds himself lionized
as an educated and sophisticated city-dweller by young and old
alike. This false evaluation of himself by others leads to its dia-

lectical opposite, a true self-evaluation: He is deprived. And thenceforth the joke on the envious Kalans is that Medza secretly worships them, at least the younger generation, a rowdy crew with "virtuous" nicknames:

> I'd have given all the diplomas in the world to swim like Duck-foot Johnny, or dance like the Boneless Wonder, or have the sexual experience of Petrus-son-of-God, or throw an assegai like Zambo . . . . The very least I could do was to conquer my fear of women (another joke on the Kalans, who of course assume . . .) [5]

These country boys in their ignorance enjoy a freedom that Medza realizes he will never, even if he should now reject his father's ambitious future plans for him, be able to recapture. But at least he ought to be able to catch up on his retarded sex life. Medza finally succeeds with an innocent girl only to find himself betrothed to her according to village custom and his future mother-in-law's strong insistence that this be observed. Meanwhile, however, he has become stubbornly and incongruously fond of his gigantic, athletic cousin Zambo.

The stray wife finally returns, and Medza succeeds in bringing her back to his own village where she will remain, perhaps for a while at least, a worthless simulacrum of love. Medza rejects, on the other hand, his own young, innocent bride as an impossible embodiment of an ideal love which, like an ideal country existence, can have no real place in his hopelessly corrupted, anxious life. After the inevitable scene with his father over the exams, Medza escapes to the city with Zambo, who in his inarticulate way is also in search of something "other," which he believes the sophisticated Medza understands. The cousins thenceforth lead, so an epilogue tells us, a life of endless wandering and companionship, a fraternal rootlessness being, so the author would seem to suggest, a condition proper to the young African soul at this time. Edima, the young girl whom Medza has rejected, eventually marries his ne'er-do-well brother and they have many children. But the childless narrator remains haunted by the story of his love for her, "which is also the story of my first, perhaps my only, love: the absurdity of life."

Like Saul who rushed off in search of his father's wild asses as a prelude to anointment, like Wilhelm Meister in turn going off to collect his father's debts, Medza too is in search of an augmented self. This is the beginning of his *wanderjahren*. His failure at school was a blessing, for it detached him from a routine he had come to think of as inevitable and sent him off quickly in search of love, a false love in the beginning, later a true. And he finds this true love only to realize that he can never keep it. Like Denis after Drumont has departed, at the end of this book Medza is at loose ends. He has learned

> . . . by contact with the country folk of Kala, those quin-tessential caricatures of the "colonized" African—that the tragedy which our nation is suffering today is that of a man left to his own devices in a world which does not belong to him, which he has not made and does not under-stand. It is the tragedy of man bereft of any intellectual compass . . . .[6]

He is, as his name suggests, a middle journey man.

Mongo Beti's most recent book, *Le Roi miraculé* (1958), trans-lated by Peter Green as *King Lazarus*, is a kind of epilogue to *Le Pauvre Christ de Bomba*. The action takes place ten years later. Le Guen, who was Father Drumont's curate at the time of his departure, is now the Reverend Father Superior of his own mission at Essazam, a backwater region similar to Tala or Kala. Things have changed among the Europeans though, and so has the protagonist-narrator changed. As this cynical new hero, Chris, puts it: "The new look in race relations is catching on . . . . Good! let's cash in on it." [7]

Le Guen's relations with the old, hyperpolygamous (twenty-three wives) chief of the Essazam are cordial—friendly chats, no proselytizing. But when this chief, fatally ill, suddenly revives following an hysterical impromptu baptism amateurishly admin-istered by his cronish old aunt Yosifa, the temptation to cash in on this event is too great for the modern missionary to resist. Le Guen gives the chief the Christian name Lazarus, expatiates on the theme in a public sermon, and then, giving the lie to the new look, goes right ahead and urges him to forsake all wives but one. Clan warfare at once ensues. Le Guen himself be-haves rudely to the administrator and is eventually forced by higher colonial authorities to resign. He has disturbed the peace. He has, in the words of the high commissioner, put himself in "an almost criminal position" by "compelling a tribal chief to renounce his ancestral way of life."

The joke of this book is, of course, that the ancestral way of life is greasy, raucous, pompous, and degenerate in every way—hardly worth preserving, save by the most cynical of administrations. There is nothing worth improving, nothing attractive in the up-country any more. Le Guen rather stupidly preserves *his* integrity as a missionary among all the cynics on both sides, but his energies are wastefully expended there, and in the end the church, having capitulated completely to the regime, insists that he resign.

The central consciousness, the chief's youthful grandnephew, is as degenerate in his own way as all the rest. Medza of the Kala story was on a mission, but young Chris in this book begins and ends unattached to anything but himself and his own interests: pecuniary, sensuous, and intellectual. He is not really a serious student, rather a dilettante, and in the village on vacation he is a mere spectator out to make a buck. (Hastily taking advantage of the chaotic situation by distilling liquor in his aunt's compound, he actually aligns himself with the greedy mercantile forces of the author's first book.)

At mid-point in the novel, the author suddenly separates himself from this alter ego, as if thoroughly sick of him, and decides to give him a minor "symptomatic" role. Mongo Beti now speaks out directly, more directly than he had spoken out since *Ville cruelle,* in the person of a new hastily improvised alter ego, Bitamo, a young man who has traveled a lot. Bitamo is a prophetic character. Although a native of the village, he has been educated everywhere, in all sorts of schools, Catholic, Protestant, and secular. He has lived and worked in cities, but is familiar with "strange primitive regions." He is an expert on local dialects and religions as well as on "the extraordinary customs of strangers and foreigners." Bitamo chastises his former schoolmate Chris for his indifference to the People's Progressive Party: "For the first time in our history, we've got a party offering us a platform of our *own* great men." But Chris demurs. And the author has since taken up Bitamo's critical role. *King Lazarus* bids a temporary farewell to literature as it welcomes an exacerbated political conscience newly arisen from the dead. Still in an ad-

versary position, Beti has turned his talents to polemical jour-
nalism as more efficacious now.

III.

Ferdinand Oyono's *Une Vie de boy* (1956) is so similar in
conception to Mongo Beti's *Le Pauvre Christ de Bomba* that it
might be regarded as a kind of continuation of the abandoned
acolyte's career. Here again an African youth as narrator exposes
the colonial world. But there are differences, attributable not
only to the distinct personalities of the authors but to the world-
liness of Oyono's colonial milieu. In this book there is no sympathetic, if misguided, central character from the European side
of things to soften and to complicate the social analysis and the
political attack. The priest who raised Oyono's "boy" is dead
before the story begins and the youth, Joseph, has just secured
the only employment open to those of his ilk. The "boy" is
colonialism's victim in a far more direct and devastating way
than is the acolyte, and Oyono's answering method is provocation of his readers' active disgust.

The Africans who work for Europeans as houseboys in Oyono's
town of Dangan are not the rowdy provincial lovers Mongo Beti
describes. The colonial controls in such a European outpost are
so tight, the indigenous occupational possibilities so limited, that
these "boys'" lives are no longer their own. They have lost all
dignity. More particularly, they have been reduced to getting
their libidinal kicks out of a fascinated, gossipy revulsion from
the grotesque details of amorous European behavior in the
tropics. The colonial women literally expose their dirty linen
and smelly lingerie for these grown-up boys to wash. No woman
was ever less of a heroine to her valet than is the Madame Joseph
works for. But one of the unwritten rules of such a depersonal-
ized system is that the "boy" must never permit the lady to see
herself as he sees her, and when the distasteful refuse of one of
her illicit nights of pleasure is by chance swept from under the
bed in the lady's presence ("Ces blancs . . . avec leur manie
d'habiller tout," quips the cook to the astonished Joseph), Joseph's
healthy days in Dangan are numbered.

For this is a brutal community. The director of the prison,
Madame La Commandante's illicit lover, is a sadist who has
two suspects beaten to death before Joseph's terrified eyes. The

chief of police is equally cruel; and when his African mistress suddenly deserts him, the chief sees this as a perfect opportunity for the commandant and his wife (now temporarily reconciled to her husband) to save face and for his friend the prison director to revenge himself on Joseph for "knowing everything." The innocent "boy" is thus charged with helping the African mistress to escape and with stealing the chief's cash box as well. Jailed, beaten, and finally admitted to the hospital for lung damage from the beatings so that he can be returned in good shape to his tormentors for more punishment, Joseph takes advantage of careless hospital surveillance and escapes to the border of Spanish Guinea, only to die near there of his punctured lung. His journal is discovered by a sympathetic African intellectual and published.

This is protest literature in the South African and American Negro traditions. Such a book is unique among novels from West Africa, in part because "settler" conditions such as those described were relatively rare. The matter-of-fact tone of the telling, however, the emotional distance of protagonist from author, are only possible in a West African presentation of the theme. Despite the nastiness and brutality of the whites depicted here, the naïve wonder and eventual cool horror expressed by the narrator are quite removed from the obsessions, the fear, and impotent rage inevitably knit into stories about societies where there is no psychic room to breathe. Ferdinand Oyono is now neither unemployed nor theoretically in exile. He is an ambassador.*

In Le Vieux nègre et la médaille (1956), Oyono exploits to the fullest his talents for attacking the colonial system through the eyes of its victims by focusing on the mordant power of incriminating detail. Oyono's satirical lens blows his carefully chosen minutiae up until they become as grotesque and revolting as the social system for which they ultimately stand. For example, here is a French high commissioner on tour:

> "It's he, the big chief," Meka said to himself. But he was at a loss for anything or anyone to compare him with. All that struck him was the voluminous underside of his chin which partially concealed the knot of his tie . . . . His every

---

* A status which often does mean de facto exile for the intellectual in West Africa today.

movement made his gullet tremble sympathetically like an old dug the color of laterite.* [8]

This technique is not only used against the Europeans in this book; it is also used to humanize the elderly victim of this book, Meka, an Uncle Tom that could be despised. Meka's bodily functions are enlarged upon, for his organic self, like Bloom's, is one of the most important preoccupations of his mental life. The story begins as Meka awakes. He rouses his snoring wife, Kelara, so that they can say their prayers together. She tells him he'd better relieve himself farther away from the hut this morning—it's beginning to smell. So he goes into the bushes where an old sow patiently waits for him to finish, as she does every morning, no matter where he is.

Today is the day chosen to inform Meka of his signal honor. Having given two sons to France for cannon fodder during World War II, he will be presented with a medal by the high commissioner himself on the occasion of his fourteenth of July visit to the town of Doum. (Also to be honored, with a better medal, so we later learn, is the Greek proprietor of the sole European café.) Meka's status in the indigenous community is based upon a whole series of foolish, magnanimous gestures towards the whites.

> Meka was often cited at the Catholic mission as an exemplary Christian soul. He had "given" his lands to the priests and himself lived in a miserable hut on the edge of town. He had had the grace to have been the proprietor of an estate which happened, one fine day, to appeal to the Good Lord. It was a white father who had revealed to Meka his divine destiny. [9]

On his way to town to be officially told of the medal, Meka stops in for a nip at Madame Titi's, a shebeen where everyone stops because drinking by Africans in the European quarter is not allowed. Here Meka is given the real African deference due his age. Most of the local wits are squatting about on their haunches, but someone gives Meka a box to sit on and opine from before beginning his deferential day.

* George Grosz would have appreciated the audacity of that metaphor

The external Meka must be transformed for the great occasion. We glimpse him having a new jacket cut to an absurd length by a cocky tailor who insists that this is the latest style. Meka is worried by the fact that the tailor chews ground nuts constantly. He wants his jacket spotless. "Peanuts don't stain, would that other things did not," says the tailor in a philosophical vein.

The brilliant central section of the book is devoted to the ceremony on the fourteenth of July itself. Meka is disclosed standing for the first time in leather shoes ("luckily I didn't wear sox too") in a (Caucasian?) white chalk circle that has been drawn by those in charge to mark his place on the parade ground. They assume that he is too stupid merely to be told where to go. Meka is, in his solitary, ludicrous splendor, cut off from the black world of spectators on the veranda as well as from the entire population of Doum (including extra relations and well-wishers from out of town), which has been herded behind barricades. The high commissioner, the one with the chin, is an hour late. Meka's feet have ceased to exist save as a series of needles down his spine and he has, in addition, an unbearable urge to relieve himself. The thought of the sow in the bushes back home is of some consolation. The sun is so hot that Meka actually turns his head to reassure himself that it's still in the sky and not seated on his back like some burning incubus. For Meka is, despite his subservience to the white world, a humorous old man with an independent turn of mind. He calls on his ancestors for the strength to endure the tortures of the sun, of the lower abdomen, and of the shoes.

In the crowd, meanwhile, Meka's wife finally comes to her senses and the story begins to turn around. Somewhere, from behind the barricades, she hears a dissenter murmur: "Me, I say they would have done better to dress him in medals . . . . That would have been more just. He might well have lost his lands and his sons for that." Kelara is at first outraged by this, then grief-stricken; finally she looks at her husband as if she were seeing him for the first time. He revolts her, and she runs away weeping for her lost sons.

Meka's conversion is a more elaborate process. He rides ignominiously to the drinking celebration after the ceremony in the back of the mission truck, aware for the first time of the local priest's real contempt for him. Once inside the corrugated hangar known as the *Foyer des Africains*, Meka drinks a great deal and, having listened to the high commissioner's speech on Franco-African friendship, is suddenly inspired to put this to the test. He makes an interminable speech of his own (avoiding the horrified gaze and gestures of the resident administrator of Doum), the gist of which is an invitation for the big chief of the whites to dine with him and his in his hut, to share the ceremonial beef that his brother-in-law has led all the way through three villages and four forests in honor of the day. There's been lots of talk about friendship, Meka concludes, but no one has ever seen white hands dipped into the pot with black. The high commissioner politely excuses himself; he is leaving Doum almost at once. But the suggestion is not abandoned. Meka's peers, relaxed by the drinks and exhilarated by the novelty of the occasion, elaborate upon the theme with great energy among themselves long after Meka himself has fallen hopelessly asleep on a bench at the back of the hall.

The Europeans leave. The police come to drive the "natives" out. The reassertion of the old order calls forth the old response, and they file out soberly, forgetting all about Meka, who by now has rolled under the bench. The medal, gradually loosened from his jacket, rolls and is lost in the dust. Meka snores on until a terrible storm awakens him. He staggers out of the collapsing jerry-built *Foyer* only to be arrested in the dark as a prowler in the European quarter. His identity unknown, Meka is brutally handled and spends what was to be his feast night in jail. Finally identified the next morning as the old man of the medal, Meka staggers home, a changed man.

He finds nature everywhere reasserting itself after the storm. All the rich odors of the forest impregnate the atmosphere, and the spirits that dwell in the things of the forest return to animate the old man's newly conscious life. All the old superstitions reassert themselves in Meka, after years of Christian belief and practice had all but washed them away. He stumbles on a root—a sign that he will fall on a good meal. He relieves himself on certain herbs which, washed by man's urine, are sure to return virility to the aged. He addresses each portentous animal that crosses his path with appropriate affectionate words and baptizes his route "the forest of return."

All the relatives and hangers-on back at his hut bewail his ill-treatment at the hands of the whites until Meka, collapsed with a strange new dignity upon his bed, gives them one thousand francs—his savings—to go and buy drinks with. These bought and consumed, the group becomes increasingly animated with a kind of bitter, defiant joy. Meka's serious brother-in-law (the one who had come such a distance with the beef) tries to divert their hilarious self-pity to some sort of effective criticism of the whites, whose fault, after all, *all* of this is. But the Mvemas prefer intoxication to political action. Forced by this behavior to admit that the strength of the ancestors has indeed left his people, that the Mvemas are too demoralized by colonization to try anything heroic now, the brother-in-law lowers his head in shame and murmurs, "poor us."

Out of the awkwardness of the situation someone facetiously suggests that when the whites honor Meka again he wear nothing for the occasion but a *cache-sexe*—then they'll have to pin the medal there. Now dishonor and embarrassment are forgotten in a burst of laughter. When in Meka's opinion the fun has gone on long enough, when there's no more palm wine to drink anyhow, the old man rises from his couch and bids them return to their daily tasks. "The whites are the whites . . . one day perhaps . . . but now . . ." mutters Meka the newly wise, "to hell with it—I am nothing but an old man."

The case against the cruelty and condescension of a European community in residence is easy to make. Insults, incarcerations, and tortures are constantly pushing things too far. But lacking the power to resist or the means to escape, the underprivileged indigenous inhabitants of such a community must simply hate, divert themselves, and with decreasing moral energy bide their time. Unless European occupation promises to approach the limit of permanence, the white man will remain a generalized negative image in the black man's mind—"they" as opposed to "we." Education, however, permits a far more debilitating form of imperialism to take hold. How difficult for the privileged African to extirpate the positive image of France from his deeply colonized heart. "Who are we, who are we anyhow, we Negroes that are supposed to be French?" [10] is the question asked at the end of Oyono's first book, a question to which he devotes his entire third.

The youthful hero of *Chemin de l'Europe* (1960) has never

called his identity into question because he has never been permitted to put his elective affinity for France into practice. At first this young man thought that his education would bring him a prestigious position in his own community, which would in turn guarantee an honorary gallicization by the whites. But having failed through circumstance to finish his formal schooling, and finding himself because of his aspirations technologically unemployed, a voyage to France itself becomes his only hope for personal fulfillment. This is a fantasy that he will go to any lengths of personal humiliation to realize.

Here then are the particulars of the case of Aki Barnabas: His father, a night watchman, reluctant at his age to go to the literacy classes that conceivably could spell success of some sort under the colonial regime, opts for Christianity. instead. Accepting a new menial job as a mission gardener, he transfers his real ambitions to the son, whom he forthwith enrolls in the mission school. Barnabas is bright. He obtains the coveted certificat d'études at an early age. His father then sends him on to the seminary. Barnabas acquiesces not because he feels a sense of vocation or because he has any desire at all to please his father, but because all secular studies higher than the certificat being at that time closed to the indigènes, "The seminary was the forbidden paradise of knowledge to which one could gain access thanks to the Trojan horse of a 'call.' "[11] But unfortunately all plans are cancelled by Barnabas' sudden expulsion from the seminary on charges of homosexuality.

The father's thwarted hopes turn to anger and succeed eventually in splitting up the family. Barnabas, now living alone with his mother, rather desperately hires himself out to a Greek merchant. For this man Barnabas must act as a kind of barker and strong man with respect to the bush folk who swarm into town each morning to do their buying and selling. Barnabas hates this job, of course, and is overwhelmed with excitement when by chance the improper behavior of a white curate makes a job as tutor for the daughter of a real French family his.

It is to the person of this Madame Gruchet that his fantasies of "arrival" now cling. He daydreams an elaborate structure of his courtship, of her divorce and return to France with him—a fantasy spun wholly out of an indifference of hers that seems "suspicious" to him. When this indifference proves to be real,

Barnabas feels betrayed, breaks his contract, and having at last decided to try directly for Europe or nothing, is content for the nonce to be nothing.

> . . . and I finally tasted the bilious pleasure of feeling myself profoundly "me"—all alone in this gluey tenacious mud, amid the howling of the wind, as if I had just been thrust outside the extreme limits of a world which formerly—in its journey towards the light—abandoned in this place that sloshy thankless part of itself in which I have just fatefully holed myself up: my country! And I continued my solitary course towards the native quarter.[12]

But *La Belle France*—ah, this is Cytherea, for which from nothing he will, despite all odds, one day embark.

> I felt for this country that I did not know, whose beauty and whose genius I had been taught to praise since childhood, such an affinity that I was driven to ask myself if I had not perhaps *been* French in some former existence.[13]

Colonization can go no farther than this.

Barnabas' African father, so repellent to him (Oyono makes him a hunchback), has died in the meantime, and has been hastily buried in the putrifying mud of his natal forest. At home without work, Barnabas' relations with his mother become more and more strained. At times he longs for the "*épaule-oreiller de mon enfance*," and at other times it is he who turns away and she who makes *him* feel guilty for refusing the comfort which she, and she alone, used to be able to give. This infantile and sporadic longing for his mother, like the romantic lust for the disagreeable white woman, like his awkward amours with an obese and sterilized prostitute, is finally subsumed under his greater unrealistic passion for France. When his inactivity becomes intolerable, he and his mother, by this time most anxious to get rid of him, attempt to solicit funds for his voyage from the grotesque old tribal patriarch, one Fimsten Vavap, whose effectiveness is metonymically reduced by Oyono to the following: "He yawned: a solitary molar, partly decayed by tartre appeared at the back of its empty palace like a spit of bile." Vavap, jealous of his sluggish authority, is most hostile to the thought of a vigorous younger generation of been-tos. He refuses Barnabas the resources of the tribe.

Strangely undaunted, Barnabas now tries for the resources of the state. A passionate letter to the colonial governor goes unanswered for months, however, and he is forced to take *ad hoc* employment, first as a scribe and then as a tour leader for romantic Africanists who come to the Hôtel de France to photograph rites that he and his friends hastily "get up" for the purpose. This last activity so demoralizes him that, after a terrible row with everybody at the hotel including the *choucroute*-eating *patronne* with a chest like "an immense octopus in the process of asphyxiating itself in a canvas bag," he decides to go to the district administrator in person.

En route to the city, Barnabas receives his first vote of confidence. In a burst of national feeling inadvertently provoked by a cynical shrimp salesman who sells spoiled fish for high prices in the interior, his fellow lorry passengers press bank notes upon him to speed his way to Europe. (Educated men in the interior, like shrimps, are a good investment.) But once *in* the city the European administrator, well-reputed for his "humanity," says that since even French B.A.'s are sweeping the streets in Paris, what chance has a Barnabas without a degree? Barnabas reminds him that only recently (since World War II) were his fellow nationals even allowed to go out for the *bachot*. But what of this? Barnabas is now too old and too impecunious to take up his books again. And when Monsieur the Humane Administrator recommends one of the good apprentice schools for "natives," Barnabas leaves the office in disgust—only to stumble upon a fantastic solution of his own.

A revivalist group called the "Spiritual Renaissance" is holding a confessional in the street. Confess enough sins, a cynical bystander assures him, and they'll even send you abroad to testify to the powers of their Lord. The book ends as Barnabas, the illuminated, begins his confident march up to the improvised white altar, inventing as he walks the first words of a promotion that will surely open up the road to Europe for him at last.

The frenetic, highly personal musings of Barnabas, rural electrifications sparked by thwarted desire, by the atrocious climate, by his poverty, and by the gloomy decay of his environment generally, as well as by the scrofulous appearance and outrageous conduct of the opportunistic people he meets—all these tell of a great contempt, a contempt for all flesh, one might say at bottom a self-contempt which shatters, like the Snow Queen's mirror in devilish hands, into a thousand pieces of jaundiced vision, into the countless exaggerated features of the flesh that animate all of Oyono's books. A healthy hatred of colonialism, turned back upon oneself as the bastard child of France produces the wens and warts of Oyono's colonial portraits, is at the source of Mongo Beti's broader caricatures as well. The politically minded may read these books and rejoice at the incriminating analogies. The poetically minded may wince delightedly at the intensity of the writing, at the explosive concreteness of the material. The authors, plainly, have suffered a great deal. In exposing colonialism they have laid bare their own nerves. The twin writers from the Camerouns are not identical, but their cries from the colonial incubator are equally loud and shrill. They are, it must be said, of a certain frustrated genius, with all that genius has to offer and to pay.

IV.

Onuora Nzekwu was born in Northern Nigeria, but his secondary schooling and teachers training took place in Onitsha (Eastern Region). He has taught both in Onitsha and in Lagos. His researches into the history of Onitsha gained him his present position as editor on *Nigeria*, a "middle-brow" (as opposed to *Black Orpheus*) magazine primarily devoted to arts, crafts, and historical and cultural affairs. Nzekwu might be taken as a kind of mean between the extremes of Ekwensi and Achebe. As an essentially popular writer, he lacks Ekwensi's ear for speech or eye for detail. This is not his interest; his is a pedagogical approach. Nor does he make use of the Western cultural tradition, in a formative way, within the texture of his books, in the depiction of "ancestral" behavior, as Achebe does. Nzekwu's appetite for sensation can be irritating if considered as calculated to sell his books abroad, but fascinating if taken to be the genuine expression of a modern mind obsessed by the more violent aspects of immemorial practices and lore.

Nzekwu's books may be taken as illustrative of the effects of the ambiguities of British colonial practice upon a bright, highly strung, and somewhat disorganized personality.* The hidden theme common to both Nzekwu's books, *A Wand of Noble Wood* (1961) and *Blade Among the Boys* (1962), is that of the supernatural revenge taken by the old dispensation upon the new. The traditional society's ways have been disturbed, violated by new patterns from the West which have been planted first by Europeans and then cultivated by "emancipated" Africans themselves. The spiritual forces behind the old community manage to break through, using *their* elected human agents in retaliation. It is important to note that in Nzekwu's books these retaliatory occurrences are presented as being really supernatural in origin— another example of his uniqueness. There is absolutely *no* evidence of irony with regard to these occurrences in the books. In addition, as atavisms they have a personal rather than a communal intent and effect, which is to say that they have an emotional impact on and affect the destinies of isolated individuals only. This is why, unlike similar mysterious and violent manifestations with a broader scope, those described by Nzekwu seem to the skeptical Western reader to be obsessional, a tumultuous inner life turned inside out.

Yet Nzekwu's apparent intentions are of a social nature, a direct lead to which may be had by considering the title of his first book, *A Wand of Noble Wood*. The image of this wand, a rod both of chastisement and of measurement as well as a sign of legitimate office, is found, so Nzekwu reminds us, in Aristophanes' *The Frogs*. It occurs in a choral speech, the gist of which is integral to the theme of the play as a whole: that Athens would do well to cease employing the baser elements of her society in high places and to give back to the tried and virtuous old aristocrats of office their proper civic status and responsibilities. They of noble wood may then chasten the vulgar roof-trees, so that if it be Athens' destiny to fall, at least there will be no loss of honor in the falling.

Nzekwu's choice of literary patron seems most appropriate.

* Certain impressions I had gained from reading their books were later corroborated by brief questionnaires that a friend in Lagos was kind enough to present to Nzekwu, Ekwensi, and Achebe. It came as no surprise to discover, for example, that Nzekwu's literary preference is for crime and mystery stories, that Achebe prefers novels by Tolstoy, Conrad, and Graham Greene, and that Ekwensi lists such disparate choices as Dickens, Dostoevsky, Rider Haggard, Steinbeck, and Richard Wright.

The theme of a debased human currency in modern Africa would have pleased the Old Comedian, and all the demigods and ancestors in their exotic masks would have seemed quite familiar to him. But there isn't much doubt about what Aristophanes is about. All is mockery in *The Frogs*, ancient gods and heroes caught in a farcical machine which grinds out critical consternation and amusement at the expense of an even more ludicrous contemporaneity. What the Nigerian is about is another question.

The first half of Nzekwu's book with the Aristophanean title is devoted to long discussions of the implications of his hero's unmarried state. Peter Obiesi, age thirty one, a magazine writer, has been forced through a concatenation of customary restrictions to maintain a bachelor's existence to which he inwardly does not at all object. This talk of traditional marriage customs under the impact of modern life takes place between Peter, his friend Reg (a newspaper reporter), and a West Indian girl (in the interests of cultural and sexual perspective). Here Nzekwu may have had the agon between Euripides and Aeschylus in mind. But does he mean his sententious, detailed descriptions of the old customs to be taken as we take Aristophanes' parodies of modern tragedy—as exaggerations which purposely overshoot the intended mark? It is difficult to take them that way. Rather it seems the droning voice of the lecturer that is heard, informing a British public of what it has failed in a hundred years or so to learn about African ways:

"As you know [the hero is speaking], children among us, are priceless possessions. To us, the primary aim of marriage is to have children, particularly boys, who will perpetuate our names. Those who show an interest in my marriage are considering my age. The essential thing to them is that I should start having my own children, with a legitimate wife of course, as early in life as convention dictates."

"You obviously don't share their views do you?" she asked.

"No. The times have changed. The old order is yielding place to the new. In the past it was necessary to have children early. Before you aged, the boys were strong enough to work on your farm, the size of which depended on the amount of free labor which was available. Larger and more farms meant more food production and therefore more wealth. The girls among them spelt wealth too. Suitors came, they paid handsome bride prices; evidence of their ability to maintain their wives. Today what do we have? A new social set-up based on cash economy. A good number of us depend on monthly salaries. If one had children he would be expected to give them school, college and if possible, university education. It is not how many children, [but] how well you have trained them to fit into present-day society, that counts." [14]

[Thirty pages later:]

"Of the desirability of having a wife I am well aware. Mine is not a question of whether I shall marry or not. It is a problem of time. It is a problem of overcoming the dilemma created by the conflict between tradition and westernism, a problem arising out of our attempts to blend present relative social practices with worthy concepts which tradition has established." [15]

And so on. We have been apprised, in the process of this discussion, of the reasons for standardization of the bride price at twenty pounds on January 1, 1939, of the necessity for elder brothers to marry before those younger, and even of the custom of breaking the kola nut as an invocation of hospitality—a practice of which a reader of almost anything from West Africa is surely aware. Breaking bread is as old as hospitality itself. These overly explicit explanations of customs are signs of anger on the part of a former colonial subject. As such they are certainly warranted, but they make poor rhetoric and worse art.

Having survived this palaver in Lagos, we are off to the Ibo township in the hinterland where the trying out of these traditional courtship patterns will take place. Helpful relatives are finally able to line up a suitable girl for Peter Obiesi. He falls in love with her—a Western practice, says the author, that a generation of young, idealistic, and "educated" Africans have taken up. Unfortunately, however, before Peter can marry his young schoolteacher and take her back with him to Lagos, an inherited curse on the girl must be revoked. They must bring a complicated set of offerings to the priest of the iyi ocha who apparently succeeds in placating this vindictive spirit by means of a sacred medicine bag.

All preliminary arrangements for the marriage having been

made, Peter returns to Lagos. His future wife is brought in ceremony to her in-laws' house and from there is expected to follow her bridegroom to the city. Then, suddenly, mysteriously, she drops dead. An evil rival for her hand had managed to slip an essential object, the white stone, from the *iyi ocha* priest's bag of wonders. The curse, therefore, acts upon her at this crucial moment, putting a tragic end to all of the hero's marital hopes. He might, however, have known that something like this would happen. The ghostly voice of his dead uncle Azoba had been constantly obtruding upon the young man's consciousness in pentateuchal utterances like the following:

> "Have we not despised our cultural heritage? . . . How many of our girls can cook well nowadays? . . . What respect is left for our traditional religion? . . . [Ancestral] spirits are taking revenge on our people for a failure to adhere to wisdom handed down to them through the generations. The gods are angry. Our people must come back to them. They must revive those aspects of our cultural life which have been dropped or allowed to go to pieces. . . ."[16]

The girl turns out to have been the innocent victim of a curse on her mother invoked for negligence in a simple commercial transaction—hardly enough to make the gods angry in this sense. But Peter? There is an interesting piece of grotesquerie in the first section involving Peter and a dangerously sick old man from his home village who is literally hanging on to life by the thread which holds a goat's heart suspended underneath his bed! The old wizard, before his "well-wishers" cut the string for him, warns Peter that women are his weakness, and that he mustn't have anything to do with anyone outside the Ado village. Peter, albeit a staunch upholder of tradition, did have an affair with that girl with the Igala tribal markings. His guilt alone, says the Western skeptic, is enough to invoke the curse. The "supernatural" always does take its revenge when there is a tortured conscience to trigger it off.

Blade Among the Boys, Nzekwu's second book, is less prosy and less spooky, and here the meaning is successfully controlled by the persuasiveness of the central characters. The author's attack on modernism here focuses on Christianity and its battle with the clan for the possession of the person, if not the real soul, of the hero. For the spirit of Patrick-Okonkwo Ikenga is so divided and confused that a profound allegiance to either institution is really impossible for him. And further, both the church and the African community make such severe demands and exact such a price for admittance to peace of mind behind their customary walls that it is psychologically inevitable for Patrick to get himself into the eventual position of being ostracized by both camps. Just a slight push from the outraged supernatural forces and he is nowhere.

Patrick's father had a reputation for being a *rechtglaübiger*, but charms hidden behind photographs on the walls of his house and a clandestine resorting to magic as protection against evil would certainly, had anyone outside the family known of these, have belied the appearance. Yet two sets of supernatural prophylaxes proved in his case to be no better than none. Patrick's widowed mother's simple concerns thus narrowed to the future possibility of grandchildren, she hastily betroths Patrick to the future girl-child of a friend of hers, *pre utero*.

Patrick's uncle has other, more complex, concerns. He believes that his nephew should take advantage of the education for money and power that the missionaries are offering as fringe benefits at this time. (For the Christian way of life itself the uncle has no use.) Patrick, on the other hand, has long entertained the desire of becoming a priest, and willingly enters the school for that reason, only to find the cynical discipline of the Catholic authorities intolerable. "Beggars cannot be choosers. You have an education on our terms or quit," a priest bluntly tells him. Patrick is eventually fired from the school after a row with the Latin teacher, and, again through his uncle, he enters into apprentice work for a railroad company, this time with the happy thought of nothing but financial gain. But he does continue to live as an exemplary Christian—for three weeks—and then he stops going to church altogether.

Patrick now becomes obsessed with women—on principle never the same one twice—and the inevitable fancy clothes. And unlike Obi Okonkwo, Patrick Okonkwo Ikenga takes easily to bribery. Working in a goods shed near Port Harcourt, he takes advantage of the fact that demands for railroad cars exceed the supply, and that palm oil merchants are willing to pay well for an early booking that will ensure a successful marketing of their perishable commodity. Patrick is not caught accepting the bribes which double his salary, although he does have a narrow escape which makes him think he is under some kind of supernatural protection. This, following hard upon an even more miraculous escape from a train wreck, during the course of which he dreams of being admitted to the Church in all the pomp of self-importance, makes him opt for the priesthood once again. But he now has no illusions about the consequences of his decision.

> If he became a priest, he thought, his kith and kin would have to disown him. Not only that, they would, through his own act, become objects of ridicule to every Ado Indigene. He considered, however, that this would be nothing compared with the very high social standing which he would occupy in the estimation of the rest of the world.[17]

His spiritual option is abruptly called into question by the news that he has fallen heir to the position of *okala*, the head of his lineage, an office his uncle has been secretly holding in trust for him all along. To refuse such an honor as *okala* is an outrage; and when Patrick does turn it down his uncle refuses even to speak to him, as Patrick himself foresaw. But he does try his best to make amends by long and consistently disappointing pilgrimages to Ado during vacations from the seminary. This closing of the doors of the clan is reinforced by the death of Patrick's mother, for which the entire Ado township turns out to blame him. Having raved on the steps of the seminary for two full days, "Fathers, give me back my son . . . why must you make him a eunuch?" this African mother finally died of a broken will.

But the mother's desire for grandchildren does triumph, ironically, in the end. Nature will not be thwarted, no matter how strict the holy fathers or how odd the son. The girl-child to whom Patrick had been betrothed does materialize into a real young lady hopelessly in love with her reluctant fiancé. She pursues him to the seminary, consults an herbalist, and one mysterious concoction, cleverly inserted into an orange, breaks down his resistance. The girl becomes pregnant and her mother informs the authorities. Patrick is expelled from the seminary and walks out into life "with unseeing eyes...a big void in his heart."

V.

Nzekwu's Patrick-Okonkwo Ikenga, like Mongo Beti's Medza, is "a man left to his own devices in a world which does not belong to him, which he has not made and does not understand . . . bereft of any intellectual compass." Here, at zero, the two West African literatures meet. The quest for identity has reached the point where man is a function of nothing—neither French culture nor African wisdom nor Christian virtue in the British style. But the center of personal despair is also the point of origin. "*Le vent se lève!*" as Valéry cried. History forces the intellect into action. An independent Africa poses problems for the emancipated individual, but these are problems of a slightly different sort.

> Poor, without friends or relations, mocked in my hopes, nevertheless I was not discouraged . . . . People said to me: Africa is becoming middle class, your Latin is still good capital, you already know enough to become somebody here. Why dwell on going to France? Put yourself in the stream of things, watch those who rise! Political affiliations will soon have it all over diplomas . . . . Watch out! You always seem to be waiting for who knows what. You've got to join up.[18]

This is the voice of Oyono's Barnabas again, in a rare objective mood, giving the author a chance to convey with irony that which Mongo Beti's prophetic Bitamo lays on the line to Chris— a sense of political urgency, a condemnation of the man of two worlds who has none. The African youths of these novels suffer from an exaggerated notion of the self as only mental, which in the Western schoolroom it is. This is a common problem. But African states are fortunate in having at their disposal the traditional communal idea. To get those, or the descendants of those, who were able to use their intellects to escape from the rigors of matchet and hoe, to return productively to the African community, African intellectuals themselves have been forced to take up the drums. The colonized heart can, with honor, return to the old village ways only by helping with special competence and perspective to transform them, either technologically or imaginatively, by the exemplary agency of art.

The loneliness of the exceptional person from the backward community who became the lonely tribesman in the regional school run according to European standards, who became the anxious ex-villager in the city or the guilty *evolué* far from home—this condition peculiar to so many African novels is obviously nowhere near as determinative as it once was.

> Novels used to be written about colonialism and the life of the *métis* [says Kane of *L'Aventure ambiguë*]. These are problems no longer. The new novels will deal with the problems of today. They will tell us, for example, what happens when an educated Senegalese boy marries a girl with no education. My first book discussed the contact and conflict between African culture and Western culture. My new book will show the synthesis of these cultures . . . . It will discuss the life of Senegal today—its tradition and its rapid development. It will be a political novel and a national novel, but it will be written from the psychological and aesthetic point of view.* [19]

The feckless times recorded by this first group of novels are over. But as long as the Western impact on Africa is felt these themes will still be sounded, more and more on communal drums, perhaps, whose talk we will not be privileged to understand. And yet occasionally the thinner convolutions of the piano solo will also be heard, taking up the theme in a language we know very well. From a city apartment or from an outpost of development in the bush, at night that lonely strain will sound —lamenting the absence of those other tam-tams that can never be heard in the same way again, lamenting the time before all of this began.

* At the time of this writing Kane's "new" new African novel had not yet appeared.

Notes

1. Ezekiel Mphahlele, *The African Image* (London: Faber and Faber, Ltd., 1962), p. 93.

2. Eza Boto, *Ville cruelle*, in *Trois écrivains noirs* (Paris: Présence Africaine, 1954), pp. 20–21.

3. C. Levi-Strauss, *Tristes tropiques*, John Russell, trans. (New York: Criterion Books, Inc., 1961), p. 308.

4. Mongo Beti, *Mission to Kala*, Peter Green, trans. (London: Frederick Muller Ltd., 1956), p. 188.

5. *Ibid.*, p. 71.

6. *Ibid.*, pp. 205–6.

7. Mongo Beti, *King Lazarus*, Peter Green, trans. (London: Frederick Muller Ltd., 1960), p. 79.

8. Ferdinand Oyono, *Le Vieux nègre et la médaille* (Paris: René Julliard, 1956), p. 117.

9. *Ibid.*, p. 19.

10. Ferdinand Oyono, *Une Vie de boy* (Paris: René Julliard, 1956), p. 12.

11. Ferdinand Oyono, *Chemin de l'Europe* (Paris: René Julliard, 1960), p. 13.

12. *Ibid.*, pp. 72–73.

13. *Ibid.*, p. 49.

14. Onuora Nzekwu, *A Wand of Noble Wood* (London: Hutchinson & Co., Ltd., 1961), pp. 34–35.

15. *Ibid.*, pp. 65–66.

16. *Ibid.*, pp. 168–70.

17. Onuora Nzekwu, *Blade Among the Boys* (London: Hutchinson & Co., Ltd., 1962), p. 143.

18. Ferdinand Oyono, *Chemin de l'Europe*, pp. 107–8.

19. Cheikh Hamidou Kane, in *West Africa*, No. 2350 (June 16, 1962), pp. 649.

BIBLIOGRAPHY

African Novels

This is a partial listing, prepared during 1964. Further bibliographical information may be had from The American Society of African Culture, 15 East 40th Street, New York, N.Y.

Abrahams, Peter. *Mine Boy*. First published in London, 1946. New York: Alfred A. Knopf, Inc., 1955. (South Africa)

Achebe, Chinua. *Arrow of God*. London: Heinemann, 1964. (Nigeria)

————. *Things Fall Apart*. New York: McDowell, Obolensky, 1959. (Nigeria) (Now in paperback.)

————. *No Longer at Ease*. New York: Ivan Obolensky, Inc., 1961. (Nigeria)

Ananou, David. *Le Fils du fétiche*. Paris: Nouvelles Editions Latines, 1955. (Togo)

Biyidi, Alexandre (Eza Boto). *Ville cruelle, in Trois écrivains noirs*. Paris: Présence Africaine, 1954. (Cameroun)

Biyidi, Alexandre (Mongo Beti). *Le Pauvre Christ de Bomba*. Paris: Robert Laffont, 1956. (Cameroun)

————. *King Lazarus*. Translated by Peter Green. London: Frederick Muller Ltd., 1960. (Cameroun)

————. *Mission to Kala*. Translated by Peter Green. London: Frederick Muller Ltd., 1958. (Cameroun)

Bolomba, G. *Kavwanga*. Namur: Collection Lavigerie, n.d. (1954?). (The Republic of the Congo)

Boni, Nazi. *Crépuscule des temps anciens*. Paris: Présence Africaine, 1962. (Upper Volta)

Conton, William. *The African*. Boston: Little, Brown and Company, 1960. (Gambia) (Now in paperback.)

Dadié, Bernard T. *Climbié*. Paris: Éditions Seghers, 1956.

————. *Un Nègre a Paris*. Paris: Présence Africaine, 1959. (Ivory Coast)

Diallo, Bakary. *Force bontè*. Paris: F. Rieder & Cie., 1926 (Senegal)

Ekwensi, Cyprian, *Beautiful Feathers*. London: Hutchinson & Co., Ltd., 1963. (Nigeria)

———. *Burning Grass*. (African Writers Series) London: Heinemann, 1962. (Nigeria)

———. *Jagua Nana*. London: Hutchinson & Co., Ltd., 1961. (Nigeria)

———. *People of the City*. London: Andrew Dakars Ltd., 1954. (Nigeria) (Now in paperback.)

Hazoumé, Paul. *Doguicimi*. Paris: Larose, 1938. (Dahomey)

Kane, Cheikh Hamidou. *L'Aventure ambiguë*. Paris: Julliard, 1961. (Senegal) (Translated as *Ambiguous Adventure*, by Katherine Woods. New York: Walker & Company, 1963.)

La Guma, Alex. *A Walk in the Night*. Ibadan: Mbari, 1963. (South Africa)

Laye, Camara. *The Dark Child*. Translated from *L'Enfant noir* by James Kirkup. London: Collins, 1955. (Guinea)

———. *The Radiance of the King*. Translated from *Le Régard du roi* by James Kirkup. London: Collins, 1956. (Guinea)

Loba, Aké. *Kocoumbo, l'étudiant noir*. Paris: Flammarion, 1960. (Ivory Coast)

Malonga, Jean. *La Legende de M'pfoumu Ma Mazona*. Paris: Éditions Africaines, 1954. (Congo)

Mofolo, Thomas. *Chaka*. Translated by F. H. Dutton. London: Oxford University Press, 1931. (Basutoland)

Mopeli-Paulus, A. S. *Blanket Boy's Moon*, Written in collaboration with Peter Lanham. London: Collins, 1953. (Basutoland)

———. *Turn to the Dark*. Written in collaboration with Miriam Basner. London: Jonathan Cape, 1956. (Basutoland)

Ngugi, James. *Weep Not, Child*. London: Heinemann, 1964. (Kenya)

Niane, Djibril Tamsir. *Soundjata, ou l'épopée mandingue*. Paris: Présence Africaine, 1961. (Guinea)

Ntara, Samuel Yosia. *Man of Africa*. Translated from Nyanja by T. Cullen Young. London: The Religious Tract Society, 1934. (Malawi)

Nzekwu, Onuora. *A Wand of Noble Wood*. London: Hutchinson & Co., Ltd., 1961. (Nigeria)

———. *Blade Among the Boys*. London: Hutchinson & Co., Ltd., 1962. (Nigeria)

Ousmane, Sembene. *Le Docker noir*. Paris: Éditions Debresse, 1956. (Senegal)

————. *God's Bits of Wood*. Translated by Francis Price. New York: Doubleday, 1962. (Senegal)

————. *L'Harmattan*. Paris: Présence Africaine, 1964.

————. *O pays mon beau peuple!* Paris: Le Livre Contemporain, 1957. (Senegal)

Owono, Joseph. *Tante Bella*. Yaoundé: librarie "au messager," 1939. (Cameroun)

Oyono, Ferdinand. *Chemin de l'Europe*. Paris: René Julliard, 1960. (Cameroun)

————. *Une Vie de boy*. Paris: René Julliard, 1956. (Cameroun)

————. *Le Vieux nègre et la médaille*. Paris: René Julliard, 1936. (Cameroun)

Plaatje, Solomon T. *Mhudi, an Epic of South African Life a Hundred Years Ago*. Lovedale: Lovedale Press, 1930. (South Africa)

Sadji, Abdoulaye. *Maïmouna*. Paris: Présence Africaine, 1958. (Senegal)

————. *Nini*, in *Trois écrivains noirs*. Paris: Présence Africaine, 1954. (Senegal)

Sellassie, Sahle. *Shinega's Village*. Translated from the Chaha by Wolf Leslau. Los Angeles: University of California Press, 1964. (Ethiopia)

Socé Diop, Ousmane. *Karim*. First published 1935. Paris: Bibliothèque de l'Union Française, Nouvelles Éditions Latines, 1948. (Senegal)

African Literature
Other Genres

A sampling of readily accessible works whose authors are referred to in the text. Three of the authors are West Indian in origin, but their works have been of inspirational importance for African literature of French expression.

Abrahams, Peter. *Tell Freedom*. New York: Alfred A. Knopf, Inc., 1961. (South Africa)

Aimé Césaire, "Poètes d'aujourd'hui 85," Presentation par Lilyan Kesteloot. Paris: Éditions Pierre Seghers, 1962.

Anthologie de la nouvelle poésie nègre et malgache. Léopold Sédar Senghor, ed. Paris: Presses Universitaires de France, 1948.

Awolowo, Obafemi. *Awo, The Autobiography of Chief Obafemi Awolowo*. Cambridge: Cambridge University Press, 1960. (Nigeria)

Clark, J. P. *Song of a Goat*, a play. Ibadan: Mbari, 1961. (Nigeria)

Damas, Leon. *Pigments*, poetry. First published 1937. Paris: Présence Africaine, 1962. (French Guiana)

Diop, Birago. *Les contes d'Amadou-Koumba*. Paris: Fasquelle Éditeurs, 1947. (Senegal)

————. *Les nouvelles contes d'Amadou-Koumba*. Paris: Présence Africaine, 1958. (Senegal)

Maran, René. *Bacouya, le cynocephale*. Paris: Éditions Albin Michel, 1953. (Martinique)

————. *Batouala*. Translated by Adele Szold Seltzer. New York: Thomas Seltzer, 1922. (Martinique)

————. *Le Livre de la brousse*. Paris: Éditions Albin Michel, 1934. (Martinique)

Modern Poetry from Africa. Edited with an introduction by Ulli Beier and Gerald Moore. London: Penguin Books, Ltd., 1964.

Mphahlele, Ezekiel. *Down Second Avenue*, autobiography. London: Faber and Faber, Ltd., 1959. (South Africa)

Nicol, Abioseh. "The Devil at Yolahun Bridge," in *African Voices*. Compiled and edited by Peggy Rutherford. New York: The Vanguard Press, Inc., 1958. (Sierra Leone)

Ojike, Mbonu. *My Africa*, autobiography. New York: The John Day Company, 1946. (Nigeria)

Poems from Black Africa. Langston Hughes, ed. Bloomington: Indiana University Press, 1963.

Senghor, Léopold Sédar. *Selected Poems*. Translated and introduced by John Reed and Clive Wake. New York: Atheneum Publishers, 1964. (Senegal)

Soyinka, Wole. *A Dance of the Forests*, a play. London: Oxford University Press, 1963. (Nigeria)

Tutuola, Amos. *My Life in the Bush of Ghosts*. London: Faber and Faber, Ltd., 1954. (Nigeria)

————. *The Palm Wine Drinkard*. London: Faber and Faber, Ltd., 1962. (Nigeria)

————. *Simibi and the Satyr of the Dark Jungle*. London: Faber and Faber, Ltd., 1955. (Nigeria)

U'Tamsi, Felix. *Brush Fire*, poetry. Ibadan: Mbari, 1964. (Congo)

Williams, George Awoonor. *Rediscovery and Other Poems*. Ibadan: Mbari, 1964. (Ghana)

Background Material

Books

Abraham, W. E. *The Mind of Africa*. Chicago: The University of Chicago Press, 1962.

Africa Seen by American Negro Scholars. Paris: Présence Africaine, 1958.

African One-Party States. Gwendolen M. Carter, ed. Ithaca: Cornell University Press, 1962.

Cary, Joyce. *The Case for African Freedom and Other Writings on Africa*. Austin: University of Texas Press, 1962.

Colin, Roland. *Les contes noirs de l'ouest africain*. Introduction by Léopold Sédar Senghor. Paris: Présence Africaine, 1957.

Cook, Mercer. *Five French Negro Authors*. Washington, D.C.: The Associated Negro Publishers, Inc., 1943.

Crowder, Michael. *Senegal, A Study in French Assimilation Policy*. London: Oxford University Press, 1962.

Davidson, Basil. *The Lost Cities of Africa*. Boston: Little, Brown and Company, 1959.

————. *Black Mother*. Boston: Little, Brown and Company, 1961.

Delavignette, Robert. *Les Paysans noirs*. First published 1931. Paris: Éditions Stock, 1947.

The Educated African, A Country-by-Country Survey of Educational Development in Africa. Compiled by Ruth Sloan Associates. Helen Kitchen, ed. New York: Frederick A. Praeger, Inc., 1962.

Evans-Pritchard, E. E. *Social Anthropology*. The Broadcast Lectures, Winter, 1950. London: Cohen & West, Ltd., 1954.

Fage, J. D. *An Introduction to the History of West Africa*. London: Cambridge University Press, 1955.

Fagg, William, with Herbert List. *Nigerian Images*. New York: Frederick A. Praeger, Inc., 1963.

Frobenius, Leo. *African Genesis*. Translated by Douglas C. Fox. New York: Stackpole and Sons, 1937.

Gide, André. *Travels in the Congo*. Translated by Dorothy Bussy. New York: Modern Age Books, 1937.

Gorer, Geoffrey. *Africa Dances.* First published 1935. London: Penguin Books, Ltd., 1945.

Hailey, Lord. *An African Survey,* revised edition. London: Oxford University Press, 1957.

Herskovits, Melville J. *Dahomey, an Ancient African Kingdom.* Two vols. New York: J. J. Augustin, 1938.

————. *The Myth of the Negro Past.* First published 1941. Boston: Beacon Press, 1958.

Hodgkin, Thomas. *Nationalism in Colonial Africa.* New York: New York University Press, 1957.

Ikeotuonye, Vincent C. *Zik of New Africa.* London: P. R. MacMillan, 1961.

Junod, Henri A. *The Life of a South African Tribe.* First published 1912. Two vols. New Hyde Park, N.Y.: University Books, Inc., 1962.

Kenyatta, Jomo. *Facing Mount Kenya.* First published in the 1930's. Introduction by Bronislaw Malinowski. New York: Vintage Books, Random House, Inc., 1962.

Kesteloot, Lilyan. *Les Écrivains noires de langue française.* Thèse presentée pour l'obtention du doctorat en philologie romane, Université Libre de Bruxelles, Institut de Sociologie, 1963.

Lasky, Melvin J. *Africa for Beginners.* Philadelphia: J. B. Lippincott Co., 1962.

Levi-Strauss, C. *Tristes tropiques.* Translated by John Russell. New York: Criterion Books, Inc., 1961.

Maurice, Albert. *Felix Eboué, sa vie et oeuvre.* Bruxelles: Institut Royal Colonial Belge, Tome 37, 1954.

Meloné, Thomas. *De la négritude dans la litterature negro-africaine.* Paris: Présence Africaine, 1962.

Moore, Gerald. *Seven African Writers.* London: Oxford University Press, 1962.

Mphahlele, Ezekiel. *The African Image.* London: Faber and Faber, Ltd., 1962.

Murdock, George Peter. *Africa: Its Peoples and Their Culture History.* New York: McGraw-Hill Book Company, Inc., 1959.

The "New Imperialism." Harrison M. Wright, ed. Boston: D. C. Heath & Company, 1962.

Ritter, E. A. *Shaka Zulu.* London: Longmans, Green and Co., 1955.

Senghor, Léopold Sédar. *On African Socialism.* Translated and with an introduction by Mercer Cook. New York: Frederick A. Praeger, Inc., 1964.

Sithole, Ndabaning. *African Nationalism*. Capetown: Oxford University Press, 1959.

Tempels, The Reverend Father Placide. *Bantu Philosophy*. Translated by The Reverend Colin King. Paris: Présence Africaine, 1959.

Thompson, Virginia and Richard Adloff. *French West Africa*. Palo Alto: Stanford University Press, 1950.

————. *The Emerging States of French Equatorial Africa*. Palo Alto: Stanford University Press, 1960.

Trautman, René. *Au pays de Batouala*. Paris: Payot & Cie., 1922.

Turnbull, Colin M. *The Forest People*. New York: The Natural History Library, Anchor Books, Doubleday & Company, Inc., 1962.

————. *The Lonely African*. New York: Simon and Schuster, Inc., 1962.

Wallerstein, Immanuel. *Africa, The Politics of Independence*. New York: Vintage Books, Inc., 1961.

West African Explorers. Edited by C. Howard, with an introduction by J. H. Plumb. London: Oxford University Press, 1951.

Wiedner, Donald L. *A History of Africa South of the Sahara*. New York: Random House, Inc., 1962.

Articles

Allen, Samuel W. "*Négritude*, and Its Relevance to the American Negro Writer," *The American Negro Writer and His Roots*. New York: The American Society of African Culture, 1960.

Baldwin, James. Ch. 2, "Princes and Powers," *Nobody Knows My Name*. New York: A Delta Book, Dell Publishing Co., Inc., 1962.

Bascom, William. "Urbanization Among the Yoruba," *Cultures and Societies of Africa*. S. and P. Ottenberg, eds. New York: Random House, Inc., 1960, pp. 255–67.

Beier, Ulli. "Public Opinion on Lovers," *Black Orpheus*, No. 14 (February, 1964), pp. 4–16.

Clark, J. P. and Andrew Salkey. A dialogue in *Africa Abroad*, a magazine program produced at the Transcription Center, London. Recorded January 21, 1964.

Drake, St. Clair, "The Responsibility of Men of Culture for Destroying the Hamitic Myth," *Présence Africaine*, XXIV–XXV (February–May, 1959), pp. 228–43.

Eiselen, W. M. and I. Schapera. "Religious Beliefs and Practices," *Bantu Speaking Tribes of South Africa*. Reprinted 1946. I. Schapera, ed. London: George Routledge & Sons, Ltd., 1937, pp. 247–70.

"L'Eveil de l'Afrique Noire," Trois conférences-débats. Robert Delavignette: "Les politiques européennes de colonisation." Georges Balandier: "Les modifications dans les structures sociales." Pierre Alexandre: "Les voies de l'indépendance." Supplément au no. 88, Juin 1958, de *Preuves*.

Fonlon, Bernard. A press report of the Kampala Writers Conference, June, 1962. Typescript. Later published in *Afrika* (August 8, 1962). Courtesy A.M.S.A.C.

Gluckman, M. "Malinowski's Functional Analysis of Social Change," *Africa*, XVII, 2 (1947), pp. 103–21.

History and Archeology in Africa. A report of a conference held July, 1953, at the School of Oriental and African Studies, University of London. London: J. W. Ruddock and Sons, Ltd., 1955.

Krige, J. D. and E. J. "The Louedu of the Transvaal," *African Worlds*. Cyril D. Forde, ed. London: Oxford University Press, 1954, pp. 55–82.

Lebel, Roland. "Tableau de l'Afrique occidentale dans la litterature française," *Afrique occidentale française, Encyclopedie coloniale*, II (1949), pp. 379–86.

Maran, René. "André Gide and l'Afrique noir." Translated by Mercer Cook. *Phylon*, XII, Second Quarter (1951), pp. 164–70.

Mercier, P. "The Fon of Dahomey," *African Worlds*, Cyril D. Forde, ed. London: Oxford University Press, 1954, pp. 210–34.

Mphahlele, Ezekiel. Report on African Literature for the First International Congress of Africanists in Accra, December, 1962. Typescript. Courtesy A.M.S.A.C.

Nicol, Davidson, "The Soft Pink Palms," *Présence Africaine*, XVIII–XIX (June–November, 1956), pp. 107–21.

Nkosi, Lewis. "Some Conversations with African Writers," *Africa Report*, Vol. 19, No. 7 (July, 1964).

"Novelist and Planner," A Profile of Cheikh Hamidou Kane, *West Africa*, No. 2350 (June 16, 1962).

Ogot, Bethwell. "From Chief to President," *Transition*, Vol. 4 (September, 1963), pp. 26–30.

Ottenberg, Simon. "Ibo Receptivity to Change," *Continuity and Change* in African Cultures. W. Bascom and M. Herskovits, eds. Chicago: University of Chicago Press, 1959, pp. 130–43.

Pageard, Robert. "Soundjata Keita and the Oral Tradition," Présence Africaine, XXXVI (April–July 1961), pp. 53–72.

Sartre, Jean-Paul. "Orphée noir," Anthologie de la nouvelle poésie nègre et malgache. Paris: Presses Universitaires de France, 1948, pp. ix–xliv.

Senghor, Léopold Sédar. "On Negrohood: Psychology of the African Negro," Diogenes, 37 (Spring, 1962), pp. 1–15.

Wallerstein, Immanuel. "The Search for National Identity in West Africa," Présence Africaine, XXXIV–XXXV (December, 1960–March, 1961), pp. 17–29.

Lectures

The following lectures on African Literature were given at the American Society of African Culture, New York City, taped, and extensively reported in subsequent issues of the A.M.S.A.C. Newsletter, Brooke Aronson, ed.

11/28/62—"African Literary Scene," Saunders Redding.

12/5/62—"Literary Trends in E. Africa," K. H. Baghdelleh.

12/12/62—"Literary Scene in Nigeria," John Pepper Clark.

12/19/62—"Contemporary Literature in Ghana," Samuel K. Opoku.

3/2/63—"Short Story Writing in Black South Africa," Bloke Modisane.

9/11/63—"African Literature of French Expression," Thomas Meloné.

10/23/63—"The Literature of Guinea," Amb. Achkar Marof.

1/7/64—"African life as Seen by the African Novelist," Amb. Mercer Cook.

Black Orpheus and the Mbari publications are available in the United States through Northwestern University Press.